Be a Successful Property Manager

R. DODGE WOODSON

McGraw-Hill

New York Chicago San Francisco Lisbon London Madrid
Mexico City Milan New Delhi San Juan Seoul
Singapore Sydney Toronto

B1248765X

The **McGraw·Hill** Companies

Cataloging-in-Publication Data is on file with the Library of Congress

Copyright © 2006 by The McGraw-Hill Companies, Inc. All rights reserved. Printed in the United States of America. Except as permitted under the United States Copyright Act of 1976, no part of this publication may be reproduced or distributed in any form or by any means, or stored in a data base or retrieval system, without the prior written permission of the publisher.

1 2 3 4 5 6 7 8 9 0   DOC/DOC   0 1 2 1 0 9 8 7 6

ISBN 0-07-147361-0

The sponsoring editor for this book was Cary Sullivan and the production supervisor was Pamela A. Pelton. It was set in Cremona by Lone Wolf Enterprises, Ltd. The art director for the cover was Anthony Landi.

Printed and bound by RR Donnelley.

McGraw-Hill books are available at special quantity discounts to use as premiums and sales promotions, or for use in corporate training programs. For more information, please write to the Director of Special Sales, McGraw-Hill Professional, Two Penn Plaza, New York, NY 10121-2298. Or contact your local bookstore.

This book is printed on recycled, acid-free paper containing a minimum of 50% recycled, de-inked fiber.

*I dedicate this book to the most important people in my life,
who are: Adam, Afton, Victoria, Jon, and Nate.*

Contents

CHAPTER   THREE

Following the Rules and Getting Maximum Profits   51

CHAPTER   FOUR

Subsidized Rental Income   75

CHAPTER TWELVE

C H A P T E R   T H I R T E E N

Financing   209

CHAPTER SIXTEEN

Protecting Yourself from Contractors and Vendors   261

About the Author

R. DODGE WOODSON has invested in and written about real estate for over 30 years. For more than 20 years, he's held the highest classification of professional real estate licensure available, Designated Broker. The president and owner of Expert Realty Services, Inc., of Brunswick, Maine, his experience in property management is vast, and includes 30 years' broadly based experience in building contracting, residential land development, and master building trades. Mr. Woodson has been a seminar leader on real estate topics, and is a state of Maine–approved presenter of continuing education materials and programs for licensed real estate professionals. A true expert in real estate, he offers tried-and-tested processes that can help anyone succeed in managing rental properties.

Managing Your Own Rental Property

Managing your own rental property can save you considerable money, but it can also be a burden. Do you have time to manage your own income property? How much experience do you have as a landlord and property manager? Are you willing to give up some of your personal time to work nights and weekends when showing apartments or scheduling repairs and maintenance? Should you manage your own rental property? This is a serious question, and it is not always an easy one to answer. Not everyone is cut out to be a landlord. There is a big difference between owning rental property and managing it. When your rental portfolio starts to grow, management duties can erode your time and patience. Many investors never stop to consider their ability to manage their properties. They look only at the cost of hiring a management firm and decide to attempt self-management, to decrease operating expenses. While these landlords are not spending money for a management firm, they may be losing more money than they are saving.

How much is your time worth? Are you willing to invest an hour in waiting for a prospective tenant who never shows up for your scheduled meeting? Many prospective tenants either don't show up, or they are late. Meanwhile, you are sitting in your car or standing around your income property without making a dime.

Will your people skills allow you to control your tenants without losing them? Property management is not an easy business. It takes special skills and a certain temperament to successfully manage income properties. You have to juggle profits with personalities. Dealing with tenants may be more than you are comfortable with.

You may find that you are an ideal manager and can save thousands of dollars by managing your own property. But, you might discover that you would be much better off hiring a professional management team to do what they do best, so that you can do what you do best.

What Does It Take to Be a Property Manager?

What does it take to be a property manager? Property managers assume many roles and balance numerous tasks, simultaneously. They must be firm, yet flexible. A good manager enjoys working with the public and is not afraid to take control of a situation. Successful managers have a strong background in the laws and principals of property management. Without this knowledge, the manager may wind up in court for violating a tenant's rights. These few examples are only the beginning of what it takes to be a successful property manager.

> ▶ *PRO POINTER*
>
> A professional manager must be willing to work nights and weekends; that is when their customers are available to do business.

The Business Side

The business side of property management can be complicated. Of course, it depends on the type and number of units you are responsible for. Managing a duplex is far easier than managing a major rental complex. Even so, many of the same tactics and principles used for large operations can be applied to small management situations.

Many real estate investors have no idea how difficult it can be to run their own rental property. If you are unprepared, being a landlord may change the way you look at rental property. After a year of bad experiences, you may never want to see another tenant.

Why do investors choose to manage their own properties? For some, the money saved from not paying a management fee is the primary reason. Others don't trust

> ✔ *FAST FACT*
>
> While property management does have its undesirable traits, it does not have to be a discouraging business. With the proper knowledge and the execution of a solid business plan, your rental management endeavors can be quite successful.

outsiders to operate their rental business at maximum efficiency. These investors want to have a hands-on position in the management of their rental portfolio. The possible reasons for wanting to manage rental units are as diverse as the investors who own rental property.

Regardless of your reason for entering the property management field, always treat your rental property as a business. Many investors have full-time jobs and buy income property in their off-hours. While this can be considered a part-time business, it should not be considered a hobby. If you don't treat your income property as a business, you will never see the rewards possible from a successful rental-income business.

When evaluating your ability to manage your own income properties, you must consider your business experience. If you lack the necessary experience, you can learn much from books like this one. The key is to establish your qualifications for the business side of managing rental property. Some investors are incredibly adept at finding and buying lucrative properties, but these same cunning investors can make horrible property managers. There is no shame in being unskilled as a rental manager. The shame is when you are out of your element and drive your otherwise profitable rental business into the ground.

▶ *P R O   P O I N T E R*

Property owners who take a hands-on approach to the management of their properties may be entitled to more tax benefits than property owners who do not participate in the management of their income properties. Talk with your tax specialist for complete details on how your choice of management options may affect your tax status.

▶ *P R O   P O I N T E R*

If you are thinking of becoming a property manager for the property of others on a part-time basis, beware. The working hours can be brutal. Pagers and cell phones can plague you with time-sensitive needs when you manage rental property. Getting your feet wet in professional property management on a part-time schedule can be very difficult to juggle with a full-time job.

The Paper Trail

The paper trail of any business is important. This holds true with property management. Most successful businesses only run smoothly when the proper paperwork is kept up-to- date. There will be lease applications, leases, inspection lists, and a pile of

RENTAL APPLICATION

Name _____

Social security # _____ Home phone _____

Current address _____

How long at present address _____

Landlord's name _____

Landlord's phone _____

Reason for leaving _____

Previous Addresses

Address_____ From_____ to _____

Landlord's name _____ Phone _____

Reason for moving _____

Address_____ From_____ to _____

Landlord's name _____ Phone _____

Reason for moving _____

Address_____ From_____ to _____

Landlord's name _____ Phone _____

Reason for moving _____

Credit References

Name _____ Account # _____

Address _____ Account # _____

Name _____ Account # _____

Address _____ Account # _____

Name _____ Account # _____

Address _____ Account # _____

(continues)

FIGURE 1.1 Rental Application

Name, address, and phone number of nearest relative, not living with you

_____

Name, address, and phone number of personal reference, not related to

you: _ _____

Names of all people planning to reside in your rental unit:

_____

I hereby give my consent for the landlord or property manager for the

property located at _____, to

verify any information on this application. I understand a request for

verification may be sent to any of the names and addresses listed above. I

further understand and consent to a credit report on my credit history

being released to the landlord or property manager.

_____

Prospective Tenant   Date

FIGURE 1.1   Rental Application *(continued)*

other papers involved with every apartment you rent. Are you willing to keep your paperwork in order? If you despise paperwork, becoming a rental manager is not a good idea. When the extensive paperwork required to run your rental business is ignored, you run the risk of losing your rental properties. If you are comfortable with staying on top of the paperwork, you should do fine in this area of property management.

▶ *PRO POINTER*

If you suffer from poor organizational skills and hate keeping up with paperwork, property management probably is not a good field for you. Consider retaining a professional management agency if you are not comfortable keeping precise records.

RENTAL LEASE

This lease is between _____,
landlord and _____, tenant, for a dwelling located at
_____, unit number _____.
Tenant agrees to lease this dwelling for a term of _____,
beginning _____, and ending _____,
for $_____, per _____, payable in advance on the first
day of every calendar _____. Rent shall be paid to _____.

Payments shall be mailed to _____, at
_____.
The first _____ rent for this dwelling is $_____. The
entire sum of this lease is $ _____. The
damage deposit on this dwelling is $ _____ and is
refundable if tenant complies with this lease and leaves the dwelling clean
and undamaged. If tenant intends to move at the end of this lease, tenant
agrees to give landlord notice, in writing, at least thirty days before the
lease expires. A deposit of $ _____ will be required for two
keys. This deposit will be refunded to the tenant when both keys are
returned to the landlord. Landlord will refund all deposits due within ten
days after tenant has vacated the property and returned the keys. Only the
following persons are to live in the above mentioned dwelling:

_____

_____

_____.

(continues)

FIGURE 1.2 Lease

Without landlord's prior written permission, no other persons may live in the dwelling, and no pets shall be admitted to the dwelling, even temporarily. The dwelling may not be sublet or used for business purposes. Use of the following is included in the rent, at tenant's own risk:

_____

_____

_____

_____

_____

_____.

Tenant agrees to the terms set forth in the attached rental policy. This attached rental policy shall be considered a part or this lease and the tenant's signature on this leases indicates his acceptance of all terms and conditions of the rental policy.

Violation of any part of this agreement, or nonpayment of rent, when due, shall be cause for eviction under appropriate sections of the applicable code and law. The landlord reserves the right to seek any legal means to collect monies owed to him. The prevailing party shall recover reasonable attorney's fees incurred to settle disputes. Tenant hereby acknowledges that he has read this agreement, understands the entire agreement, agrees to the entire agreement, and has been given a copy of the agreement.

_____

Landlord   Date

_____

Tenant   Date

FIGURE 1.2 Lease *(continued)*

MOVE-IN CHECKLIST

Please inspect all areas of your rental unit carefully. Note any existing deficiencies on the form below. The information on this form will be used in determining the return of your damage deposit. Please be thorough, and complete all applicable items.

Tenant: _____

Rental unit: _____

Item _____

Location of Defect _____

Walls _____

Floor coverings _____

Ceilings _____

Windows _____

Screens _____

Window treatments _____

Doors _____

Light fixtures _____

Cabinets _____

Countertops _____

Plumbing _____

Heating _____

Air conditioning _____

Electrical _____

(continues)

FIGURE 1.3 Move-in Checklist

Trim work _____

Smoke detectors _____

Light bulbs _____

Appliances _____

Furniture _____

Fireplace _____

Hardware _____

Closets _____

Landscaping _____

Parking area _____

Storage area _____

Other _____

_____

_____

Comments

_____

_____

_____

_____

Inspection completed by: _____

_____

_____

　　　　　　　　　　Tenant　　　　　　　　　　　Date

FIGURE 1.3   Move-in Checklist *(continued)*

Good Marketing

There is an old saying that makes a lot of sense, It goes like this: "You can sell a bad product with good marketing, but you can't sell a good product with bad marketing." There is a lot of truth to this statement.

Most investors never consider themselves as working in the sales and advertising business. But successful investors are creative and accomplished in both of these fields. If your rental units are vacant, you are not receiving income from them. This defeats the purpose of owning income properties. In most places, rental competition can be fierce. If you are not able to put together a good marketing plan, you may fall behind the competition.

This is not to say that you must have a degree in marketing or advertising. What you must have is an awareness of the public's desires and needs. If you know what people want, you can work to meet their desires and enjoy a profitable rental operation. This requires market research and the ability to be flexible. A dry, boring advertisement is not going to attract many desirable tenants. You must learn to put some zip in your ads to entice the type of tenant you want.

> ✔ **FAST FACT**
>
> With the proper advertising, you can target your demographics to obtain the tenants you want.

The skills needed for marketing can be learned by anyone with reasonable intelligence. It will simply be a matter of investing your time and effort to perfect your marketing plan. Advertising can be perfected through test ads. If you are willing to devote time and a little money to advertising and sales techniques, you can reduce your vacancy rate and ride high as a landlord.

The Public

> ✔ **FAST FACT**
>
> Generating calls to fill vacancies is expensive. You cannot afford to discourage prospective tenants, simply because it is inconvenient.

How do you feel about dealing with the public? Some people do not enjoy frequent contact with strangers. If you are one of these people, property management will be a tough business for you. As a property manager, you will be required to deal with people you have never met and may not like. The public can be cruel, especially if you are their complaint department.

When you assume the responsibility of running your own properties, you must also take on the duty of public relations. It may be inconvenient when a tenant calls to see your advertised vacancy, but you must make time to take the call.

If you hate playing politics, being your own property manager will not be fun. You must use tact and diplomacy to keep your buildings running smoothly. There will be times when you must hold your temper with irate tenants. A screaming property manager is rarely in control. As the Captain of your rental ship, you must maintain control and avoid the many obstacles that could sink your boat.

▶ *PRO POINTER*

Turning pro in the property management business is a big decision. Landlords who manage their own properties have more authority and control than property managers who work for landlords. Assess your personality carefully before you throw your hat into the ring of professional property managers.

Computerized Records

Computerized records are about the only way to go in today's business world. Not too many years ago, many people resisted computers, myself included. But now, being computerized is nearly as important has having a telephone. How do you feel about computers? Computers are not mandatory equipment for a successful property manager, but they make the job much easier. If you are running a large number of rental units, computers are almost essential.

Maintenance Matters

Property managers must coordinate and supervise the maintenance of rental properties. Do you know a closet auger from a pipe wrench? A closet auger is used to clear stoppages in toilets. Pipe wrenches are used to assemble and disassemble plumbing pipes and fittings. You don't have to know how to use these tools, but you must know enough about each trade involved in the maintenance of a building to talk intelligently with the providers of services.

If your plumber tells you that your old boiler needs a new domestic coil, it will be helpful to know what the plumber is talking about. Domestic coils provide hot water for home use. If you don't know any better, you could logically think your tenants are cooking and bathing in grungy boiler water. While the domestic coil is in the boiler, the water passing through the coil is potable (drinking) water. My point is that you need a reasonable understanding of the maintenance procedures for the buildings you manage.

Tax Factors

Being your own manager means doing your own bookkeeping or hiring it out to an independent bookkeeper. If you have been spoiled by having a professional management firm keep your records for you, you may be dissatisfied with the requirements you will face as your own manager.

An Attorney

Nearly all property managers need an attorney at one time or another. Legal matters abound in the property management field. It is wise to leave the legal implications of the business to lawyers who specialize in this field of expertise. If you don't have the personality for dealing with legal confrontations, you could find you are in the wrong business. Hiring a good attorney can ease this burden for you. But, you may still find yourself in court more than once.

▶ *PRO POINTER*

It is a good idea to establish a solid relationship with a tax expert before you venture into a property management business. The expert you choose is likely to recommend computer software that will make keeping your tax records easier. Having the right tax professional can have a profound impact on the amount of money you are able to leave in the bank at the end of the year.

Time Management

Time management is critical in making the highest profits in the shortest time possible. Your time is a very valuable asset. To run your business smoothly, you must learn to make the best use of your time. It is easy to get caught up talking with tenants, tradesmen, and the like. If you allow yourself to spend too much time on casual conversation, you lose time that could be producing profits. Poor time-management skills will severely hamper your effectiveness as a property manager.

▶ *PRO POINTER*

As you seek profits from property management, you must be aware that your time is valuable and that wasted time can result in lost profits. Keep a log of your daily activities to establish an overview of how productive your time is. You may not like what you find at the end of two weeks. However if you use the log as a tool and make needed adjustments, you can see higher profits.

Benefits

The benefits of self-management are numerous. Once you learn to run your own rental business, you can make more money. This money will not always come easily, but the opportunity is there. By acting as your own manager, you should retain a minimum of about ten percent of the gross rents that would have been paid to a management firm. In all likelihood, your savings will be even greater.

The job of property manager will take a portion of your time. While some investors will see their time as being too valuable to manage their own properties, others will enjoy the diversion. There are definitely advantages to being your own manager. With a little effort and research, you can become a profitable property manager.

Questions

There are a multitude of questions to ask yourself before committing to a career as a property manager. Whether you plan to manage only your own properties or to go full speed ahead as a property management firm, you must determine if the career path is right for you. Following are some questions to ask yourself:

- Do you enjoy working with people?
- Are you well organized in your daily routines?
- Are you computer literate?
- Do you have maintenance and repair abilities?
- Are you available to take phone calls after business hours?
- Are you willing to work nights?
- Are you willing to work weekends?
- Do you lose your temper easily?
- Are you familiar with the laws of property management?

How many traits are required to be a successful property manager? There is no set number of traits or skills required. Obviously, the more you know and the more you apply to your business requirements, the better off you are likely to be. Very few people possess all of the elements required to be a supreme manager. However, there are ways to compensate for your weaker areas. For example, you can consider hiring an employee for some of the work that you are not as well-qualified for. Retaining professional help, such as lawyers and certified public accountants, is another way to overcome your shortcomings. Ponder these points:

- Do you enjoy doing research work for your ventures?
- Do you want to be a rental manager?
- Are you willing to invest your time in long-term goals?
- Do you possess strong time-management skills?
- Can you separate emotions from business?
- Would you like to save 10% of your gross rental income?
- Do you believe rental management is easy?
- Are you a good negotiator?
- Do you have sales skills?
- Will it be cost effective to manage your rental property?
- Can you be firm without being overbearing?
- Do you believe your rental endeavors are a business?
- Are you meticulous in your paperwork requirements?
- Would you like to learn more about property management?
- Are you excited about being your own manager?

Your mind may be swimming in questions at this point. This is good. The more you think, the more likely you are to come to a viable conclusion. How will you find answers to your questions? Many of the answers will come to you as you do a self-evaluation of your skills, traits, and personality. More questions will be answered as you read the chapters that follow. The key is to arm yourself with as much information as possible to make a wise decision before committing to a lifestyle change.

Managing Someone Else's Rental Property

Managing someone else's rental property may require special licensing in your community. This is certainly something to check on before putting an ad in the paper offering your services as a professional property manager. Rules and laws vary from location to location. Your local licensing board should be able to tell you if a special license is required for operating a professional property management firm.

Can you make a living as a property manager? Many people do, and some of them earn very comfortable livings. Where you live can have a lot to do with your income potential. People who live in rural farmland are not as likely to live full time from their earnings as a property manager when compared to those who live in heavily populated urban areas.

Open your local phone book and look in the advertising section under the classification of "Real Estate" and "Property Management". How many ads do you see? This will give you some idea of the competition you will be facing.

✔ **FAST FACT**

Many real estate brokerages have their own property management divisions. This is a common practice throughout the country. These competitors have an edge. If a person has moved out of a home and has the home on the market for sale, it is reasonable to assume that the listing brokerage has an edge in getting the rental management of the property if it does not sell in a timely manner.

What Type of Management Will You Offer?

What type of management will you offer potential clients? Your answer to this question will help to establish your path to prosperity. I always like to make a plan and then work the plan. Without the proper planning, your odds of success suffer.

Management Options

- Are you willing to manage commercial properties?
- Should you stick to residential rental units. If so, should you limit the size of the buildings that you are willing to look after?
- How do you feel about managing mixed-use buildings? These are typically buildings that have commercial space on the ground level and residential rentals on subsequent floors above the commercial space.
- Have you considered managing private communities?
- Do you want to manager community association properties?

Commercial Properties

Managing commercial properties can be extremely lucrative. There is a reason for this. The work is demanding, the skills needed are numerous, and the pressure can be extreme. Without a long and successful track record as a commercial manager, getting properties to manage will be very difficult.

▶ *PRO POINTER*

Large companies and developers who retain commercial property mangers seek out seasoned professionals. If your goal is to manage commercial properties of large sizes, consider taking a job at a firm that does this type of management to learn the ropes. Jumping into this arena on your own as a rookie is likely to spell financial disaster.

Residential Rental Properties

Residential rental properties are a great place to begin your career as a property manager. If you are seeking the "Earn-While-You-Learn" plan, this is the safest place to find it. From single-family homes to apartment buildings, the residential route is easier and more assessable to inexperienced property managers.

Mixed Use

Mixed use buildings combine residential and commercial management in one building. This can be okay for learning managers. For example, if you take on a building that has a restaurant on the ground floor and three apartments on the second floor, you will probably do all right. Personally, I prefer residential management over commercial management, but there is better money in commercial management and a mixed-use building can be a good opportunity to cut your teeth on.

Private Communities

Private communities have many nuances.

My father used to manager a private lake community. The organization had its own maintenance department, its own police department, and many other elements of a small town. City managers have their hands full. I have known a number of people in urban management, and most of them didn't follow that career path to its end. The pressure and time demands are intense. You will likely need the appropriate education and track record to have any shot at this type of management.

Community Associations

Community associations can be similar to private communities. Size matters when it comes to this type of management. You may be charged with managing thirty condos or fifty townhouses. This is manageable. However, if you get into large community associations, like some that I have been involved with in Virginia, you are essentially running a miniature city.

Think about some of the elements that you will be responsible for managing and maintaining if you take on a community association of moderate size. Let me throw out just some of what you will be likely to deal with, depending on the geographical location.

- Road repairs
- Snow removal
- Grass cutting and landscaping
- Waking trails
- Tennis courts
- Swimming pools
- Parking lots
- Fences
- Irrigation
- Insect control
- Pest control
- General building maintenance and repair
- Tree removal
- Trash removal
- Water and sewer service maintenance

There is a long list of potential responsibilities associated with private communities. If you choose to explore this endeavor, talk with the powers at be and establish clearly what you will be responsible for. Then, make very sure that you are up to the task.

The Law

There are numerous laws affecting the management of rental properties. The laws vary from state to state and may be based on the number of rental units you manage. As a property manager, you must develop a working knowledge of these laws. You don't have to earn a law degree, but you must learn enough of the law to stay out of trouble. Start by establishing a working relationship with a solid attorney who specializes in real estate law.

There are several ways you can tutor yourself in real estate and rental management laws. But, there is no substitute for having proper legal representation. You can read books to gain insight into the laws. You could consult with an attorney to create a checklist of rights and wrongs when it comes to property management. Seminars are another way to enrich your legal knowledge on matters that pertain to your rental

business. In addition to all these ways, you
could attend part-time courses in a local
college to sharpen your skills in acceptable
property management practices.

The more you educate yourself in the
legal aspects of property management, the
fewer problems you will have down the
road.

✔ FAST FACT

As a professional property manager, you should have all of your
legal agreements prepared by a
practicing attorney.

Generic Agreements

If you have ever looked at generic rental agreements, the type available in stores, you
might have noticed they are not all inclusive. These form documents leave much to
be desired in protecting you and your property owners from bad tenants. Many landlords use these form agreements as a template to create their own lease or rental
agreement. Unless you have an attorney review and approve your homemade document, you may be in violation of the law. It is not uncommon for states to prohibit the
average person from drafting a contract agreement. Even licensed brokers are very
restricted in what they may draft into an agreement, without the review and approval
of an attorney. As a professional property manager, you should have all of your legal
agreements prepared by a practicing attorney.

Discrimination

Discrimination is a major consideration in the legal ramifications of property management. There are many types of discrimination that you may be guilty of if you don't
know the law. Some types of discrimination may never be considered by you to be
discrimination, until you are charged with it. By this time it's too late, and you are
headed for court.

Take the time to obtain the necessary
posters to display in your office. When you
open a business, there are a host of posters
required to be displayed in your place of
business. Many of these posters are available from the United States Department of
Labor. They are free of charge, but

▶ PRO POINTER

You can expect to post about one
dozen different posters to comply
with legal requirements. Your
lawyer can also assist you with
this phase of your business.

required to be posted. Financial fines for failing to display these posters can be significant, so don't overlook these requirements. What the Department of Labor does not supply can be obtained from your local state agencies. You can expect to post about one dozen different posters to comply with legal requirements. Your lawyer can also assist you with this phase of your business.

Eviction

Eviction is an ever-present consideration in any rental business. For the unsuspecting landlord, eviction can be one of the worst nightmares ever experienced in managing rental property. If you do not follow the proper steps in an eviction process, the tenant may have grounds to sue you. There are people who have become professionals at using the court systems to live in an apartment, rent-free, for months. If

---

FINAL NOTICE TO VACATE

Be advised, this is your final notice to vacate these premises. All of my attempts to resolve your breech of our lease have gone unanswered. You have five days to vacate this property. If you have not delivered the property to me within five days, eviction proceedings will be started. Eviction is not an enjoyable experience for anyone. I am giving you this final notice to allow you the opportunity to leave these premises under your own power. If you fail to vacate, I will take all actions available to have you removed from the property.

Date: _____

Time: _____

_____

Landlord

FIGURE 2.1   Final Notice to Vacate

you consider that it could take four to six months to get a non-paying tenant out of a building, you will see how expensive eviction can become. Add to this expense a violation of the tenant's rights and you may lose much more.

Deposits

Deposits made by tenants are another area where there is always a risk of trouble. Do you need a separate escrow account for each tenant's rental deposit? Can you put

▶ *PRO POINTER*

Different states have different laws on the process of eviction. Don't wait until you have a bad tenant to remove to find out how the eviction laws in your state work. Talk with your attorney before you open your business to establish the best procedures and protection to use in avoiding evictions and perfecting them when necessary.

SAMPLE OF SECURITY DEPOSIT RECEIPT

Landlord hereby acknowledges the receipt of a security/damage deposit from the tenant in the amount of $_____. This deposit will remain in an escrow account during the term of the lease/rental agreement. Landlord has the right to apply this deposit to the costs incurred to offset any damages or financial responsibilities incurred, due to the tenant's lack of performance as agreed upon in the lease/rental agreement dated _____, between the landlord and tenant. If the tenant complies with the lease/rental agreement and does not cause damage to the landlord's property, this deposit will be returned to the tenant within 48 hours of the tenant's vacating the property. If the terms of the lease/rental agreement are breached by the tenant, or if the tenant causes damage to the landlord's property, the landlord may retain any portion of this deposit necessary to compensate the landlord for financial burdens caused by the tenant.

FIGURE 2.2   Sample of Security Deposit Receipt

all of the rental deposits into one escrow account? Do you need an escrow account, or can you commingle the deposits with your personal funds? Before you start taking people's money, you had better know what to do with it.

Your local jurisdiction probably has rules and laws that pertain to escrow accounts. Check with your attorney to be sure that you comply with all local requirements.

It is never wise to commingle deposits with your personal funds. Other questions may arise around deposits. Here are some of them to consider:

- When are you required to return the deposit to a departing tenant?
- Is there a time limit in which you must return the deposit or notify the tenant of your intent and reason for retaining the deposit?
- What events allow you to legally retain the deposit?
- How are your arrangements with your clients when it comes to dealing with deposits?
- Will tenant earn interest on their deposit money while you are holding it in escrow?
- How much of a deposit are you allowed by law to collect?
- Can the deposit be applied to unpaid rent?

These are simple questions, but many investors and some property managers don't know how to answer them. The law is filled with facts every landlord and property manager should know and work with. If you violate the law long enough, there will come a time when it catches up with you. Ignorance of the law is no defense. It is your responsibility as a business person to know and obey the laws governing your business.

Insurance

As with any other business, your rental business will require various forms of insurance to operate safely. When you act as a property manager, the responsibility for insurance coverage is up to you. Although your state or local jurisdiction may have minimum insurance requirements that you must meet. Depending on the size and type of your operation, there are several types of insurance that may be needed. Liability insurance is always needed. Worker's compensation insurance will be required if you have employees who are not close relatives who waive their right of coverage.

Fire insurance certainly should be considered mandatory if you own the property that you are managing. The list for possible types of insurance is long and we will address them in depth as we move into later chapters.

When you are running properties that you own, your tenants may be required to carry insurance, but it is your responsibility to request proof of their insurance. For example, if you require all tenants with water beds to provide insurance to protect your property in the event of an accident with the bed, you should have a copy of their insurance on file. Simply stating such a requirement in your lease is not enough, if disaster strikes. You may have a legal case against the tenant in such circumstances, but the odds of the tenant having enough money to repair the damage are not good. When managing the properties of others, you will likely be responsible for staying on top of the same type of proof of insurance.

Organization

All businesses run better and more profitably with optimum organization. Whether you have a battered, two-drawer filing cabinet or a high-tech computer, the key is having your business organized. If you don't already possess good organizational skills, set a goal to improve your habits. There is extensive paperwork and record-keeping involved with property management.

> ✔ **FAST FACT**
>
> Good organization and time management go together well to make you a more profitable investor, landlord, or property manager. When you harness the power of effective time management, you can make more money, without working any harder. The key is working smarter with an organized environment and concise time management.

Being well organized will not only make your day-to-day activities more fruitful, it will make surviving a tax audit much easier. Having all of your records in good standing will be handy if your clients want you to account for your time and expenses.

Market Research

Market research may be one of the most commonly overlooked factors than can increase any landlord's income. If you are working as a professional property manager, your client is likely to expect you to take care of the market research. How do you decide how much to charge for rental units? When you buy a building or sign it up for management purposes, do you assess the market demand for its apartments? If you are not delving into extensive market research, you may be missing big profits.

Market research can determine the type of rental business you will develop and how it will run. If you have a building comprised of all one-bedroom apartments, you can expect a high turn-over of tenants. If you want a high turn-over, to allow for more rapid rent increases, this is fine. If you want stable tenants, with less time spent preparing, showing, and renting vacant apartments, the building with all one-bedroom apartments is not such a good deal. This is only one example of how effective market research can steer your business.

Market research can also tell you how much the public is willing to pay for rental units. If the surrounding, comparable properties are demanding high rents, the building you are working with should be able to produce high rents. If you are contemplating an increase in rental amounts, market research can tell you how high you can raise the rent, without losing tenants. With the power you can gain from thorough market research, you cannot afford to ignore it.

Pricing

Setting a price for rentals is a matter to be taken seriously. If you set the price too high, you will have an empty building. If you pick a price that is too low, the profits on the building will suffer. Finding the right price is easy when you rely on accurate findings from market research.

▶ **PRO POINTER**

Setting a price for rentals is a matter to be taken seriously. If you set the price too high, you will have an empty building. If you pick a price that is too low, the profits on the building will suffer. Finding the right price is easy when you rely on accurate findings from market research.

When it is time to set rental figures, don't just pick numbers out of the air. Too many investors determine their desired rental amounts by looking at profit projections on a spreadsheet. Of course, the goal is to make money, but the amount of money made will often be dictated by current market conditions. Just because you want to see a net gain of $3,000.00 each month, you may have to settle for $2,500.00. You can set your rental rate at any amount when you are renting your own income property, but if you don't have tenants, you will not show a profit. When you are managing property for clients, picking the wrong pricing points can put you out of business quickly. In either case, your numbers have to be realistic and profitable if you want to keep doing what you are doing.

Market conditions play a key role in the decision on how much rent is too much. If the market is flooded with vacant apartments, you can expect lower rents if you want to maintain a full tenancy. When the demand for housing exceeds the supply, you can cash in with higher rents.

✔ *FAST FACT*

To survive through the real estate cycles, you must monitor, project, and adapt to the ever-changing market conditions.

Marketing

Without effective marketing, you cannot maximize rental income. You may get by with dry classified advertising, but a well written ad will pull a higher number of quality tenants. Your marketing will set the trend for the type of tenants you attract. With targeted marketing you can aim your advertising dollars at a selected audience.

Creative marketing allows you to prosper, while other investors flounder. If you unleash your imagination, you can create a situation where you have more prospective tenants than empty apartments. This can hold true even in poor economic times. The market research we discussed earlier will be a factor in your marketing. With adequate research and a winning plan, you can alleviate the worries of vacancies.

	MARKETING MEMOS			
Ad Number	Ad Placed In	Calls Received	Number Of Showings	Number Of Leases Signed

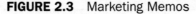

FIGURE 2.3 Marketing Memos

PHONE CHECKLIST FOR PROSPECTIVE TENANTS

1. How many bedrooms do you need   _____

2. Do you prefer a ground-level unit?   _____

3. How many people will occupy the property?   _____

4. Do you have pets?   _____

5. How much parking space do you require?   _____

6. Do you work in this area?   _____

7. Do you require laundry facilities?   _____

8. Are you new to the area?   _____

9. Do you have a water bed?   _____

10. Do you work in this area?   _____

11. When would you like to see the property?   _____

12. Will your spouse be attending the showing?   _____

13. Have you seen the exterior of the property?   _____

14. May I have your name and phone number?   _____

15. Do you have any other questions?   _____

Comments

_____

_____

_____

_____

_____

_____

FIGURE 2.4   Phone Checklist for Prospective Tenants

Phone Work

How you handle your telephone work can have a dramatic effect on the success of your marketing. Advertising expenses and vacant apartments put a strain on cash flow. When the phone rings with a prospective tenant on the other end, you must make the most of the call. Your phone behavior may alienate the prospect and result in wasted time and advertising money. If you don't capitalize on each acceptable tenant, you are throwing your advertising dollars away.

When prospective tenants call, they will have questions for you to answer. To pre-qualify tenants, you should have some questions of your own to ask of the tenants. When you are able to pre-qualify prospective tenants in the initial phone call, you save hours of wasted time. The time saved can be invested in making new deals or in recreation. In either case, it makes sense to eliminate undesirable tenants as quickly as possible.

By creating a checklist, you will have all of your questions at hand when a tenant calls. The checklist will ensure that you don't forget to ask key questions. While the checklist adds to your paperwork, the benefits outweigh the time spent on the checklist. Phone tactics may not seem important, but they are.

✔ *FAST FACT*

If you learn how to screen tenants on the phone, you will have more time to devote to other aspects of your rental business. Phone manners and methods are important steps in running a profitable rental business.

Showing Property

When the time comes to show rental units to new tenants, you must assume the role of a salesman. As real estate brokers say, "There is a difference between showing real estate and selling it." This rule holds true in renting apartments. If you don't preach the features and benefits of a property, the tenant may move on to the building down the street. The first person to use effective sales tactics will secure the tenant.

▶ *PRO POINTER*

Sales tactics vary with different types of property. For example, you might pitch the large, family-oriented lawn when you are showing a single-family home. In an apartment building, you might pitch the onsite gym, the swimming pool, and so forth. When showing a commercial space for a small store, you would talk about traffic counts and visibility. Adapt to what you are showing.

There are many books available that can help you to take on a sales attitude. You do not have to use high-pressure tactics or demean your character to be a good salesman. The most important part of any sale is gaining the customer's confidence. If you present a trusting image, your customer is very likely to do business with you.

The telephone checklist mentioned earlier will come into play with your sales maneuvers. People like to be called by their names. If you recorded the prospect's name on the phone checklist, you will be able to address the prospective tenant or client by name when showing a property or discussing your services. The background information you gathered on the telephone will serve to break the ice. This information gives you a known area to open a conversation around.

How you dress and what you drive will have a mental affect on your prospective tenants. If they are wearing jeans and driving a sub-compact car, your luxury car and silk suit may intimidate or degrade them. It is important to match your appearance and presentation to the level of the person you are dealing with. No one likes to feel that they are of a lower class than the person they are dealing with. If you allow tenants to feel as though they are on equal ground with you, your sales efforts will be much more effective.

If you can develop sales skills, you will be well on your way to becoming an envied landlord or property manager. Other investors will struggle to fill their vacancies while you make it look easy. As you have gathered by now, you must wear many hats to be a successful property manager. All of these tasks require different business principals and practices, but they are what separates the winners from the losers.

Applications

Rental applications can save you months of grief. The information contained in a rental application is invaluable when screening tenants. With the proper wording, you will be authorized to check the prospective tenant's credit rating and references. You can subscribe to credit reporting agencies to obtain important financial information on prospective tenants. If a tenant passes muster on these two points, it doesn't guarantee a good tenant, but it improves your odds.

Some investors don't believe in using these helpful forms. They meet with people and decide if they will make good tenants based on a gut reaction. Regardless of the extent you investigate a tenant, it is always a risk that you will get a bad one. With the expense of removing a problem tenant, anything you can do to reduce your risks is worthwhile. Rental applications can save you from months of lost income and legal fees. As a part of your business practice, you should incorporate the use of a rental application into every apartment you rent. This is especially important if you are offering professional property management services.

Screening

Getting a bad tenant is worse than not getting a tenant at all. As part of your business duties, you must carefully screen each prospective tenant before making a commitment to them. This requires putting on yet another hat. All of a sudden, you must play detective. Unfortunately, bad tenants are not ashamed to lie to you. If you take the information on a rental application at face value, the purpose of the application is defeated.

There are people in this world who have learned to have a free place to live off unsuspecting landlords. These professional deadbeats are hard to distinguish on looks alone. If they were not good at fooling people, they wouldn't be able to get by for so long on so little. You must make a hard rule in your business play book to carefully screen all prospective tenants before entering into an agreement with them.

If you hope to be a good property manager, you cannot be bashful. You must dig deep into people's backgrounds and personal lives to ensure that they will make good tenants. If you get squeamish at the thought of asking someone how much money they make, you had better hire a professional management firm for your properties and stay out of the business.

RENTAL AGREEMENT

This rental agreement, dated _____, is between
_____, tenant, and_____,
landlord, for the rental unit located at _____.
Under this agreement, the tenant agrees to rent the above-mentioned
dwelling on a month-to-month basis, with a monthly rental amount of
$_____.
The monthly rent will be due and payable on the first day of each month,
starting on the first day of _____, 20_____. A damage
deposit is required at the signing of this rental agreement. The deposit will
placed in an escrow account. The amount of this deposit shall be
$_____,
If the rental unit is returned to the landlord in a clean and good condition,
this deposit will be refunded to the tenant within _____ days of
vacating the property. An additional deposit of $_____, will be
required when keys are issued to the tenant. This deposit will also be
placed in escrow and returned to the tenant within _____ days from
the date the tenant returns said keys to landlord. Tenant or landlord may
terminate this agreement with a 30-day written notice to the other party.
The attached rental policy shall be made a part of this agreement and shall
be binding on all parties.

Tenant acknowledges reading and understanding this agreement and the
rental policy that is a part of this agreement. Tenant's signature below
indicates acceptance of all terms and conditions of this rental agreement
and the rental policy.

_____   _____

Landlord   Date   Tenant   Date

FIGURE 2.5   Rental Agreement

Agreements

Whether you use a rental agreement or a lease, you should have all terms of your agreement with a tenant in writing and signed by all parties. Oral agreements are legal, but they are largely unenforceable. If you are forced into going to court, only your written documents will be of value. When a judge is deciding your case, most of the decision will be based on hard evidence. Your written agreement will substantiate your position and serve as hard evidence. This additional paperwork may take a little extra time, but it should be a rule you live by.

Addendums

Most experienced landlords and property mangers have come to recognize the value of a written lease, but many still leave themselves open by not requiring written addendum agreements. Anytime there is a change in the terms of an original lease, you should require a written addendum to identify the changes. Without these addendums, you may be helpless in court.

For example, let's say that you rented a unit to a single man. He gets married and his bride has a dog. You allow the bride and the dog to move into the rental unit, without a written addendum changing the terms of the original lease. During their stay, the couple's dog destroys the apartment. Since the man didn't have a dog when he rented the apartment, the lease did not address his responsibility in regards to pet damages. Further, the dog doesn't belong to him. It belongs to the wife, who is not even on the original lease. Where does this leave you or your client who you are managing the property for? It leaves you in a situation where long litigation and a questionable outcome of a court case controls your financial destiny.

You can avoid this type of situation with addendum agreements. If you had required an addendum that changed the terms of the original lease when the woman and dog were allowed to move in, you would have grounds to defend your legal actions against the couple. In the above example, your position is weakened by the lack of an addendum. As a strong business owner, you must stay up to date on your paperwork.

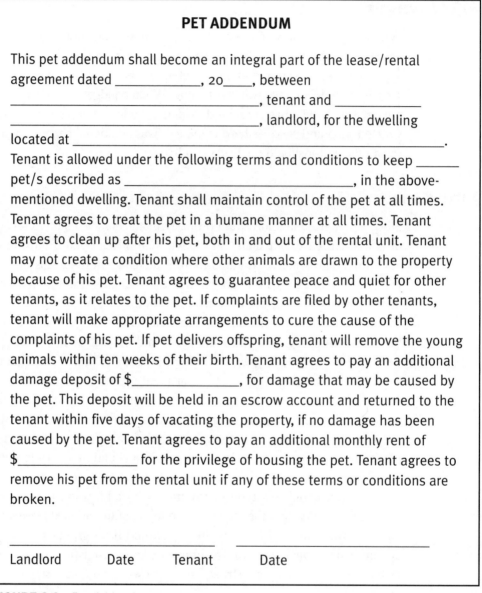

PET ADDENDUM

This pet addendum shall become an integral part of the lease/rental agreement dated _____, 20____, between _____, tenant and _____ _____, landlord, for the dwelling located at _____.
Tenant is allowed under the following terms and conditions to keep _____ pet/s described as _____, in the above-mentioned dwelling. Tenant shall maintain control of the pet at all times. Tenant agrees to treat the pet in a humane manner at all times. Tenant agrees to clean up after his pet, both in and out of the rental unit. Tenant may not create a condition where other animals are drawn to the property because of his pet. Tenant agrees to guarantee peace and quiet for other tenants, as it relates to the pet. If complaints are filed by other tenants, tenant will make appropriate arrangements to cure the cause of the complaints of his pet. If pet delivers offspring, tenant will remove the young animals within ten weeks of their birth. Tenant agrees to pay an additional damage deposit of $_____, for damage that may be caused by the pet. This deposit will be held in an escrow account and returned to the tenant within five days of vacating the property, if no damage has been caused by the pet. Tenant agrees to pay an additional monthly rent of $_____ for the privilege of housing the pet. Tenant agrees to remove his pet from the rental unit if any of these terms or conditions are broken.

_____   _____
Landlord   Date   Tenant   Date

FIGURE 2.6   Pet Addendum

RENTAL ADDENDUM

This rental addendum shall become an integral part of the lease/rental agreement dated _____, between the landlord, _____, and the tenant, _____, for the real estate commonly known as _____. The undersigned parties hereby agree to the following:

_____

_____

_____

_____   _____

Landlord   Date   Tenant   Date

FIGURE 2.7   Rental Addendum

CO-SIGNER ADDENDUM

Addendum to rental agreement/lease dated:_____, between _____ and _____. This addendum shall become an integral part of the above- mentioned agreement for the rental unit located at _____. The undersigned has read and understands the above-mentioned document and agrees to abide by the agreement in the capacity of a co-signer. In affixing his signature below, the co-signer may be held accountable for all terms and conditions of the rental agreement/lease described above.

_____

Co-Signer   Date

FIGURE 2.8   Co-Signer Addendum

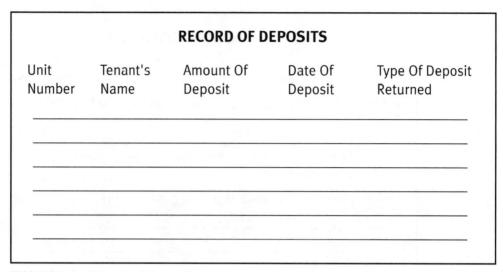

FIGURE 2.9 Record of Deposits

Deposits and Escrow Accounts

Handling other people's money is always serious business. When it comes to security deposits and escrow accounts, you must act in a professional manner. This is true of managing your own properties or

the properties of others. If you approach this responsibility in a haphazard manner, you could wind up in deep trouble. Before you begin taking deposits, consult with an attorney to establish the requirements of the law in your area. There is a good chance you will be required to maintain an escrow account for the keeping of deposits.

Checklists

Move-in checklists are one way of protecting the property you are offering for rent. If you have each new tenant complete and sign a move-in list, you have an established record of the condition the property was in when the tenant took occupancy. This simple little form can save the day when a dispute arises over a damage deposit. If you don't have a move-in list on file, you may be hard pressed to prove a tenant has done damage to your property when you complete a move-out checklist. I know it means more paperwork, but the property management business runs on precise paperwork.

MOVE-OUT CHECKLIST

Tenant: _____

Rental unit: _____

Item	**Location of Defect**
Walls	_____
Floor coverings	_____
Ceilings	_____
Windows	_____
Screens	_____
Window treatments	_____
Doors	_____
Light fixtures	_____
Cabinets	_____
Countertops	_____
Plumbing	_____
Heating	_____
Air conditioning	_____
Electrical	_____
Trim work	_____
Smoke detectors	_____
Light bulbs	_____
Appliances	_____
Furniture	_____
Fireplace	_____
Hardware	_____
Closets	_____
Landscaping	_____
Parking area	_____
Storage area	_____
Other	_____

Comments _____

Inspection completed by: _____

_____
Landlord   Date

FIGURE 2.10   Move-Out Checklist

Supervision

Tenants require supervision. You cannot move tenants into your property and forget about them. Even if the tenant is paying the rent regularly, you should arrange to visit the rental unit at least twice a year. When you have a lease prepared, it should contain language allowing you access to the apartment at anytime, with reasonable notice to the tenant.

By monitoring tenants, you solve two potential problems at the same time. You are able to keep an eye on how the tenant is treating the property. If negligent

---

NOTICE
INTENT TO ACCESS YOUR RENTAL UNIT

Be advised, your landlord requires access to your rental unit on

_____, at _____ a.m./p.m. As stipulated in

your lease, this notice is your formal notification of the landlord's intent to

enter your dwelling. If you wish to be present during this access, you are

welcome. If you would like to attempt to arrange a more convenient time

for the entry, please contact your landlord by calling _____.

In the event you are unable to be available for this access, your landlord

will be present during the time your rental unit is open. In addition to this

notice, an additional notice has been mailed to your address. Thank you for

your cooperation.

Date_____

Time_____am./p.m.

Notice posted by_____

FIGURE 2.11   Notice of Intent To Access Your Rental Unit

damage is occurring, you can catch and correct it early. In addition, you can maintain good tenant relations at the same time. By showing an interest in the tenant's living conditions, the tenant should be more respectful of you and the property that you are responsible for. This is a procedure that provides multiple benefits and doesn't cost any more than a little of your time.

Property Maintenance

Rental property requires routine maintenance. Without regular maintenance, the property and its equipment will lose value and cost more money to repair. This is an area where many professional management firms charge additional fees. If they must arrange and oversee repairs, they often charge a percentage of the cost of the repair for their services. As a self-manager, you avoid paying these extra fees, but you must invest your time in the job. If you are handy, you may be able to complete many of the routine maintenance duties personally. When you perform the work yourself, you save even more money. If you offer these services as a professional manager,

✔ **F A S T F A C T**

Depending upon the value of your time and your ability, you may do well to learn to perform your own maintenance duties. Many of the routine maintenance calls are simple and do not require extensive tools. If you learn to be your own handyman, your bank account can build to a tidy sum.

MAINTENANCE EXPENSE LOG

Unit Number	Building Address	Date Of Expense	Nature Of Expense	Amount Of Expense

FIGURE 2.12   Maintenance Expense Log

remember to build in some income to compensate you for your time in working with the people arranged to do the maintenance.

Whether you plan to do the work or just oversee it, you should know something about what's going on. If you have no knowledge in the area of property and equipment repairs, you are a potential victim to unsavory contractors. If you take the time to learn the basics or maintenance and repairs, you can keep your contractors honest. There are many fine books available to help you develop a working knowledge and vocabulary on these subjects.

Collecting Rent

Collecting rent is one duty many investors hate, and there are plenty of property managers who don't look forward to knocking on doors for a rent check. They want the

---

FRIENDLY REMINDER

I wanted to take this opportunity to remind you that your rent for

_____, 20_____ is past due. I trust this is the result of

an oversight. If you have already mailed your rent, please disregard this

notice. If you have not mailed your rent, please do so immediately. If your

rent has not been received by _____, 20_____, you will be

assessed a late charge, as allowed by your lease. I don't wish to charge

you for being late, but the late-fee policy must be enforced on all tenants

to be effective. Thank you for your prompt attention to this matter. If for

some reason you are unable to pay your rent, please call me to discuss

your circumstances. I can be reached from _____a.m. to _____p.m. by

calling _____.

Date_____

_____

Landlord

FIGURE 2.13   Friendly Reminder

PAST-DUE RENT NOTICE

Please take notice, your rent, that was due on _____, 20_____, is
past due. Unfortunately, you will be assessed a late charge for allowing
your rent to become delinquent. If you have already mailed your rent,
please disregard this notice. If you have not mailed your rent payment, this
is your formal, and final, notice of your past-due rent. If your rent is not
received within the next 48 hours, collection and eviction actions will be
taken. If you are having trouble paying your rent, I will be happy to talk
with you to see if we can come to amicable terms. If you dispute this
notice, I will gladly meet with you to discuss the circumstances. If you do
not pay your rent or contact me within the next 48 hours, you will be
notified by the appropriate legal channels of the upcoming proceedings. I
can be reached between _____a.m. and _____p.m. at

_____.

Date:_____

Time:_____

_____
Landlord   Date

FIGURE 2.14 Past Due Rent Notice

money, but they don't want to go get it. There are times when a property manager
must aggressively seek the rent payment. With good tenants, rent collection is as
simple as checking the morning mail, but not all tenants pay their rent on time.

I have seen countless investors put off rent collections for months, just to avoid
contact with their tenants. When tenants are not paying rent, you cannot afford to
wait. If you are forced to take legal action, the collection process can take long enough
by itself. When you procrastinate on initiating the collection procedure, you are only
worsening the situation. Follow the terms of your agreement with the tenant and stay
within the law, but get your rent on time, or get rid of the tenant.

NOTICE TO PAY RENT OR QUIT

To _____, tenant in possession:

  You are hereby notified that the rent is now due and payable on the premises now held and occupied by you, being those premises situated in the city of _____, county of _____, state of _____.

Commonly known as _____ .

  Your account is delinquent in the amount of $ _____, being the rent for the period from _____ to _____.

  You are required to pay said rent, in full, within _____ days. If rent is not paid, you must vacate and deliver the above-mentioned premises, or legal proceedings will be instituted against you to recover possession of said premises, to declare the forfeiture of the lease or rental agreement under which you occupy said premises and to recover rents and damages, together with all fees allowed by the lease or rental agreement in effect.

Dated this _____ day of _____, 20_____.

_____

Landlord

PROOF OF SERVICE

I, the undersigned, being of legal age, declare under penalty of perjury that I served the notice to pay rent or quit, of which this is a true copy, on the above-mentioned tenant in possession in the manner indicated below:

On _____, 20_____, I served this notice in the following manner:

_____

Executed on _____, 20_____, at _____.

By: _____

Title: _____

FIGURE 2.15   Notice To Pay Rent Or Quit

This job seems to be hardest for landlords who become too friendly with their tenants. It is alright to be cordial to your tenants, but don't become best buddies. Trying to collect rent from a distressed friend is a tough job for anyone. Evicting a close friend is even harder. Keep your relationship with your tenants on a business level. This is somewhat easier to do as a professional manger than it is as a property owner who self manages a building.

Expenses

As you move along in your property management business, you will have to take control of operating expenses. Annual maintenance is just one example of operating

---

ANNUAL MAINTENANCE REMINDER

Item_____

Date for Attention _____Completed_____

Clean heating system _____
Clean Chimney _____
Service heating system _____
Clean air conditioning unit _____
Service air conditioning unit _____
Inspect water heater _____
Inspect toilet tanks _____
Inspect faucets _____
Inspect caulking at fixtures _____
Inspect attic _____
Inspect basement/crawlspace _____
Inspect safety equipment _____
Inspect parking area _____
Inspect lighting _____
Inspect for fire hazards _____
Inspect porches _____
Interview tenants _____

FIGURE 2.16 Annual Maintenance Reminder

expenses. These expenses are what stand between you and your net profit. If the operating expenses for your property or management business are excessive, your net income will be minimized. As the chief bean counter, the job of balancing your budget is all yours. When using a professional management team, you could yell and scream at the manager for his poor handling of operating expenses. When you are your own manager, there is nobody to get upset with, except yourself. And when you are the professional manager, you are the poor, unfortunate one that property owners will be yelling at when profits are down.

▶ *PRO POINTER*

Fine tuning the cost of operating your business is a goal you should set early. Create a working budget and track your expenses on a monthly basis. If you follow your operating expenses closely, you will notice abrupt changes in time to do something about them. If you wait until tax time, it will be too late to make adjustments for the past year.µ

Keeping Records

Keeping financial records is an area of business that you may wish to hire out to an independent firm. Unless you are good with numbers, keeping the books for multiple rental properties can be distracting. To do this job right, you must be alert and avoid mistakes. If you are not an experienced bookkeeper, it may pay to have someone else to the job for you. Before hiring an employee to do the job, investigate the many independents specializing in bookkeeping. While subcontractors may appear to cost more than an hourly employee, when you factor in all the expenses of an employee, subcontractors are often less expensive.

When you don't want to share your financial information with anyone else, you can do the books yourself. A computer, with the right software, will make a huge difference in the time you spend keeping good records. With today's software, you can get by with a limited knowledge of accounting principals. If you plan to keep your books manually, spend the necessary time to learn the proper procedures. Mistakes in your bookkeeping can be costly at tax time.

Operating Capital

It will be up to you to determine how much operating capital is needed to run each of your buildings or your management business. Making this decision will require the

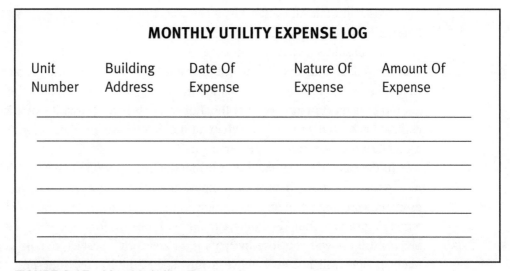

FIGURE 2.17   Monthly Utility Expense Log

evaluation of many factors. If you have owned a building for awhile, you can pull from historical facts. By examining the past performance of the property, you can get a good idea of your future needs. If you are embarking on a new building, historical data may not be as accurate. The previous owner may not have kept accurate records and may not have run the building the way that you will.

If you are just going into business for yourself as a property manager, you will have little, if any, known data to work with. Most of your budget will have to be created using estimates. There is risk here. When you are projecting your needs, estimate on the high side to avoid losses during the year.

Employees

As your rental business grows, you may develop a need for employees. You might desire a secretary or a part-time maintenance worker. Before you hire any employees, you must determine how much they will cost you and how much they are worth to you. This is not always as easy as it sounds.

When you look at how much an employee costs you, you must look at much more than their hourly wage. You will be responsible for tax payments and other employee-related expenses. In most situations, you will be required to carry worker's compensation insurance on your employees. There is also the expense of employee benefits. If you pay your employees for holidays, vacation time, or even lunch breaks, these costs add up. All of these expenses must be added to the employees' earnings to establish their true cost.

As a business owner, you must assess these expenses and determine if they are warranted. It is difficult to know just how much an employee is worth to you in many circumstances. With your maintenance worker, figuring the worth of the employee is not too difficult. You look at what the individual does and what it would cost to hire a contractor to do the same job. When all the factors are accounted for, you can draw a conclusion to the value of the employee.

In the case of a secretary, your evaluation may not be as clear cut. The duties of a secretary are much harder to compare than those of a maintenance worker. For example, you could hire an answering service to answer your phones. The cost of an answering service should be only a fraction of the cost for a secretary. However, how much business will you lose by having an answering service handle your phones? Many people will not even leave a message if they know they are talking to an answering service. In addition, it is unlikely that the service will be prepared to answer a caller's questions. Properly trained, your secretary may be very competent at expanding your business through phone contact.

The questions pertaining to employees have plagued business owners for years. The complexity of the questions often seem to have no answer. As the owner of the business, you will have to make the decision on if and when to hire employees.

Subcontractors

For some businesses, subcontractors solve the employee dilemma. In the case of a maintenance worker, you may be far better off to hire independent contractors to do your maintenance and repair work. You will pay more per job for their work, but you will only pay them when you need them. If you must pay the in-house maintenance person to be on standby, your costs may well exceed those of the subcontractors.

I mentioned earlier how retaining an independent bookkeeper can be a financially sound move. If you have a specific part of your business that you are unable to do, subcontractors may be the best solution. As good as subcontractors can look, they are not without their problems and responsibilities.

You must be sure the contractors are properly licensed and insured for the work they perform. Another problem with subcontractors can be their reliability. Since these contractors are working for other people as well, your work may not get done in a timely fashion. Ultimately, you will have to address your business needs and cure them in the way that best fits your business plan.

SUBCONTRACTOR AGREEMENT

This agreement, made this _____ day of _____, 20__, shall set forth the whole agreement, in its entirety, between _____ hereafter referred to as Contractor, and Subcontractor.

Job location: _____

Subcontractor: _____, referred to herein as Subcontractor.

The Contractor and Subcontractor agree to the following.

ORIGINAL CONTRACT

Contractor has entered into a contract, hereinafter referred to as the original contract, dated _____, with the owner wihich includes the work to be performed under and pursuant to this subcontract agreement.

SCOPE OF WORK

Subcontractor shall perform all work as described below and provide all material to complete the work described below.

Subcontractor shall supply all labor and material to complete the work according to the original contract with the owner and the attached plans and specifications. These attached plans and specifications have been initialed and signed by all parties. The work shall include, but is not limited to, the following:

_____
_____
_____
_____
_____
_____

(Page 1 of 5. Please initial _____.)

(continues)

FIGURE 2.18   Subcontractor Agreement

COMMENCEMENT AND COMPLETION SCHEDULE

The work described above shall be started within _____ (____) days of verbal notice from Contractor, the projected start date is _____. The Subcontractor shall complete the above work in a professional and expedient manner by no later than _____ (____) days from the start date. Time is of the essence in this contract. No extension of time will be valid without the Contractor's written consent. If Subcontractor does not complete the work in the time allowed, and if the lack of completion is not caused by the Contractor, the Subcontractor will be charged _____ ($_____) dollars per day, for every day work extends beyond the completion date. This charge will be deducted from any payments due to the Subcontractor for work performed.

CONTRACT SUM

The Contractor shall pay the Subcontractor for the performance of completed work subject to additions and deductions as authorized by this agreement or attached addendum. The contract sum is _____($_____).

DUE DATE FOR RECEIPT OF PAYMENTS FROM OWNER

The due date for receipt of payment from the owner is _____.

PROGRESS PAYMENTS

The Contractor shall pay the Subcontractor installments as detailed below, once an acceptable insurance certificate has been filed by the Subcontractor with the Contractor. Contractor shall pay the Subcontractor as described: _____

_____

The Subcontractor shall be paid upon 7 days after receipt of each progress or final payment by the owner or 7 days after receipt of the subcontractor's or material supplier's invoice, whichever is later. Payments are subject to retainage for uncompleted performance. Retainage shall be paid prior to thirty days after final acceptance of the work. All payments are subject to a site inspection and approval of work by the Contractor. Before final payment, the Subcontractor shall submit satisfactory evidence to the Contractor that no lien risk exists on the subject property and Subcontractor shall supply an executed lien waiver.

(Page 2 of 5. Please initial _____.)

(continues)

FIGURE 2.18 Subcontractor Agreement *(continued)*

WORKING CONDITIONS

Working hours will be _____ a.m. through _____ p.m., Monday through Friday. Subcontractor is required to clean work debris from the job site on a daily basis and leave the site in a clean and neat condition. Subcontractor shall be responsible for removal and disposal of all debris related to the job description.

REIMBURSEMENT FOR DAMAGES OF COST

Subcontractor shall reimburse contractor for any actual damages or costs incurred by reason of subcontractor's failure to prosecute the work diligently, including any liquidated damages assessed by owner pursuant to the original contract.

TAKEOVER BY CONTRACTOR

Should subcontractor fail or neglect to proceed diligently, timely, competently, or in a competent manner, or should subcontractor by delaying, interfering with, or jeopardizing the timely or satisfactory completion of the work under the original contract, then and in that event contractor, in its sole discretion, reserves the right, after giving 48 hours notice, written or oral, to take over the work and complete such work at the cost and expense of subcontractor, without prejudice to contractor's other rights or remedies for any loss or damages sustained, and in the event of such takeover, subcontractor agrees that no material, machine, or tools belonging to subcontractor shall be removed from the job until completion. Previous demands made on subcontractor not followed by a takeover shall not be deemed a waiver of contractor's rights to do so.

CONTRACT ASSIGNMENT

Subcontractor shall not assign this contract or further subcontract the whole of this subcontract, without the written consent of the Contractor.

LAWS, PERMITS, FEES, AND NOTICES

Subcontractor shall be responsible for all required laws, permits, fees, or notices, required to perform the work stated herein.

(Page 3 of 5. Please initial _____.)

(continues)

FIGURE 2.18   Subcontractor Agreement *(continued)*

WORK OF OTHERS

Subcontractor shall be responsible for any damage caused to existing conditions or other contractor's work. This damage will be repaired, and the Subcontractor charged for the expense and supervision of this work. The Subcontractor shall have the opportunity to quote a price for said repairs, but the Contractor is under no obligation to engage the Subcontractor to make said repairs. If a different subcontractor repairs the damage, the Subcontractor may be backcharged for the cost of the repairs. Any repair costs will be deducted from any payments due to the Subcontractor. If no payments are due the Subcontractor, the Subcontractor shall pay the invoiced amount within _____ (_____) days.

WARRANTY

Subcontractor warrants and guarantees the work and materials covered by this subcontract and agrees to make good, at its own expense, any defect in materials or work thay may occur or develop prior to contractor's release from responsibility to owner for such materials or work.

INDEMNIFICATION

To the fullest extent allowed by law, the Subcontractor shall assume full responsibility for its employees, officers, agents, and business invitees. Subcontractor hereby agrees to indemnify and hold and save Contractor harmless from and against any claim, demand, action or cause of action that may be asserted by any person arising out of any damage, loss, expense, injury or death suffered by any of subcontractor's employees, officers, agents, and business invitees and regardless of the sole or concurring negligence of the contractor. Subcontractor shall indemnify contractor and owner against any and all loss, damages, cost, expenses, and attorney fees suffered or incurred on account of any breach of the obligations and covenants any any other provision or covenant of this subcontract.

(Page 4 of 5. Please initial _____.)

(continues)

FIGURE 2.18   Subcontractor Agreement *(continued)*

LEGAL ACTION

Should legal action be required, this agreement shall be interpreted under the laws of the State of _____. Any dispute, controversy, or claim arising out of or relating to this agreement, or the breach of this agreement, shall be subject to the jurisdiction of the courts of _____ County, in the State of _____. The parties hereby designate the venue of _____ County, in the State of _____, as the forum for the resolution of all disputes, controversies, or claims arising out of or relating to this agreement, or the breach of this agreement. The Subcontractor consents to and acknowledges personal jurisdiction over the Subcontractor by such Court and the Subcontractor agrees to be subject to the personal jurisdiction of the State of _____.

If there is any portion of this agreement that the Subcontractor does not understand fully, the Subcontractor is encouraged to seek competent legal counsel prior to executing this contractual agreement.

This agreement, entered into on _____, 20____, shall constitute the whole agreement between Contractor and Subcontractor.

_____

_____

_____

_____

Contractor _____ Date _____

Subcontractor _____ Date _____

(Page 5 of 5. Please initial _____.)

FIGURE 2.18   Subcontractor Agreement

Projecting the Future

Another of your responsibilities as a property manager will be projecting the future. For any business to run profitably on a continual basis, it must have a sound business plan. As the owner of the business, you are responsible for coming up with a winning plan.

Projecting the future of real estate and rental activity is not as hard as you might think. History has a tendency to repeat itself. Knowing this, you can use historical data to help you predict coming market conditions. While your projections may not be dead on, you may be surprised how effective your planning is. Real estate runs in cycles. Housing needs tend to follow patterns. By looking into the past, you can get a glimpse into the future.

A trip to city hall can reveal growth plans in the community that will attract new people to the area. This type of research can provide insight to the long-range future. Something as simple as tracking the help-wanted ads in the local paper can give you an idea of the needs for the near future. By projecting the future, you can build a business plan. You may have to alter your plans to accommodate unforeseen shifts in the market, but over a ten-year period, your projections should ring close to the truth.

The Cornerstone

The cornerstone to success in your rental business will be you and your actions. If you treat your rental activity as a business, you can prosper. If you treat your endeavors as a hobby, you may never see a substantial profit. This chapter has outlined many of the basic business principals and practices used in efficient property management. The remaining chapters will expand on and add to this list.

When you make the decision to manage your own property or the properties of others, you must go into it with a serious demeanor. Competition can be fierce and the world of property management can be unforgiving. Remember, whether you have two tenants or twenty tenants, you are running a business. Look at your actions and ask yourself if they are on a professional level. Would you pay someone to manage your properties the way you are doing the job? If you answer this question with a yes, you are on the right track. If you answer with a no, you should reconsider your decision to self-manage your income properties.

Following the Rules and Getting Maximum Profits

If you have been in the rental business for long, you have probably noticed that tenants seem to have more rights than landlords. This may not be fair, but it is a fact. I have seen landlords become hostages to their tenants, not physically, but financially. For you to avoid being the one out in the cold, you must maintain control if you are the property owner. As a property manager, you can use the tips found here to keep your clients happier.

If you are fair and reasonable, it would seem your tenants should return the gesture, but they don't always do that. Have you ever had a tenant vacate your unit in the middle of the night? Has a tenant ever moved your appliances with him when he left? These are only two questions about problem tenants. I could probably could write an entire book on the subject of the misfortunes of landlords I have known, myself included.

Tenant Rights

Tenants do, and should, have rights. As a landlord and property manager, you may not infringe upon these rights. If you do, you may find yourself in jail. At the least, you could be required to pay a heavy fine for violating a tenant's rights. I am not an attorney and will not attempt to tell you what you legally can and cannot do. What I will do is give you ideas to run by your lawyer. If the attorney approves of the suggestions, feel free to use them.

What Is Control?

Control does not have to mean physical dominance or legal rights. A person can be in control without any threat to the people being controlled. Respect generates the most lasting form of control. If you hold a gun to someone's head, you are in control as long as you have the gun. If you turn to leave, the other person may take control by attacking you from behind. On the other hand, if you are in control by the approval of the other person, there is little risk of being stabbed in the back. Gaining control from respect takes time, but it is the best type of control to have. As it relates to being a property manager or landlord, control is usually maintained with written agreements and consistent actions.

✔ **FAST FACT**

Gaining control from respect takes time, but it is the best type of control to have.

With all of my years of experience in real estate, I have seen many forms of control. Some worked, and some didn't. My experience with managing other people's property has shown me a lot. The experience gained from running my own buildings has cost me a lot. This chapter should give you an edge. It is compiled from many years of hands-on field experience, both as an owner and a manager.

▶ **PRO POINTER**

Having a written rule is of little use if you fail to enforce it. Making exceptions to the rule, for chosen tenants, will erode the effectiveness of the rule for other tenants.

You, the Owner

As the owner of rental property, you may have more latitude in what you are able to do than a professional management company would have. The laws on discrimination vary depending upon specific factors. For example, as the owner of a single-family home, that you rent to tenants, you can be more selective in your choice of tenants than you could be with a twelve-family apartment building. However, if you own several single-family homes, you can be placed in a different class. Before you get too consumed with control, check with your attorney to see if your control measures are legal.

You, the Manager

There is a big difference between being just the landlord and being the property manager. When you are a professional manager handling the property of others, you have a buffer for the property owner. You are not personally making all of the rental rules, but you may still be involved in a lawsuit caused by your actions.

RENTAL POLICY

1. Tenant shall keep all areas of his rented portion of the property clean.

2. Tenant must not disturb other people's peace and quiet.

3. Tenant may not alter the dwelling, without landlord's written permission.

4. Parking of vehicles must be confined to only those areas designated for the tenant.

5. The tenant must keep the parking area assigned to him clean and unsoiled by oil drippings.

6. Tenant may not perform major repairs on motor vehicles while the vehicles are parked on the premises.

7. Landlord has the right to inspect the dwelling with 24 hours verbal notice given to the tenant.

8. Landlord has the right to access the rental unit to have work performed on the property.

9. Landlord, or his agent, may show the dwelling to prospective tenants or purchasers at reasonable times, with 24 hours verbal notice to the tenant.

10. Tenant must receive written permission from the landlord to use a water bed or other water-filled furniture.

11. Tenant shall pay all costs of repairs and or damage, including, but not limited to, drain stoppages, they or their guests cause.

12. Tenant shall prevent the plumbing in the rental unit from freezing.

13. Tenant shall provide landlord with a completed move-in list, to be furnished by the landlord, within five days of taking occupancy of the rental unit.

14. Tenant shall inform landlord of any defects or safety hazards that may cause damage to the property or the occupants.

15. Pets are not allowed, without the written permission of the landlord.

16. Violation of any part of this rental policy or nonpayment of rent as agreed shall be cause for eviction and all legal actions allowed by law.

FIGURE 3.1 Rental Policy

The law is very strict on rental management. Before you spread your shoulders and take a bad attitude, know your limitations. If you are not familiar with the laws pertaining to rental management, attend classes, read books, and talk with your lawyer until you do understand what is required of you. Ignorance is not a suitable defense in court.

Now that you have been advised of the possible repercussions of your actions, let's consider how you can stay in control, and out of court. Going to court is a losing proposition, even when you win. It cost money, and sometimes lots of it, to bring action against a tenant or to defend yourself from a suit filed against you. If you do find yourself in court, the written word will rule the day. All of your actions that might result in a legal confrontation should be documented in writing. This can mean everything from a signed, written lease to a phone log.

There is another advantage to written agreements. They remove confusion. Confusion is a major cause of conflict between tenants and their managers. If your tenants know the rules, most of them will play by them. You cannot give vague instructions and then punish tenants who couldn't read your mind.

Written documents not only help you win court battles, they can keep you out of court. When you can produce legitimate written documentation to support your position, people will not want to fight you in the courtroom. All in all, the proper paperwork is one of your best tools for staying in control, and out of court.

> **✔ FAST FACT**
>
> The judicial system runs on paperwork. The more documentation you have, the less likely you are to lose your battle.

Forms That Can Keep You in Control

With the help of your attorney, you can maintain much of your control, at least legally, with forms. Once the master form is made, you can use the same basic form for all your tenants. You can either photocopy the master form or store it in your computer for multiple uses. Let's take a close look at what some of the most common forms used to stay in control of rental property are.

Tenant Application Forms

Tenant application forms should be completed by every prospective tenant, before you make a decision to rent your unit to the tenant. This is usually the first form you will use with new tenants. The tenant application form, when completed, provides you with detailed information on the prospective tenant.

The form will give information on the tenant to be used in your approval process. The form normally contains information on where the tenant has lived in the past. It should provide information on the tenant's social security number, employer, credit references, and financial status. The application may ask a number of other questions to enable you to make a sound decision on if the tenant meets your criteria.

One of the most important aspects of the form will be language giving you permission to investigate the prospect's credit history. Without the individual's permission, you cannot pry into his credit rating. Every property manager should verify the credit standing of prospective tenants. People with excellent credit ratings can turn bad, but if they have good credit at the time you check, your odds are better for collecting your rent.

If you have enough rentals to justify the expense, you should consider joining a credit reporting bureau. These agencies make it easy to run a credit inquiry. If you do not have the volume to support the overhead expense of a credit agency, at least call all the references given on the application. Be advised, not all references will be on the up and up. Some people give the names of family and friends for references.

When you call to check references, be a little sneaky. Unless the phone is answered professionally, giving a company name, do a little probing. Ask what the relationship is between the reference and the applicant, before you tell them why you are calling. People that give false references often use them for more than rental applications. You may trip the reference up and cause them to spill the beans. If they say Joe used to work for them, but Joe gave you their name as a landlord, you have exposed Joe as a potential fraud. Look below the surface to protect yourself from the professional deadbeats sometimes encountered in the rental business.

Rental Policy

After establishing a rental policy, you should create a form detailing all the rules and regulations you plan to enforce. This might cover the ownership of pets or waterbeds. It may refer to how many parking spaces the tenant is entitled to. Who is responsible for overflowing toilets? Unless you have an agreement, in writing and signed by the tenant, you will be responsible for paying the plumber and any damages incurred from the stopped-up toilet.

Many landlords require their tenants to be responsible for overflowing toilets, if the cause of the problem was the tenant's fault. For example, assume the toilet in a second-floor apartment overflows and floods the apartment below it. A plumber will have to clear the stoppage in the toilet. Someone will have to clean up the mess and make restitution for damages caused by the water. If the plumber finds a rubber ducky in the toilet, it should be the tenant's responsibility to cover the costs of repairs and damages. If the problem was caused by faulty pipes, the landlord should bear the burden of costs. These types of details will often have to be worked out on a building-by-building basis with the property owner.

The plumbing example is only one example of how this wording can give you an edge. The same principal could be applied to broken windows. If the tenant breaks the glass, the tenant pays to repair it. The rental policy might cover any alterations to the property that the tenant is, or is not, allowed to perform. How would you feel to enter an apartment and find the living room walls painted with a blaze orange paint?

> ▶ **PRO POINTER**
>
> Have all prospective tenants review your rental policy before you allow them to sign a lease. It is a good idea to have the tenant sign the rental policy. This ensures to anyone involved in settling a dispute that the tenant has seen the document.

> ▶ **PRO POINTER**
>
> Avoid the use of generic legal forms. Have a competent attorney draft working legal agreements for you and your business.

Make sure your rental policy covers every conceivable point you can muster. Have all prospective tenants review your rental policy before you allow them to sign a lease. It is a good idea to have the tenant sign the rental policy. This ensures to anyone involved in settling a dispute that the tenant has seen the document.

Leases

Leases are one of the next forms used when a tenant passes your application screening. Leases are also one of the most important forms you can use to maintain control of rental property. Leases, as with all other legal forms, should be prepared by an attorney. It is possible to buy leases in some stores, but these generic leases do not afford the benefits of a custom lease, prepared by your lawyer.

A rental lease should be comprehensive, leaving nothing to the imagination. It should obviously dictate the terms and conditions of your rental agreement with the tenant. You may include your rental policy in the lease or refer to it as an exhibit that is made a part of the lease. The amount of the rent and how it should be paid must be in the lease. Security and damage deposits should be covered in the lease. The term of the rental is another fact that the lease should include. If you can think of it, it should be in the lease. If you can't think of it, hopefully your attorney will.

The Check-In Form

Check-in forms protect you if you are compelled to retain a damage deposit when a tenant vacates your property. You should have each new tenant complete a check-in form as soon as the tenant takes occupancy. The form should have a room-by-room description of items for the tenant to inspect. Items such as walls, ceilings, cabinets, plumbing, and related items should all be on the form. If you provide appliances, they should be described on the form.

Have the tenant inspect the rental unit and complete the check-in form. If the prospective tenant finds holes in the bedroom wall, there should be a place on the form to note the deficiency. If the range or refrigerator is missing, it should go on the form. Your check-in form should cover every item you will consider in evaluating the retainage of a damage deposit.

If you are forced to keep someone's deposit, you may have to justify your actions. If you go to court with a completed check-in form, signed by the tenant, you have a good chance of winning your case. If the walls were in good shape when the tenant moved in, but they are a mess now, you should win your case to keep the damage deposit.

Pet Addendums

If you will be allowing some of your tenants to keep pets, you should have a pet addendum form. This form can be made a part of your lease and it will specify the terms and conditions of allowing pets in the property. The addendum may require the tenant to comply with rules that are above and beyond those of the standard rental policy.

✔ **FAST FACT**

Many landlords require additional damage deposits from tenants with pets. It is also not unusual for landlords to charge pet-owning tenants a higher rent than tenants without pets. Any rules and conditions applying to pets should be installed in the pet addendum.

WATERBED ADDENDUM

This addendum shall become an integral part of the lease/rental agreement dated _____, 20_____, between _____, tenant and _____, landlord, for the property located at _____.
Under the terms and conditions of this agreement, tenant may use a waterbed in his rental unit. The terms and conditions for the use of a waterbed in the above-mentioned dwelling are as follows: Tenant must allow landlord to inspect and approve the quality and installation of the waterbed. Tenant shall provide the landlord with proof of insurance naming the landlord as first insured for damages caused in regards to the waterbed. The minimum amount of liability coverage acceptable to the landlord is $100,000.00. In addition to the insurance coverage, tenant agrees to make an additional damage deposit in the amount of $_____.
This deposit will be held in an escrow account and returned to the tenant within five days of vacating the property, if no damage has been caused in conjunction with the waterbed. Tenant agrees to remove his waterbed immediately, if any of these terms or conditions are broken.

_____   _____

Landlord   Date   Tenant   Date

FIGURE 3.2   Waterbed Addendum

Other Addendums

You can create other form addendums for almost any purpose. One common addendum is used to address the issue of water-filled furniture. People with waterbeds are often made to pay additional damage deposits or to purchase insurance to protect the landlord's property, and the property of other tenants. You can use addendums to cement agreements on any subject. This concludes the most common forms used to move a tenant into your rental unit. Next, we will look at some forms that are helpful after the tenants have taken occupancy.

Rent Payment Coupons

Rent payment coupons are used by many property managers to facilitate faster collection of rents. Since most people are accustomed to paying their bills from payment books or monthly statements, rent coupons can be beneficial. They can help remind a tenant to pay rent on time. It does not cost much to have rent coupons printed and anything that may make tenants pay their rent on time is worth a try.

Access Forms

If your lease is properly worded, it will allow you access to your rental unit at anytime, so long as reasonable notice is given to the tenant. You may need access for maintenance duties or to show the apartment to a prospective purchaser. For what-

▶ *PRO POINTER*

If your lease allows you to charge a late fee for past-due rent, this fact should be outlined in a late rent form.

ever the reason, when you need to get into an occupied apartment, access notices should be delivered. By creating access forms you are well prepared to give formal notice of your intent to enter the premises.

Late Rent Forms

Some people will be late in paying their rent. You should use forms to notify these people that their rent is overdue. This form can be friendly, but it should be firm enough to get the tenant's attention. If your lease allows you to charge a late fee for past-due rent, this fact should be outlined in a late rent form. Don't hesitate to send these forms to tenants. The late rent form is the beginning of your paper trail for eviction. Hopefully you will never have to evict a tenant, but if you stay in the business long enough, there will come a time when eviction is the only way to deal with a problem tenant.

Vacate Forms

The reverse side of eviction is when tenants move out on their own motivation. Since you will appreciate some notice prior to a tenant's departure, it is a good idea to provide tenants with a form to notify you of their intent to move out of a rental. Your lease should cover the acceptable reasons for early termination and the notice required to be given to you by the tenant. These forms simply make it easy for the tenant to comply with the terms of your lease.

Change Order Forms

Your lease may allow for rental increases at set intervals or other changes in the lease during its time of enforcement. When a change is made during a lease's term, you should use a change order. The change order will be a form describing the nature of the deviation from the signed lease. By having your tenant sign the change order, you have proof of the tenant's acceptance of the changes.

> ✔ **FAST FACT**
>
> Not enough property managers use change orders. Too many managers allow changes to be made with nothing more than a verbal agreement. This is fine, until there is a problem. When a conflict arises, without a signed change order, you have little chance of defending your position in the battle.

Pay Rent or Quit Forms

When tenants have not paid their rent in the allotted and agreed upon time, you should issue a pay rent or quit notice. These notices inform the tenants of your plans to pursue legal actions to collect the money due you. It will tell the tenants that if they don't pay their rent, they must move. This is an important form in the eviction procedure.

Perform Covenant Forms

If you have a tenants breaking the rules of your rental policy, you should serve them with perform covenant notices. This form will notify tenants of their non-compliance with your rental rules and regulations, as dictated by the signed lease and rental policy. The form will give tenants some period of time to conform to the rules before further action is taken. This form can be instrumental in the execution of eviction proceedings.

NOTICE TO PERFORM COVENANT

To _____,
tenant in possession:

   Please take notice that you have violated the following covenant in your
lease/rental agreement: _____
You are required to perform the aforesaid covenant or to deliver up
possession of the premises now held and occupied by you, being those
premises situated in the city of
_____, county of
_____, state of _____, commonly
known as _____.
If you fail to do so, legal proceedings will be instituted against you to
recover said premises and such damages as the law allows.

   This notice is intended to be a _____ notice to perform the aforesaid
covenant. It is not intended to terminate or forfeit the lease/rental
agreement under which you occupy said premises. If after legal
proceedings, said premises are recovered from you, the landlord will
attempt to rent said premises for the highest possible rent, giving you
credit for sums received and holding you liable for any deficiencies arising
during the term of said lease/rental agreement.
Dated this _____ day of _____, 20_____.

_____
                                                                                       Landlord

PROOF OF SERVICE

I, the undersigned, being of legal age, declare under penalty of perjury that
I served the notice to perform covenant, of which this is a true copy, on the
above-mentioned tenant in possession in the manner indicated below:
On _____, 20_____, I served this notice in the following manner:

_____
Executed on _____, 20_____, at _____.
By: _____
Title: _____

FIGURE 3.3 Notice to Perform Covenant

Terminate Tenancy Form

Most leases provide the landlord with rights to terminate the tenancy granted in the lease. Normally there will be a clause requiring the landlord to give sufficient notice to the tenant, prior to terminating the lease. Forms made to terminate tenancy will keep you within your legal rights when terminating a tenant's occupancy, in compliance with the terms of the signed lease.

Not the Cure-All

Forms are very helpful in maintaining control of your rental property, but they are not a cure-all miracle. Without the proper forms and paperwork you are very likely to find yourself on the losing end of a tenant conflict. With the proper forms, acknowledged by all parties, you have a much better chance of settling disputes out of court, or in court.

By combining the proper use of selected forms with good management skills, you can gain and retain control of a building. If you sit in your office with a deaf ear to your tenants, no amount of forms will save you. You must take an active interest in the management of rental property if you are going to run the buildings well.

> ✔ *FAST FACT*
>
> When you are dealing with the public, as all property managers do, you must develop people skills. These people skills are the most effective when coupled with sales skills.

The Basic Skills

With basic skills and intelligence, you can enjoy a profitable future as a property manager. However, the job comes with its share of problems. Few people enjoy arguments and adversarial meetings. As a property manager, you will be placed in the position to perform tasks most people wouldn't consider attacking. If you went out on the street and asked a pedestrian if he or she would go to your building and collect past-due rent from a hard-nosed tenant, what do you think the individual would say? How much money would you have to offer to convince the person to knock on a door and ask for money a tenant either doesn't have or is unwilling to give up? For many people, you could not pay them enough, within reason, to handle such a job.

NOTICE TO TERMINATE TENANCY

To _____, tenant in possession:

You are hereby required within thirty days from this date to remove from and deliver up possession of the premises now held and occupied by you, being those premises situated in the city of _____, county of _____, state of _____, commonly known as _____.

This notice is intended for the purpose of terminating the lease/rental agreement by which you now hold possession of the above-described premises, and should you fail to comply, legal proceedings will be instituted against you to recover possession, to declare said lease/rental agreement forfeited and to recover rents and damages for the period of the unlawful detention.

Please be advised that your rent on said premises is due and payable up to and including the date of termination of your tenancy under this notice. This notice complies with the terms and conditions of the lease or rental agreement under which you presently hold said property.

Dated this _____ day of _____, 20_____.

_____
Landlord

PROOF OF SERVICE

I, the undersigned, being of legal age, declare under penalty of perjury that I served the notice to terminate tenancy, of which this is a true copy, on the above-mentioned tenant in possession, in the manner indicated below:

On _____, 20_____, I served the notice to the tenant in the following manner: _____

Executed on _____, 19_____, at _____.

By: _____

Title:_____

FIGURE 3.4 Notice to Terminate Tenancy

NOTICE
FINAL NOTICE

Be advised, this is your last opportunity to resolve your breach of our lease. You have been mailed many notices. All previous notices have gone unanswered. Other means of communication have failed to produce a response from you. If you do not comply with the terms of your lease within the next 48 hours, legal proceedings will be started to resolve this matter. If in doubt, refer to your lease. You will see that you may be held responsible for the fees incurred in these legal proceedings. If you fail to comply with your lease, all legal actions allowable by law will be used to correct this situation. It is not my desire to proceed legally, but you are leaving me with no options. If I have not been contacted by you within the next 48 hours, the next notifications you receive will be from my attorney. Please contact me immediately to avoid legal action. I can be reached from _____a.m. to _____p.m. at _____. A copy of this noticed has also been mailed to you at this address.

Date:_____
Time:_____

_____
                                                                Landlord

---

FIGURE 3.5   Final Notice

Do you know many people with the ability to remove problem tenants, even if the tenants will have no place to go? There will probably come a time in your career when you must be cold-hearted. It can be difficult to remove human emotions from your business, but to make money, you sometimes have to. There are many ways to approach the job of property manager. You can be soft-spoken and friendly. You can be loud and abrasive. Most managers

✔ **FAST FACT**

As a property manager, collecting late rent is an accepted part of your job.

fall somewhere between these two extremes. In whatever manner you use to do it, you must remain in control.

What Not to Do

There are some requirements for what you must not do when gaining or retaining control. The most important rule is to not violate a person's legal rights. I know I have mentioned this often, but you might be surprised how many so-called professional managers flagrantly violate the laws pertaining to property management. Don't do it; if you violate a tenant's rights, you could face imprisonment and strong fines. Other activities to avoid are numerous. For now, let's concentrate on what you should do.

Getting Off to a Good Start

To get off to a good start, you must assume a position of control in your first dealings with tenants. Since the first contact between a property manager and tenants is frequently on the telephone, you must perfect your phone tactics. The first impression a tenant will perceive of you will be from your phone manners. If you are unorganized and hesitant on the phone, it will reflect an air of incompetence. Tenants will have little respect for an incompetent property manager.

When you are well prepared and fluent on the phone, you impress the caller. The prospective tenant will create a mental picture of a person who is professional in their rental management duties. By making a good impression on the phone, you are getting off to a good start. The tenant will acknowledge your business skills and will see that you treat the rental of your property as a business, not an unorganized hobby.

When You Show a Vacant Unit

When you show a vacant unit you will have the opportunity to size up your prospective tenant. The tenant will be checking you out at the same time. In the first few minutes of your meeting, impressions will be made. Many factors can influence the flow of control. Little gestures will go a long way in putting you in the driver's seat.

Don't be late for your meeting with the prospective tenant. When someone is late for a scheduled appointment he is automatically on the losing end. Being late indicates a lack of professionalism and it gives the person who arrived first an edge. There will be a psychological swing in the momentum of control if you are late. Tenants may feel that they have the upper hand. You should be on time and animated for the meeting.

If you do not show an enthusiastic interest in renting the property, the tenant will be less likely to rent from you. By exerting a positive outlook, you may be able to make a better deal with a tenant. If you look disinterested or desperate, the tenant may move to beat you in negotiations for the price of the rental. By giving a confident appearance you reduce the chances of the tenant trying to beat you down on your price.

> ✔ *FAST FACT*
> By exerting a positive outlook, you may be able to make a better deal with a tenant. If you look disinterested or desperate, the tenant may move to beat you in negotiations for the price of the rental. By giving a confident appearance you reduce the chances of the tenant trying to beat you down on your price.

Presentation of Paperwork

As you know, the paperwork involved in the rental business can become extensive. Some tenants will be intimidated from the mass of papers requiring their signatures. Many property managers lose good tenants by not presenting their paperwork in the proper manner.

The forms required to run a successful rental business are extensive and can seem imposing. If you are forceful and inconsiderate when asking tenants to sign these forms, they may look to rent some other property, where the formalities are not so formidable. Many tenants will feel all of your legal forms are tying their hands

> ✔ *FAST FACT*
> Many tenants will feel all of your legal forms are tying their hands and putting you in total control. If the tenants feel they are being tied too tightly by your paperwork, they may not sign them. If they do sign them with these back-of-the-mind feelings, you can have management problems from the start. These tenants will feel you are taking advantage of them. After awhile these feelings will fester into resentment.

and putting you in total control. If the tenants feel they are being tied too tightly by your paperwork, they may not sign them. If they do sign them with these back-of-the-mind feelings, you can have management problems from the start. These tenants will feel you are taking advantage of them. After awhile these feelings will fester into resentment. You are after respect, not resentment.

When you present the forms in the right way, you can convince the tenant that the forms are as much for their protection as for yours. Since the presentation of paperwork is so important to good tenant relations, successful management, and maintaining control, I am going to give you some examples of how you might present some of your legal instruments.

Getting Your Forms Signed

Most tenants will not object to filling out a rental application. Tenants expect any good business owner to check into the past history and credit ratings of new tenants. When it comes to signing a lease, you may hit some resistance. While tenants will be expecting to sign a lease, they may not be willing to sign yours.

If you have worked with an attorney to develop a custom lease, the lease will favor your position. Smart tenants may catch the language in the lease that puts unusual demands upon them. For example, assume your lease holds the tenant responsible for all plumbing repairs. A clause of this nature is not normal and it is not fair to the tenant. Landlords are expected to pay for repairs and upkeep to the rental property, unless the tenant is responsible for causing the need for such capital outlays.

If you have a clause requiring the tenant to pay for damages caused by the tenant, such as in the example of putting a rubber ducky down the toilet, you shouldn't have much trouble getting the tenant to sign the lease. But, suppose the tenant balks at the clause, what do you say? If you say it is your building and your rule and that the tenant can take it or leave it, the prospective tenant will probably leave it. This approach may cost you a good tenant and a great deal of lost time.

If you explain the reasoning behind the insertion of the clause, you can convince most tenants to accept your rule. You might tell the tenant that the clause helps you to keep your rents at a lower amount. Tell the tenant that if you are forced to pay for the abuses of your tenants, you must charge a higher rent to offset the additional expenses.

Further explain how the rule helps the responsible tenants and only affects the tenants who do not respect the property. Explain how charging higher rents to cover your costs for repairs and damages caused by problem tenants only serves as a hardship on good tenants. Tell the tenant that this clause will have no affect on anyone who does not do something to damage your property. If after this type of presentation the tenant still refuses to abide by your rules, you probably don't want the tenant. By taking the time to explain the purpose and meaning of the clause, you can gain respect from the tenant, at the same time as you are gaining control.

Convincing Your Tenants to Complete Check-In Forms

Your check-in forms are an important block in your paperwork foundation. With a completed and signed check-in form in your files, it will be easy to pinpoint the reasons to justify retaining a damage deposit. Without check-in forms you will have to argue your case with the tenant. The tenant may say the wall was full of picture holes when the apartment was rented. You, of course, will say it wasn't. Who's right? You will know you are right, but proving the truth to a judge, without check-in lists might be very difficult.

You could give the form to tenants and demand that they complete and return it within three days. The tenant may, or may not, comply with your demand. There is a simple way to manipulate the tenant into wanting to complete the annoying form. It all boils down to presentation.

If you are extremely aggressive in your request for the form, the tenant may delay delivering it, just to spite you. For best results, try the following approach. Explain to the tenant how you take a personal interest in all your tenants and in the condition of your rental units. Go on to explain how the completed check-in form provides two services to the tenant, yes, to the tenant.

Tell the tenant how you want to make living conditions as comfortable as reasonably possible. Give them a list of helpful phone numbers to get settled in with.

✔ **FAST FACT**

A lot of property managers give new tenants check-in forms to complete, but never follow up on the return of the form. It doesn't do you any good to present the form if you do not recover a copy of the completed form for your files. Many tenants will take the form for granted. In the hustle and bustle of moving in, the form will be left in a drawer. It will be up to you to see that you get a copy of the completed form for your files and protection.

✔ **FAST FACT**

The presentation for your paperwork can make all the difference in the world when it comes to gaining and maintaining control. By being forceful and demanding, you are less likely to see favorable results and you will not be building a good relationship with your tenant. By turning your presentation around and showing tenants how they benefit from your paperwork, they are much more likely to cooperate. By using the softer approach, you get your form signed quickly and gain respect from the tenant. You win in all directions; you get the form signed, you gain respect from the tenant, and you establish control, while building a good tenant relationship.

HELPFUL INFORMATION

This form is for your convenience. We know it can take awhile to get adjusted to a new home, and we will be happy to help you with questions you may have about the community. Thank you for renting with us.

Phone Numbers

Police (non-emergency) _____

Police (EMERGENCY) _____

Fire Department _____

Ambulance _____

Emergency Room _____

Hospital _____

Doctor _____

Telephone Company _____

Utility Company _____

Water & Sewer District _____

Resident Manager _____

Landlord _____

Notes

_____

_____

_____

FIGURE 3.6   Helpful Information

Explain how the completed form will alert you to deficiencies in the rental unit, so that you can render the necessary repairs. Then explain how the form protects a tenant financially. Point out how the tenant's damage deposit is at stake for any damage done to the unit while the rental unit is leased to the tenant. Show the tenant that by completing the check-in form the condition of the unit at the time of occupancy is duly noted.

Go on to explain how the form protects tenants from losing damage deposits for damage caused by a previous tenant. It will be easy to show tenants why you need the form completed and how it will benefit them to process the form expediently. Once tenants understand the form is protecting them from being falsely accused for damages they didn't cause, they will jump at the chance to put the form on file with you.

Sales Skills

Sales skills are an invaluable asset to a property manager. You may not think of yourself as a salesman, but you should. Your job requires you to rent vacant units. You are not selling the units, but you must sell the tenant on renting your unit, instead of your competitor's. Sales skills produce evident results when doing certain aspects of your job. When you are creating a marketing plan, you see the advantage of having sales skills. When you are probing prospects for information, a background in sales will produce noticeable results. Showing vacancies will produce better results when you incorporate sales ability into your actions. For all of these parts of your job, sales ability can be easily identified as a plus.

When you are thinking about gaining and maintaining control, you might not consider sales skills to be important. If you don't believe these skills are advantageous in dealing with people, you are wrong. While you are not directly selling anything in this phase of your job, you are working to maintain control and profits. The easiest way to maintain control is to get people to agree with you. The best skills available for making people agree with you are sales skills. This can translate into higher profits.

These skills may not be what you think of when you think of a salesman. When dealing with control, you do not need to use high-pressure sales tactics. In fact, subdued suggestions and careful use of the proper words will get you much further in your quest for control. A skilled salesman can imply actions and plant thoughts that will make their prospect respond in the desired manner. Good salespeople can make a prospect perform in a prescribed manner, while the prospect is thinking it was his idea. These subliminal messages are sent through carefully structured words and actions.

Role Playing

If you have an understanding friend or spouse, you can practice your sales skills through role playing. If you have been in the business very long, you know the areas where you have the most trouble with your tenants. If you are new to the business, reading this book will alert you to many of the problems you can expect to arise. Have your friend assume the role of the problem tenant. You, of course, will be the property manager. This learning process will work best if you read books on the subjects of sales and managing people. After you have read the books, practice the procedures on your friend. I will give you a few examples of how the game might be played.

Example One

Here is example one. Your problem tenant comes to you with a grievance. He is complaining that his kitchen faucet continually drips and keeps him awake at night. What will you say or do? Some landlords and managers will promise to have the problem taken care of right away. For the moment, this promise appeases the tenant and he leaves feeling satisfied. However, if the plumber doesn't show up for days, the tenant is right back in your face, complaining with more intensity than before. If this type of situation continues, tempers flare and both you and the tenant become angry at each other. The landlord still has to fix the leak, but even after it is fixed, there are still hard feelings between the landlord, the tenant, and you.

A better approach to this problem is to tell the tenant you will contact the plumber as soon as possible and have the plumber schedule a time that is convenient with the tenant to repair the faucet. It would be a good idea to place a call to the plumber while the tenant is standing in front of you. You know the leak is wasting water and will have to be fixed, you might as well handle the problem quickly, to avoid bad feelings from the tenant.

When you take this approach, the tenant sees you take action. He knows you are responding to his request and doing the best you can, as a manager, to have his problem corrected. Then if the plumber doesn't show up for days, the tenant will be angry with the plumber, not with you. This is only a slight manipulation, but it is effective. You will not be the bad guy; after all, the tenant saw you take immediate action. The tenant cannot blame you for the actions of an undependable plumber.

Example Two

Here is example number two. Suppose a problem tenant comes into your office to dispute a late charge you assessed against him for past-due rent; how would you handle the situation? The tenant comes in steaming mad and refuses to pay the late fee. He tells you that you are a money-grabbing, selfish manager. The tenant is flinging his arms around in gestures and ranting uncontrollably. What should you do?

You could answer the tenant's bizarre behavior with similar behavior. If you do this, you will wind up in a shouting match that will not solve the conflict. You could be meek and agree to forget about the late charge, but this would cause you to lose control of the situation. If you give in once, you can be labeled as a softy, that any tenant can take advantage of.

Let the tenant go through the motions to relieve his pent-up frustration. Unless the tenant storms out of your office, he will run out of breath at some point, and you will have an opportunity to talk. The first few words you say will influence the way the matter will be settled. Choose your words carefully.

When you get the chance to talk, address the tenant in a firm voice, from a strong posture. Tell him you will be happy to discuss the matter with him in a business-like manner, if he will just settle down for a few minutes. You are telling him you will discuss the matter, but you are dictating the terms on how the discussion will go down. When the tenant realizes you are willing to talk about the late charge, he may feel some victory and should calm down.

When you have the person calmed, ask him to excuse you while you pull his file. Even if you know the details of the late charge by memory, pull his file. This gives you time to think and it allows time for the tenant to relax. Once you have the file, the tenant will know you are taking the matter seriously. Sit down and review the file. Tell the tenant that according to your files, his rent payment was late and the late charge was assessed in accordance with the terms of the lease. Expect a brief explosion from the tenant at this point.

Give him a few moments to vent his fury and then ask him if he is ready to continue your meeting in a professional manner. By not lowering yourself to the tenant's level, you are maintaining control and wearing down the tenant. If he is normal, it will not take long for him to realize he is being childish in his actions. Your next step should be to ask the tenant if your files are inaccurate. Ask him when his records indicate his rent was paid.

If the rent was paid late, the tenant will have to admit to breaching his rental agreement. Once you have maneuvered the tenant into admitting he paid his rent late, you are half way home. Next, ask him if there were extenuating circumstances that forced his rent to be late. In doing this, you are showing compassion and defusing the irate tenant. If he says there was no good reason for paying his rent late, ask if he remembers the clause in the lease pertaining to late payments. He should say he does and he knows you have the file in your hands that contains the lease. You are slowly putting the guy into a box.

First, you got the tenant to admit paying his rent late. Then, you had him agree to knowing he would be charged a fee for paying his rent after the agreed upon time. Now it is time to move in for the kill. Ask the tenant to put himself in your position. Tell him how you depend on his rent payment to make your books balance for the property owner. Go on to explain how you are not some rich real estate mogul, but only a working property manager, whose livelihood depends on the timely payment of each tenant's rent.

By now you have the guy thinking. Expand your speech to impress upon the tenant how you believe in being fair and playing by the rules. Ask the tenant what he would do if he was the manager. Ask him if he would charge a late fee to delinquent tenants when they caused him hardship in meeting his monthly obligations. By working the conversation in this direction, you can trap the tenant into agreeing to pay the late charge and understanding why you enforce the clause.

Certainly, there will be tenants who will not play along. There will always be people you cannot deal with, but they are the exception, rather than the rule. The old "wouldn't you agree" tactic is very effective. You might close this problem tenant down by saying, " I believe it is important to a person's character and integrity to live up to their promises, wouldn't you agree." What is the guy going to say, no? He will agree with you. As soon as he does, you say, " Well, when you accepted my rental policy and lease, you promised to pay late fees when your rent was not paid on time. Are you telling me now that you are not a man of your word?" The tenant will quickly defend his honor of being a man of his word. When he does, you've got him. At this point there is no way he can leave your office with his head up, unless he pays the late fee.

By learning to steer people into giving the answers you want to hear, you are in control. This control is best gained by using sales skills. There are many good books available to help you master your sales skills. When it comes down to gaining and maintaining control, sales skills will be one of your most effective tools. When you combine written agreements with sales skills, you become a good property manager.

✔ **FAST FACT**

Good people skills are necessary for prosperous management of rental property. Sales skills take the edge off the job. When you learn to manipulate people, your job becomes easier.

What Is the Best Way to Be Effective?

Each individual will find different ways to be an effective property manager. There is no single way that works best in gaining and maintaining control and higher profits. You must experiment and find ways that work for you. Written agreements are a given. They must be in place to ensure control. Good people skills are necessary for prosperous management of rental property. Sales skills take the edge off the job. When you learn to manipulate people, your job becomes easier. A positive attitude is beneficial in dealing with the control of your building and tenants. Genuine interest in your tenants will improve your success. It is hard to sell anybody on anything if you don't believe in what you are selling. You can get away with hiding behind a smile for awhile, but if the smile is a fake, you will be exposed in the end.

Control is what you make it. If you work at improving your performance as a manager, control will come. As you gain control, you should see higher profits. When you have the respect of your tenants, you are in control. I believe the best place to begin in establishing control is with your tenants. They may just be tenants, but their rent pays your bills. Don't put yourself on a pedestal. Someone will knock it out from under you. Be real, and be honest. There will be people you cannot agree with, but the people you do develop relationships with will make up for all the ones that didn't.

Subsidized Rental Income

If you decide to participate in programs offering subsidized rental income, there are a few facts you should know. This chapter is going to give you those facts in easy-to-follow comparisons of the pros and cons associated with subsidized housing programs.

Subsidized rental income is guaranteed money, but it does not always come easily. Most programs require a rental property to meet certain minimum standards, before you can participate in the programs. The tenants you get under these programs are not always the most desirable tenants, but they can be some of the best tenants you can find.

> ✔ **FAST FACT**
>
> Don't make the mistake of thinking that all tenants who require subsidized housing are deadbeats. Some of these tenants are the cream of the crop for a property manager.

When many landlords think of Section 8 (one of the primary subsidized programs) tenants, they think of poor people who will make horrible tenants. It is often assumed that tenants receiving housing assistance are lazy and irresponsible. This is not always true. Elderly tenants are often involved in subsidized housing and these senior citizens can be model tenants. People with physical disabilities are another example of tenants receiving subsidized rental assistance. These people can be the kind of tenants that any landlord would be proud to have. Your job as a property manager can be a breeze when you have the right Section 8 tenants.

If you have predetermined ideas about subsidized rental income, you may be surprised with what you can learn from this chapter. When you want to maximize the rental income of a property, you must investigate the advantages offered from subsidized rental income. If you have set your mind against tenants receiving financial help, you are doing yourself, and some fine tenants, a disservice.

What Is Subsidized Rental Income?

What is subsidized rental income? There are many government programs in existence to help people from all walks of life to cope with rising rental rates. These programs work in various ways. Basically, subsidized rental income is the income a landlord receives from one of these programs to complement the rent paid by a tenant. The subsidized rental income is guaranteed money. It is there, every month, like clockwork.

How Do Subsidized Programs Work?

How do subsidized programs work? Subsidized rental programs function in many ways. Rather than give you a broad-brush description, I am going to detail the most common programs available. To obtain more information on these programs, you can contact your local housing authority. If you prefer, you can contact the U.S. Department of Housing and Urban Development (HUD). You can visit the HUD website at: www.hud.gov. To contact HUD by mail, write to:

Assistant Secretary for Housing
Federal Housing Commissioner
Department of Housing and Urban Development
Washington, D.C. 20410-8000

Lower-Income Rental Assistance

The Lower-Income Rental Assistance program is best known as Section 8. This program is designed to help low-income people obtain safe, sanitary housing in private accommodations.

How the Program Works

The Lower-Income Rental Assistance program covers the gap between what a tenant can afford to pay and the market rate for available rentals. The rent charged for approved accommodations must meet the criteria of the program. Eligible tenants are required to pay a percentage, up to forty percent, of their income towards the rental amount of living quarters. The program pays the difference between this amount and the required for approved rent. For tenants to qualify for this assistance, they must meet certain criteria.

Building Requirements

For buildings to meet the requirements of this program they must meet safety and sanitation requirements set forth by HUD. A building will have to be inspected and approved before your Section 8 tenants can be approved to reside in the rental units.

Getting a building to conform to Section 8 guidelines is not usually a major problem. Most any rental unit that is up to modern standards will meet Section 8 requirements. For buildings that are not acceptable to Section 8 standards, property owners should consider bringing their buildings up to the standards for Section 8 tenants. The guaranteed rental payments from the program are an excellent incentive for making property improvements.

▶ *PRO POINTER*

I have managed buildings where the Section 8 tenants scrubbed the floors in hallways. This was a common area, but the tenants kept the halls neat and clean. There can be problems with subsidized tenants, but many of these tenants make model residents for rental properties.

Meet Requirements

In order for you to participate in a Section 8 program, a building must meet certain requirements. It must provide decent, safe, and sanitary housing to the tenants. The interpretation of the words decent, safe, and sanitary can vary, depending upon who is setting the standards. When you want to work with subsidized tenants, the interpretation of these words will be done by the people administering the program.

To have a building placed on the agency's approved list, the building must be inspected by a representative of the

✔ *FAST FACT*

If your building fails its inspection for approval to be rented in a subsidized program, you have two options. You can leave the building in its present condition and not rent to subsidized tenants. Or, you can make the necessary alterations to conform to the inspector's checklist.

agency. This is typically done after a qualified tenant has expressed a desire to rent your unit. Section 8 tenants shop for their housing in the same way other types of tenants do. When they find a unit they like, they ask the landlord or property manager to allow them to rent the property. At this point, the property must be approved by the program's administrator, which is usually the local housing authority.

Once you request approval to rent your property to subsidized tenants, an inspector will be dispatched to evaluate your building. The building must be in conformance with local codes and ordinances. For example, you will be expected to have smoke detectors and adequate hall lighting installed. The inspection will go smoothly if your property is of average condition and is not in violation of building and fire codes.

If your building fails its inspection, you have two options. You can leave the building in its present condition and not rent to subsidized tenants. If you choose to, you can make the necessary alterations to conform to the inspector's checklist. After you make the changes, the building will be inspected again. If your building is approved, it is time to negotiate the rental amount for the unit.

> ✔ **FAST FACT**
>
> Section 8 programs allow for property owners to receive fair-market rental rates, in most cases. Rental amounts are based on HUD fair-market rents, but there is some latitude for adjustments. The best way to determine how much rent a specific unit can pull is to have the rental unit evaluated by the officials who administer subsidized housing funds.

Negotiating Rent

Negotiating an acceptable rent with the administrator of the program should not be difficult. The programs usually allow enough latitude in rental figures to pay a fair market rent. The amount of rent you will receive will be negotiated with the administrator in the same way that you would haggle with an average tenant.

These programs provide information on the ceiling they have to work with on rental amounts. When some landlords see these rental amounts, they get excited. At first look, it may appear you can make much more money with Section 8 tenants than you can with average tenants. It is possible to enjoy a higher net income with Section 8 tenants, but the figures are not quite what they seem.

In the first place, the rental amounts you see are the highest amounts acceptable to the program. You are not guaranteed of receiving the highest amount. The rent you receive will be negotiated and could be much lower than the upper limit allowed by the program. Generally, the amount will parallel the fair market rents for your area.

Secondly, the rental amounts shown as a ceiling include an allowance for utilities. This allowance can reduce the amount of money you thought you would get with the Section 8 program. Once you come to terms on the amount to be charged in rent, it will be time to complete a lease agreement.

Signing the Lease

When you rent to a Section 8 tenant, you will be signing a one-year lease. The lease will be fair and you will have the comfort of knowing that most of your money will be coming from the subsidizing agency. You can think of the agency as a co-signer for the tenant.

> ✔ **FAST FACT**
>
> Section 8 tenants are entitled to a one-year lease. This lease can be the property owner's lease with a HUD addendum or a HUD-approved lease form.

Some of the Advantages of Providing Subsidized Housing

There are many good reasons to participate in subsidized housing. The advantages offered to you are numerous. Let's take a look at a few of these advantages.

Maximum Rents

When you participate in subsidized housing programs you are usually able to receive maximum rents. If you are able to negotiate for market-rate rents, and you should be able to in most cases, you will be making just as much money with Section 8 tenants as you would with any other tenant. And, much of the rent is guaranteed to be paid.

Low Vacancy Rates

When you open your doors to income-assisted tenants, you lower your vacancy rate. You automatically have a larger base of prospective tenants to pull from. Your units will be leased for a year and many of the tenants will renew their leases. If you treat the tenants right, they have little reason to relocate.

Almost Guaranteed Income

Much of your income will be guaranteed when you have a lease with HUD-sponsored tenants. The tenants will be responsible for a small percentage of the rent, but HUD will pay most of the rent. The portion of the rent paid by HUD will be there for you on time, every time. If the tenants fail to pay their portion of the rent, you may use the same procedures you would employ with average tenants to collect your rent. If the tenants just won't pay, you can evict them.

✔ **FAST FACT**

When you are working with Section 8 tenants, you are allowed to require security deposits up to the maximum amount allowed under state and local laws.

The Other Side of the Coin

There can be a dark side to the subsidized rental programs. While the programs offer many advantages, there are some aspects of the programs that are not appealing. What are the disadvantages? Well, let's see.

The Inspections

The inspections performed on a building to qualify it for subsidized tenants can be a hassle. If you maintain good living conditions for your tenants anyway, the inspections will not be much bother. If your building is not kept up, the inspections will require an investment of time and money in the property.

The Paperwork

As with any government program, there is plenty of paperwork to be done with subsidized tenants. Some of the paperwork seems unnecessary, but most of it works to your advantage. While there is paperwork to be completed, the volume is not much more than what you should maintain with any tenant. There can be a delay in filling a vacancy while you are waiting for the paperwork to be processed.

The Quality of the Tenants

The quality of the tenants you receive in subsidized housing is probably the biggest fear of most landlords. Landlords have a tendency to assume that all of the tenants they get through the program will be bad. This, of course, is not always the case.

It is a fact that the tenants will be low-income individuals; they must be to qualify for financial assistance. Some of the tenants may be more ignorant than other tenants you could rent to. Since the tenants are not paying all of the rent, it is possible they will be less responsible than a standard tenant. All of these factors could lead you to believe that you are opening your doors to undesirable tenants.

Yes, you could get bad tenants. The Section 8 tenants are screened for financial consideration, but they are not rated in the area of responsibility and dependability. It is up to you to investigate the tenant, just like you would with any other tenant. If you perform an adequate background investigation, you can remove all but the most remote chances of getting burned. And remember, if these tenants do turn out to be bad, you can evict them.

What Type of People Will You Get as Tenants?

The type of people who are eligible for these programs are as diverse as the properties they occupy. You could be dealing with people from all walks of life. I have seen excellent Section 8 tenants and I have seen subsidized tenants that I wouldn't rent my doghouse to. The key to success in dealing with these tenants is a thorough background investigation. If you select your tenants carefully, you will have no more problems than normal, and probably less.

Elderly Tenants

In my experiences I have seen numerous elderly people being helped with subsidized housing. I sold a twelve-unit building that housed seven elderly tenants using Section 8 services. Some of these tenants had lived in the building for more than twenty years. These ladies took better care of that building than most people do their own home. In essence, the building was their home. Not only did these tenants maintain impeccable apartments, they scrubbed the floors in the hall.

When the building was purchased, the new owner weeded out the Section 8 tenants. He did this in an attempt to collect higher rents and to avoid some of the responsibilities he had as a Section 8 landlord. In less than eighteen months, all of these excellent tenants had moved out of the building. New tenants came in and problems began to arise. By the end of the next year, the twelve-unit building stood empty and boarded up. The new owner lost the building to bankruptcy.

This building had maintained tenants and a positive cash flow for years. During the prosperous years the building housed Section 8 tenants. Under new management, the building went into depression and finally into bankruptcy. The Section 8 tenants didn't cause this failure. In fact, they may have been what kept the building healthy during its earlier years. I know from first-hand experience that you can get some superior tenants through subsidized housing programs.

Disabled Tenants

Disabled tenants are another possibility when you try to identify the type of tenant you will be working with in a subsidized program. Remember, these programs help people with low-incomes, and not all people with low-incomes are lowlifes.

A person who is unable to produce a high income because of a disability is not a low-class citizen, at least not because of an inability to make a lot of money. If you are prejudiced about people, based on their income, subsidized housing will not work for you. If you treat each individual as a person, and not as a worthless life form, you can find some very good tenants in the subsidized housing pool.

Drug Dealers and Such

I'm not going to lie to you about some types of tenants that you may encounter. You may wind up with drug dealers, thieves, pimps, and a host of other undesirable tenants when you participate in subsidized housing. Of course, you could end up with this same caliber of tenant in any event. As I said earlier, if you do your homework before leasing your unit, you can avoid most of the bad tenants.

Will Section 8 Tenants Give Your Building a Bad Reputation?

Some people perceive Section 8 tenants as second-rate tenants. The people who feel this way will dub the property owner as a slumlord. It is safe to assume that a building's reputation may be affected by Section 8 tenants, but the people who matter will not harbor bad feelings. Many people will see the property owner as a gracious landlord and a person willing to help disadvantaged people. I don't believe your reputation, or the reputation of your building, will be damaged by housing Section 8 tenants.

What Are the Risks of Renting to Section 8 Tenants?

The risks of renting to Section 8 tenants are not much more than the risks associated with any other type of tenant. In some ways, your position is stronger when you rent to Section 8 tenants. The program is well worth looking into.

Some Words of Advice

I would like to give you some words of advice. Give strong consideration to working with subsidized housing programs. When these programs are used properly, you can maximize your rental income and help unfortunate people at the same time.

Take the time to sift through this chapter and consider the many benefits your property owners could receive from being Section 8 landlords. Talk to your competitors and see if they have experience in working with subsidized tenants. Meet with your local housing authority and get all the details on the programs available to you.

Don't jump in with both feet. If you decide to give Section 8 tenants a chance, do so in moderation. Once you allow these tenants into a building, you must let them stay for a year, unless they violate the covenants of your lease. Start with one subsidized tenant and see how the deal goes. If you like what you see, recruit other Section 8 tenants. If you are unhappy with your new tenant, tighten your screening procedures and choose the best tenants for the buildings that you are managing.

Keep an open mind towards the programs. Do not conjure images of bad tenants stealing cleaning supplies and appliances. To avoid undesirable tenants, perform complete investigations on each tenant, before you agree to take them in. Play by the rules. Just because these tenants are Section 8 tenants doesn't mean you can ignore or abuse them. If their faucet is dripping, fix it.

My Opinion

In my opinion, Section 8 tenants can be the best tenants you will ever have. In my experiences with Section 8 tenants I have seen all types of people. Many of these people were not top-quality tenants. However, I have found a large number of Section 8 tenants to be responsible and desirable.

As it relates to profits, I have seen Section 8 tenants turn troubled buildings around. The steady, dependable income from subsidized housing programs is a tremendous boost to some buildings. This is especially true in areas where average tenants are not typically ideal tenants. In selling buildings, I have seen the positive impact made by having the building filled with Section 8 tenants. When a prospective buyer is buying a building with Section 8 tenants, it is known that a majority of the rental income is guaranteed. This guaranteed income is attractive to a new buyer.

I have also seen the negative affects of subsidized housing. I have seen the system and the tenants abused. I have known landlords who did not fare well with Section 8 tenants. My dealings have revealed people who would not buy a building, simply because it housed Section 8 tenants.

There is always more than one way to view an opportunity. Depending upon your point of view, subsidized housing can be great, or it can be a disaster. The final decision will be up to you. I believe you owe it to yourself and your clients to at least investigate the possible gains associated with subsidized housing.

Getting Low-Interest Loans and Grants

If you are a property owner and a property manager, and many managers are owners, you could benefit from low-interest loans and grants. How would you like to receive thousands of dollars to improve your rental property as a gift? Suppose you could obtain improvement money for your building without ever having to pay it back; would this interest you? Can you imagine being able to borrow rehab money at interest rates of only a fraction of the going rate? Does all of this sound too good to be true? Well, buckle up for a wild ride, because there are programs available to help you do a lot with a little, and you are about to discover them.

There must be a catch to free money and cheap money. Well, all of what you are about to learn is possible and there are no strings attached. You don't have to worry about big guys in long, black limousines coming to break your kneecaps. You don't have to surrender your soul. All you have to do to enjoy the benefits of low interest loans and grants is to work with Uncle Sam. No, you don't have to join the military. Our government has numerous programs available to help landlords. These programs exist to help you improve the quality of your rental property.

If you have any interest in receiving money to invest in your rental property,

> ▶ **PRO POINTER**
>
> Investigate what types of special loan programs are available in your area. See if there is grant money available to revitalize neighborhoods in your region. There could be hidden treasure in your backyard.

you must investigate the many government-backed programs available. These programs make it possible to improve your property when other methods would be impossible. Why would the government do this? The government's motivation is the revitalization of neighborhoods.

Programs Change

Before we begin, I feel compelled to tell you that the programs I am about to explain change from time to time. The programs are fluid; this book is not. Before you rely on any of the following information, check the present status of any program that you may be interested in.

To investigate new programs, changed programs, and discontinued programs, you can check with your local housing authority and HUD. Your local housing authority should be the best resource for you. Why the local authority? Even though many of the programs are associated with the government and HUD, they are often originated for landlords at the local level.

Not all communities are approved for all programs. This is another good reason to check with your local housing authority. With this said, let's explore some of the programs that may be available and of interest to you.

Community Development Block Grants

Community Development Block Grants are given to entitled communities to apply to a vast array of community development activities. These activities may include neighborhood revitalization, economic development, and other community improvements.

The grants must be used for purposes that will benefit low-income and moderate-income people. The grants are designed to prevent and eliminate slums. A percentage of the funds from these grants must be used to benefit the low-income and moderate-income citizens. The funds may be used for the rehabilitation of residential properties, among other activities.

There are also community development block grants for states and small cities. This type of grant falls under the "non-entitlement" category.

> ✔ **FAST FACT**
>
> Many investors have made bundles of money by purchasing rundown properties and fixing them up for rental use and resale. You might find that rehabbing rental properties will fit your investment profile.

Rental Rehabilitation

The rental rehabilitation program is ideally suited to landlords of residential properties. This program is designed to encourage the rehabilitation of rental property. The program also offers rental subsidies to aid lower-income tenants. These grants are awarded to selected communities. The funds may be used for the improvement of rental property.

There are limitations on the type of improvements you may use this money for. If you are correcting substandard conditions, you can use this money. When you are about to repair major systems, that may fail if not repaired, you can take advantage of these funds. Essential improvements are approved for the use of this money. Some energy-related work is approved. Alterations to allow handicapped people access to the rental units are okay.

Once you have used these funds and completed the work, you must rent a substantial percentage of the rental units to low-income families. Your rents must be set at market rates and may not be limited by rent controls. These grants may are limited to certain neighborhoods. If rents in your neighborhood are likely to escalate more rapidly than the general rental market, you may not be able to use these funds.

There are three considerations that will be examined before these funds are awarded to an area. The income of tenants will be examined to determine a need. The age of existing rental units will be considered. The final consideration is the living conditions of existing rental properties. This aspect is weighted double in the formula used to decide what areas receive the grant money. The specific areas of concern include the following:

- Plumbing facilities
- Kitchen facilities
- Overcrowding within the properties
- The cost of rents

Consider the possibilities available with this type of program. A savvy investor can use grant money to pay for up to one-half of all approved expenses in renovating a building. Plumbing and kitchen facilities are high on the priority list of this program. Kitchens and bathrooms are also high on the priority lists of prospective tenants. Consider your options with this plan.

Rehabilitation Loans

The rehabilitation loans program is available to aid in financing real estate renovations. These loans may be made to anyone who can demonstrate the ability to repay the loan. Special consideration is given to applicants with low or moderate income.

Rehabilitation loans are available for single-family homes, multi-family housing, mixed-use properties, and non-residential real estate. These loans are meant to reduce the destruction of basically sound structures. This type of loan may be used for insulation and weatherization projects.

In addition, the loans are available for bringing properties into compliance with building codes and standard living conditions.

A loan from the rehabilitation loan program will have maximum limits, but they are realistic. As a borrower of these funds, you may have up to twenty years to repay the loan. Low-income borrowers will repay the loan at a low interest rate.

Manufactured Home Parks

The manufactured home parks program provides federal mortgage insurance to finance the construction or rehabilitation of manufactured home parks. While this, at first glance, may not seem to be a program for landlords, it can be. As an investor, you might consider buying a manufactured home park. If you do, you become the landlord of all the lots. This program is normally thought of as serving builders and developers, but there is room for landlords in the program, as well.

To qualify for this program, the manufactured home park must have a minimum number of rental lots. Mortgage amounts are restricted. The loan amount for each lot will vary from area to area. HUD must approve the location of the manufactured home park. Further, market conditions must show a demand for this type of housing. HUD insures mortgages made by private lending institutions for the purposes of building or rehabbing manufactured home parks. The lender originating the loan must be approved by the Federal Housing Authority (FHA).

Multi-Family Rental Housing

The multi-family rental housing program exists to provide federal mortgage insurance to finance the construction and rehabilitations of rental property.

HUD insures mortgages made by approved, private lending institutions for the construction and rehabilitation of rental property. To qualify, a property must contain a minimum of five residential rental units. As part of the selection criteria, buildings affected by these funds should have the ability to accommodate families at reasonable rates.

Multi-Family Rental Housing for Moderate-Income Families

The multi-family rental housing for moderate-income families program is designed to provide mortgage insurance to finance rental or co-op multi-family housing. This housing is intended for the occupancy of moderate-income families and may be designated for the elderly.

The money for your project will come from a private lending institution, but it will be insured by HUD. Money may be borrowed to build or to substantially improve multi-family rental and co-op housing. There must be a minimum of five units in the project to qualify for money from the program. The residents for the project must be moderate-income families or displaced families.

The project may be comprised of detached or semi-detached dwellings. The units may be accessible by stairs or elevators. For most investors, HUD will insure up to ninety percent of the loan amount.

Some Other Programs

There are many HUD-backed programs available to property owners. The programs described earlier are the ones generally of the most interest to investors and landlords, but there are still more programs to look at.

Mortgage Insurance for Housing the Elderly

The mortgage insurance for housing the elderly program is in place to finance the construction or renovation of rental housing for the elderly or handicapped. This program is designed to assure a supply of rental housing suited for the elderly or handicapped. This program requires the property to have a minimum of five units. The program considers people of age 62, or older, as elderly.

Housing Development Grants

The housing development grant program makes money available for building or renovating rental property, co-ops, and mutuals. Its purpose is to increase the availability of rental housing, in areas where there are severe shortages. All projects participating in this program must reserve at least twenty percent of the units for families with low-incomes. These units must remain available to low-income tenants for twenty years. The units may not be converted to a use other than low-income rental for at least twenty years. These grants cannot exceed fifty percent of the project's cost and will not normally include the cost of acquisition of the subject property.

Property Improvement Loan Insurance

The property improvement loan insurance program provides federal insurance for loans used to finance property improvements. The program can be used for improvements, alterations, and repairs. Single-family homes, multi-family housing, and non-residential properties are all potentially eligible for the plan.

> ✔ **F A S T   F A C T**
>
> The rehabilitation mortgage insurance program can help you to finance the improvement of single-family homes and small multi-family buildings, with less than four units.

Rehabilitation Mortgage Insurance

The rehabilitation mortgage insurance program can help you to finance the improvement of single-family homes and small multi-family buildings, with less than four units.

This program insures loans to finance the rehabilitation of existing properties. It also helps when you are refinancing an existing debt in the process of doing rehab work. Further, you can use this program when acquiring a property to rehab.

Flexible Subsidy

The flexible subsidy program provides federal aid to assist multi-family projects with financial problems. This program can assist in restoration work and maintenance matters. The program can provide immediate cash to correct deferred maintenance and replacements. The subsidy program can

> ✔ **F A S T   F A C T**
>
> If you learn to work with housing programs available to you, it is possible to greatly increase your net worth. When you are creative, you can generate a handsome salary for yourself. Low-interest loans and grants are strong tools in the right hands.

assist with financial deficiencies and the replacement of reserve and operating capital. Improved management is another goal of the flexible subsidy program.

Are You Surprised?

Are you surprised at all the ways your government can help you with your rental property? Many landlords go through their entire career without ever having the knowledge to take advantage of these programs. A few investors learn of the programs and go on to perfect their use. These few investors turn a government program into a money machine. Of course, some investors abuse the system. The gamblers that abuse the system, on the hope they won't be discovered, hurt the programs. If you learn to work with these programs, you can greatly increase your net worth. When you are creative, you can generate a handsome salary for yourself. Low-interest loans and grants are strong tools in the right hands.

What Can You Do with These Programs?

What can you do with these programs? There are numerous possibilities for the use of these programs. You could convert your existing building into specialized housing for the elderly. In doing this, you may see a considerable increase in your rental income. You might rehab your building to build net worth and to see nice profits by using grant money.

Final Words

As you can see, the programs shown to you here can provide wealth. If you expand your operations to include contracting, maintenance, and other service-related businesses, you can begin to stack up the cash. Even if you have no interest in playing all the roles, you can do very well doing what you do best, landlording. Look into these programs and see if you can find a use for any of them. Contact your local housing authority and confirm the terms, conditions, and availability of the programs you are interested in. Times change, and so do government programs.

Improving a Property

When you are considering improving a rental property, you have much to think about. When the question of making non-essential improvements arises, you must evaluate the financial feasibility of the venture. Making the right improvements to your property can improve your cash flow and the property's value. Making the wrong improvements can drain your bank account, without providing financial rewards.

Many investors fall into a trap when it comes to capital improvements. They are convinced that their attempt to improve their property will be profitable. The improvements may have been recommended by tenants or amateur advisors. If the investor does not prove the viability of the project money may be lost, and lots of it.

What Are Capital Improvements?

For the purposes of this chapter, capital improvements are improvements that will cost more than five-hundred dollars. Normally these improvements are not mandatory. They could include painting the exterior of a property or installing new siding. Extensive remodeling to kitchens and bathrooms is an example of a capital improvement. Having a new roof installed is a capital improvement. Installing a new roof may or may not be essential, but in either case, it is a capital improvement. The same rule applies to the replacement of a heating system and other similar situations.

When a landlord makes a capital improvement to a building, it is usually in an attempt to generate a stronger cash flow or a higher appraised value. The intent is good, but the results are not always what are hoped for. To be successful with major improvements you must research market conditions and plan carefully. It is easy to dump several thousand dollars into a property without any noticeable increase in income or value. When this happens you have spent your money with little hope of seeing a return on it. This is bad business and can cause you serious financial distress. You can eliminate the risk of losing big money by investing some of your time in research, before making improvements.

Research

What type of research is needed prior to committing to capital improvements? There are a few different angles to look at when it comes to large improvement investments. Much of the research will depend on the type of improvement you are contemplating. If you are planning an improvement to increase cash flow, you must research market conditions and demand. If you are improving your property to increase its value, you must assume the role of an appraiser or hire a professional appraiser. If you are attempting to gain better cash flow and a higher property value, you must combine your research duties.

> ▶ *PRO POINTER*
>
> With any type of improvement you must assess the cost of making the improvement. This research will be done by soliciting bids from the needed contractors. You will also have to make projections for the performance of your improvement. This part of your homework will be speculation, based on as much available data as you can find. By the time you are done with your planning you should know within a reasonable margin of error how effective your improvement will be in meeting your goal.

Rate of Return

When you are projecting the rate of return from improvements, you must set realistic goals. If you remodel rental units to give them a modern appearance you should be able to obtain a higher rent for the units. However, you will not be able to collect more rent than the market will bear. If you project your increased income based on a percentage of your improvement investment, you could be sorrowfully disappointed.

You may be able to project your equity gain as a percentage of the improvement expense, but not the income performance.

It is easy to get caught up in the excitement of punching numbers into the computer and grinning at their results on your spreadsheet. But, if these numbers are not realistic, there will be little joy after the improvements are made. There are some attempted improvements that may cause your cash flow or property value to decrease.

The key to reaching realistic goals is setting them with accurate information to work from. Personal opinions are not worth much in business. You may love the idea of painting your building pink and blue, but an appraiser will probably have

> ✔ **FAST FACT**
> You must base your decisions, projections, and goals on factual information.

a different opinion. From a business standpoint, the appraiser's professional opinion is the one that will count. You must base your decisions, projections, and goals on factual information.

Cash Flow and Property Value

The two basic reasons for capital improvements are to increase cash flow or a property's value. Ideally, your improvements should fill both of these desires. Most improvements that increase your property value will allow the opportunity for better cash flow. Improvements that are done to increase cash flow may not show a significant impact on your property value. When you are planning to make improvements, you must decide what you want the improvement to do. Then you must predict how well the improvement will perform its intended task. Let's look at some specific examples of each type of improvement.

Cash-Flow Improvements

The primary objective of cash-flow improvements is to generate higher rents. Since many rental properties are appraised using formulas built around the building's income, these improvements often increase a property's value, as well as its cash flow. For residential income properties with less than five rental units, the results will not be as favorable as they are with larger buildings. Most buildings with four units, or less, are appraised with the comparable-sale method. This is the same type of appraisal method that is used for single-family homes. This does not allow as much opportunity for increased cash flow to determine the building's value. We will get into the differences in appraisals a little later on. For now, let's concentrate on the improvements themselves.

The effectiveness of cash-flow improvements will be determined by three basic factors. These factors are as follows:

- The present condition of a property
- The condition of competitive properties
- The market demand

If your apartments are dingy and dark, a fresh coat of paint could make a big difference in the amount of rent a tenant is willing to pay for the unit. On the other hand, if the apartment's paint is satisfactory, freshening it or changing the color may have no effect on the rent you can request.

A Poor Decision

A poor decision on what improvements to make can crush your profit potential with a building. Suppose all the apartment buildings in your area have painted wood siding. They are all in good condition and attractive. Your building is comparable to the competitive properties in its present condition. You decide that installing vinyl siding on your property will make it easier to maintain. You further believe that by adding vinyl siding, you can recover the cost in increased rent. If you make this improvement, you are unlikely to collect any additional rental income.

As long as all the available rental units are clean and neat, tenants will not care if their building has vinyl siding or painted wood siding. They will not be willing to pay a higher price to live in your building, just because it has new vinyl siding.

If the surrounding, competitive properties are all equipped with appliances, adding appliances to your units should command a higher rent. In contrast, if none of the local landlords supply appliances, adding appliances to your building might cause the increased rent to price you out of the marketplace. No matter how nice your rental units are, if people can't afford them, you will not see any additional income. By being the only building offering appliances with the rental unit

> ✔ *FAST FACT*
> You must be careful not to over-improve your building to a point where tenants will not, or cannot, pay the increased rent to offset the cost of the improvement.

COMPARATIVE PROPERTY DATA SHEET

Address _____

Style _____ Rents _____

Amenities _____ Number Of Rooms _____

Number Of Bedrooms_____ Number Of Bathrooms _____

Siding _____ Heat Type _____

Type Of Hot Water _____ Water (public/private) _____

Sewer (public/private) _____ Basement (yes/no) _____

Utilities paid by landlord _____

Security _____ Storage _____

Laundry facilities _____

Deposit required_____ Pets allowed _____

Parking facilities _____

Proximity to shopping _____

School system _____

General condition of rental units _____

FLOOR PLAN

1ST _____

2ND_____

3RD_____

BASEMENT

Living Room _____

Dining Room _____

Family Room _____

Bedrooms _____

Bathrooms _____

Kitchen _____

Comments _____

Other pertinent information:

_____

_____

FIGURE 6.1 Comparative Property Data Sheet

you should attract more tenants. This will reduce your vacancy rate, but may do nothing for your rental amount.

Increased-Value Improvements

Improvements made to increase a property's value can influence the building's cash flow, but they may not. For example, building a garage for your tenants should increase the value of your property. There could be an equity gain from the construction if you act as the general contractor or build the garage yourself. However, if your building is already producing rents at the upper end of the market demand, you may not be able to raise the rents to cover the cost of your improvement. You could accumulate equity with this type of improvement, but you will have to spend liquid cash to do it. Even if you build the garage yourself, you will have cash invested that cannot be extracted from the building. These improvements can cause you to lose your rental property.

Almost any increased-value improvement that is worthwhile will increase your cash flow. If an improvement will not boost your net income, don't do it. Increased-value improvements are most effective when you are dealing with old, rundown properties.

> ▶ **PRO POINTER**
>
> If you buy a building to rehab, you can build substantial equity with increased-income improvements. Buildings that have been abandoned, damaged by fire, or that have not had routine maintenance for years are the best bets for increased-value improvements.

Replacing a Roof

Unless a roof is leaking, don't replace it. The only reasons for replacing a roof are to prevent leaks or to change the appearance of a particularly ugly roof. If a roof is a mismatched, multi-color eyesore, it might be worth replacing. If the roof is leaking and cannot be repaired, it will have to be replaced.

Tenants will not be willing to pay a higher rent to live in a building with a new roof. As long as the existing roof doesn't leak and isn't a beacon of ugliness, tenants will not care if it is new or not. An appraiser may allow a little extra value for a building if it has a new roof, but not enough to cover the cost of the job. In general, don't invest money in roof replacements unless you are forced to.

New Paint Jobs

The paint on a building should be kept in good condition. If the paint is cracking and peeling, it should be replaced. If the paint is in good shape, leave it alone. A white building will produce as much rent as a brown one. Unless you have a horrendous paint job now, repainting a building to change its color will be a waste of money. Tenants will not pay extra for the new paint and appraisers will not adjust their reports much for the new paint job.

Gutters

Installing gutters on a property will not be very cost effective. Appraisers may allow some extra value for the gutters, but not much. Prospective tenants are not likely to have gutters on their list of must-have items when searching for an apartment. Gutters can solve basement flooding, ice build-ups on walkways, and other water-related problems. While they are beneficial, gutters do little for your cash flow or appraised value.

> ▶ *PRO POINTER*
>
> Tenants will enjoy having a deck for sitting on, cooking out, and entertaining. The tenants may be willing to pay extra for the privilege of a deck.
>
> From an appraiser's point of view, decks and porches add value. When you combine increased desirability, increased value, and increased cash flow, you have a winning improvement.

Adding Porches and Decks

Depending on the property and the location, adding porches and decks can increase your cash flow and your property's value. Porches and decks can also set your building apart from the competition and attract more tenants. You will not experience a huge equity profit by adding these features, but you shouldn't lose any money either.

Of the two investments, decks should produce a better rate of return than porches. They are less expensive to build and they still add a touch of difference to your building. Tenants will enjoy having a deck for sitting on, cooking out, and entertaining. The tenants may be willing to pay extra for the privilege of a deck.

From an appraiser's point of view, decks and porches add value. When you combine increased desirability, increased value, and increased cash flow, you have a winning improvement. This is not to say that adding decks or porches to all buildings will be successful. In this and all the examples, you must temper the examples with regional differences, market conditions, and your own personal situation. There is no hard and fast rule to lock in on. There are averages and historical data to point you in the right direction, but the final outcome will be decided through your personal research.

New Siding

Many landlords consider installing vinyl siding when the time comes to paint their existing wood siding. This is a reasonable consideration. Vinyl siding does reduce long-term maintenance cost. If you are going to have a major expense in preparing and painting your existing siding, deciding to install vinyl could be a good alternative. However, installing vinyl over perfectly good wood siding is not likely to produce positive results.

Your appraisal report will show a higher value with new vinyl siding installed, but it will not compensate for all the money you have spent. Tenants won't care whether the property has vinyl siding or wood siding. The return on your investment will come mostly from reduced maintenance expenses. If you plan to keep the building for years to come, consider vinyl siding when it's time to paint the wood siding. If you will be selling in the next few years, painting is probably the best choice. You will have to weigh the expenses and make your own decision.

Paving Your Parking Area

Paving your parking area will improve the appearance of your property. It will also increase your property value to some extent. A paved parking lot will probably not increase your cash flow. Tenants will normally accept a well-kept graveled parking lot as quickly as a paved one. Unless there are personal reasons, such as snow removal, to consider, save your money for a more profitable improvement.

Increasing Your Parking Area

In cities, parking space can be very valuable. If you can alter the grounds of your property to create additional parking you may be well rewarded. Tenants might welcome a higher rent if they receive the benefit of convenient parking. Appraisers will be generous when evaluating the additional parking space, if it is a commodity competitive buildings don't have.

Again, we are back to your personal evaluation. If you have adequate parking for all your rental units it would be silly to replace your lawn with gravel or pavement. If your tenants are paying a monthly fee to keep their cars at an off-premises parking lot, you should cash in on it by creating your own additional space. The value of parking will vary greatly between locations. It is much easier to find parking in Maine than in it is in Massachusetts.

On-Site Playgrounds

If you cater to families with children, building an on-site playground could keep your units full, while your competitor's are empty. The cost of a simple play area is not enormous, but the results can include happy tenants, stronger cash flow, and a lower vacancy rate. The playground will not do much for your appraised value, but the other redeeming qualities make it worth considering.

There is a downside to having your own playground. There is a liability factor that must be addressed. If a child is injured on the playground, you may be held accountable. Before you invest in a playground, talk with your attorney and insurance company. The risks may be more than you can afford to gamble.

Fencing Your Property

Installing a fence around the perimeter of your property can serve many functions. It can act as a kiddy corral. The fence will allow your tenants with pets to have a safe place to let their pets get some exercise. Even a small fence will discourage outsiders from running through your lawn and abusing your building. For all its benefits, your fence investment will be hard to recover. Some tenants may pay more to live in a unit with a fenced yard, but they are a minority. Appraisal reports will not show enough equity gain to pay for the fencing. The choice is yours, but fencing is rarely a good investment.

Replacing Your Windows

If you own an old building, you might be considering replacing the windows. This is an expensive proposition, but it can pay for itself in reduced heating and cooling cost. If your windows are drafty and poorly insulated, new windows can make a notable difference in your utility bills. If your tenants pay for their own utilities, they may inspect the windows of a property before agreeing to rent it. The public is aware of energy costs and the value of tight, well-insulated windows. When your building has new energy-efficient windows, tenants may rent your unit instead of the next guy's. However, they may not be willing to pay a higher rent for your unit, based solely on the better windows.

If you do a sales job on them, you may be able to justify your higher rent to the tenants. But, if their net out-of-pocket expenses will be the same in either building, you will need more than new windows to secure the tenant. When your building is appraised, the new windows will make a difference in the property's value. It is doubtful, however, that the appraisal will reflect a high enough gain to offset the expense of the windows.

The biggest advantages to replacement windows will be reduced operating expenses. Your utility costs will be lower and, if they are vinyl-clad windows, your maintenance costs will be less. If you are hoping to pay for the windows with higher rents, don't hold your breath. If you anticipate recovering your investment from a higher appraisal, you might, but I doubt it. You will recover some of your window investment, but probably not all of it.

If you are replacing the windows to make your building more appealing to a potential buyer, they will. A savvy buyer will notice the windows and appreciate their value. They may not be willing to pay the long dollar for the windows, but if they can get your building at a reasonable price, the windows may be the catalyst to making a deal. Many improvements can increase the desirability of your property to potential purchasers. While these improvements may make your building sell faster, they may not bring you a higher sales price. It will be unlikely for you to sell the property for more than its appraised value.

> ✔ **FAST FACT**
>
> Energy costs are escalating. Making rental properties more cost-efficient to heat and cool should be in the back of any property owner's mind with a long-term plan for holding a property.

Replacing Exterior Doors

The replacement of exterior doors can be compared to replacing windows. You can gain energy savings and possibly increased security. The value of the investment is also comparable to that of windows.

Adding Security Features

Adding security doors, lights, alarms, and related equipment can produce a stronger income. Depending on the building's location, tenants may be willing to pay a higher rent for increased security. Equity gain will be minimal with security equipment, unless it is normal for the area. In locations with a high crime rate, security features enhance your property's rental ability. The building will pull and hold tenants if they feel comfortable.

On average, beefed-up security is not a good investment, as far as a direct return on your investment goes. When you assess your personal situation, you may find there is no need for increased security. On the other hand, it may give you the marketing tool you need to reduce your vacancy rate. Prepare your opinion of the pros and cons before buying a security system.

Painting the Interior of a Property

Most landlords expect to paint their rental units each time they become vacant. This is routine maintenance. It is important to keep the walls and ceilings of your building attractive and bright. It is not necessary to go through the entire building painting all the walls and ceilings, just to change the color. Unless there are extenuating circumstances, there should be no reason to paint the interior of your rental units, except between tenants. If you have tenants who have been with you for many years, it might be a good gesture to give them a fresh coat of paint, but this is the exception, rather than the rule.

Hallways need to be painted more often than rental units. Halls take a lot of abuse. The hallways are also the first part of a building's interior seen by people. These halls cast the first impression of a building's condition. While you may not recover the cost of regular painting in increased rent or property value, you will enjoy a more stable tenancy record. Plan to paint your halls as often as needed and to paint your apartments between occupants. Confine your painting expenses to necessities, rather than desires.

Light Fixtures

Most landlords never think about their light fixtures. They are so used to seeing them that they accept them for what they are. Tenants and appraisers may see them in a different light, so to speak. Light fixtures can date your building. Outdated light fixtures signal an old building. Selectively upgrading your light fixtures can make your property more desirable. Take a look at your units and see if the fixtures are old and dingy-looking. Do they impress you as ancient artifacts? If so, consider budgeting a little money to update them, along with the rest of your improvements.

When landlords make capital investments they often overlook the little items that expose the building for what it is. Giving your property a modern facelift is good, but follow through with the job. If you are transforming an old building into a modern place to live, don't forget the light fixtures. You may not see a cash-on-cash return for your investment, but the overall effect will be good.

Floor Coverings

Floor coverings need to be replaced periodically. When replacing them out of need, the act is one of maintenance. When replacing them out of desire, the logic of the act can be considered questionable. Often a good cleaning will make a world of difference in the appearance of carpet and vinyl floors. Sanding wood floors and adding a new sealant can make them look new again. Weigh your decision to replace flooring carefully.

New floors will enable you to rent or sell your building faster. They will also have some positive impact on the property's value. But, the cost can be prohibitive and the rate of return can be poor. There are many grades of carpeting, carpet pads, and vinyl flooring to choose from. With conscientious shopping, you can save money on your flooring purchases. Selecting the proper grades will be a matter of money and use. Your halls will have to endure much more traffic than the bedrooms of your units. When you have to replace flooring, do so with a watchful eye.

With so many grades and choices, it is easy to invest more in flooring than you can recover. Also remember that it only takes one bad tenant to ruin your new flooring. The combined effect of many cosmetic improvements may enhance your cash flow, but it is hard to raise the rent only because you have installed new carpeting. Appraisers expect rental property to have satisfactory floor coverings. They will not raise your appraisal dramatically because of the installation of new flooring. Be sensible with the money you spend on flooring; it can be tough to recover the investment.

Appliances

If you supply tenants with appliances, you must keep them in good repair. With regular maintenance, appliances can last for many years. Sometimes they last so long that they should be replaced. Like light fixtures, appliances can tell the age of your building. How often do you find Harvest Gold and Avocado Green appliances in new buildings? If a washing machine has a handle and rollers on it, you should consider replacing it. Appliances influence the opinions of tenants. Battered appliances tell the tenants the rest of the building is probably beat too.

While you won't see much equity gain or increased cash flow from replacing appliances, there comes a time when they must be replaced. Choosing that time is up to you. As long as the appliances function properly and are not too old, you can leave them alone. If you

✔ **FAST FACT**

Tenants use their appliances frequently. They will appreciate modern appliances, but probably will not pay a lot more for them.

are making improvements to change the image of your units, appliances could be high on your list of changes to make. As long as you have working appliances, an appraiser will not deflate your property value by much. Most of the benefits you derive from appliance replacements will not be noticed as a direct result of the replacement, but they will be present.

Window Treatments

Window treatments may not seem like a capital improvement, but if you have several large, multi-family buildings, it can cost thousands of dollars to outfit them with window treatments. Some landlords

▶ **PRO POINTER**

When units are vacant, window treatments can reduce break-ins and vandalism. From the street, the apartments will appear occupied, even when they aren't.

provide window treatments for their tenants and others don't. If you don't, maybe you should. By providing window treatments you control the appearance of your rental units from the outsider's view.

When units are vacant, window treatments can reduce break-ins and vandalism. From the street, the apartments will appear occupied, even when they aren't. If you don't provide window treatments, your tenants may elect to hang bed sheets on the windows. This degrades your property and hurts the first impressions of prospective tenants. These two reasons are enough to justify the consideration of supplying your tenants with window treatments.

Window treatments are another improvement where it is difficult to assess your payback. They may allow you to achieve a slightly higher rent, but the extra income will be minimal. An appraiser may give additional value for the curtains, but you can't count on it. If you decide to install window treatments in your building, you will have to accept the fact that you will not be able to track your rate of return on the investment. The venture should draw more tenants, reduce losses to theft and vandalism, and reduce tenant turnover. Whether your gamble will pay off is to tell.

Large-Scale Projects

Large-scale projects involve heavy investments in remodeling, rehab work, and additions to a property. Examples might include the following:

- Building private storage areas for your tenants
- Adding a coin-operated laundry
- Remodeling all of the kitchens or bathrooms
- Adding bedrooms
- Adding entire rental units to a property

These large-scale projects can make you, and they can break you. When you are talking big projects, you are talking big money. When there is big money involved, there are big risks present. Let's examine some big-league projects and see how they might affect your building.

Storage Areas

Storage areas have become a thriving business. There are personal storage facilities with units to accommodate everything from small possessions to vintage automobiles. The price a person has to pay for these storage facilities is nothing to laugh about. There is some serious money being made by the owners of private storage businesses.

As a landlord, you are in an ideal position to get a piece of the storage pie. As more and more people are forced to remain tenants for longer, they need more room for storage. Most people don't need a garage to house an antique car, but they do need a place for their stuff. Christmas decorations, outgrown toys, abandoned exercise equipment, and a bevy of other articles need a place to reside. You can let your tenants go down the street and rent a storage cubicle, or you can provide them with an on-site storage area, for an additional rental fee. This is a tremendous opportunity for you to increase your cash flow.

Whether you convert your building's basement into storage or you build a new facility, the rewards can be great. If your mind is racing with thoughts of chicken-wire enclosures, forget it! People will pay handsomely for secure storage, but they will not offer much for the old-fashioned wire enclosures. If you want to make money from storage rental you will have to spend money on the development of a suitable facility.

When you consider how much you may be able to rent your storage units for, the idea becomes very interesting. Call local storage facilities and check their rental rates. This will give you a good idea of what you can charge. Remember, it will be more convenient for your tenants to have onsite storage, so you may be able to charge more than a facility that is a mile away. How would your building's net income look if you factored in this type of additional income? You are in the perfect position to find customers to rent your storage facilities. Your tenants are ideal prospects for the rental fees. Give this idea a lot of thought; I think you will like it more as you run the numbers.

Laundry Facilities

Are your rental units equipped with individual laundry facilities? Do you have a laundry room that your tenants share? Tenants must wash their clothes somewhere. If you are not providing free laundry facilities, many of your tenants are spending money each week at the local Laundromat.

By creating a coin-operated laundry room you can cash in on their dirty clothes.

Why let the business down the street take your tenants' money when you could be taking it? The cost to the tenant would be the same, but by having facilities onsite, their laundry duties would be much more convenient. You would be providing the tenants with a service and making money while doing so.

> ✔ **FAST FACT**
>
> Coin-operated laundries can produce exceptional net income. In commercial-grade, residential properties, increased income translates into increased property value. You initial investment may be steep, but the payoff should more than outweigh the expense.

Bath and Kitchen Remodeling

Bathrooms and kitchens are two rooms in a rental unit that will influence many people to make a decision to rent the unit. If these rooms are modern, clean, well-appointed, and desirable, you are well on your way to renting your unit. The costs involved with major remodeling can become intimidating. You will have to evaluate your decision to take on a large project carefully. If your research shows promise, these two rooms are the place to direct your remodeling efforts to.

> ▶ **PRO POINTER**
>
> Recently remodeled kitchens and bathrooms can demand a higher rent. They can also have a favorable impression on your building's appraised value. In addition, they will often reduce your vacancy rate. At the same time, you eliminate many of your repair calls when you upgrade these two rooms. Do thorough projections to see if your property warrants major remodeling. If it does, I think you will be pleased with the results.

Bedrooms

The value of a residential rental unit is often established by the number of bedrooms it contains. Typically, a three-bedroom apartment will rent for more than a two-bedroom apartment. If you can make conversions to your existing units to generate more bedrooms, you should be able to generate more cash. Old buildings are frequently spacious in their room sizes. They can also offer the opportunity for bedroom conversions. To accomplish this goal you must be creative. It is not easy to add a bedroom to an existing apartment, without adding additional space. In the conversion procedure you must make do with what you have. Here are some questions to ask yourself:

- Walk through your buildings and look for wasted space. Is there a dining room that could be converted to a bedroom?
- Is it feasible to divide the apartment up into a different design to generate a new bedroom?
- Is there an attached, covered porch that could be converted into a bedroom?
- Would it be possible to combine a closet with some wasted hall space to add a bedroom to your units?

If you can find a way to make a new bedroom, without ruining the function of the rest of the rental unit, go for it! Be aware of the building codes pertaining to bedrooms. If you must have an emergency egress window, some locations will not be suitable for your new bedroom. If your building is served by a septic system, make sure you will be able to add the bedroom without upgrading the septic system. When you get into expanding septic systems, you can run up a tall bill quickly.

Adding New Units

If your land is large enough, you may be able to add new units to your existing building. You will have to check for zoning regulations and other local laws that may affect your plans. The expense of building new rental units will be considerable, but you already have the land. Adding new units will give you the opportunity to make more money, but be sure the market demand will support them. If the rental market is glutted with vacant units, adding more units to your building could be a financial flop.

Rehab Work

Many investors make their living by rehabbing rental properties. They buy buildings in need of major work and make their money in the improvements. When these investors do the work themselves, they can make a year's income on a single building. If they only act as the general contractor, they may make more than most people do in a year. Much of their earnings will depend on the extent of the work done to the property. Logically, the more they do, the more they make.

By using low interest loans and grants, landlords that do rehab and remodeling work can take an abandoned building and turn it into a money machine. This is not light work. It requires experience, dedication, and hard work to be successful in the rehab business. This type of project also requires a strong credit rating and a willing lender. The money involved for large rehab projects is formidable.

When done properly, rehabbed buildings can make the owner large sums of money. They can produce excellent rental income. They can often be sold for a tidy profit. Many times they can be refinanced to extract cash, while producing income and tax benefits. As you get further into your new career, rehab work may be worth investigating, but don't attempt it until you are well prepared. If you don't know what you are getting into, rehab work can spell the end of your real estate career.

How Big Of A Gamble Are Capital Improvements?

Capital improvements are a gamble, but you can hedge the odds. When you do enough research you can remove most of the risks associated with investing in capital improvements. For example, let's say you are thinking about remodeling all of your bathrooms and kitchens. This project is going to be expensive. You have no idea if you will see a fair equity return for the money invested in the remodeling. What should you do?

You could flip a coin for the answer, but there is a better way to decide. You can hire a professional appraiser to give you a before-and-after opinion of value. Have the appraiser come in and appraise the property in its present condition. Provide the appraiser will a detailed set of plans and specifications for the proposed improvements. Ask the appraiser to give you a value on the property if these improvements are made.

Appraisers are accustomed to working with plans and specifications to obtain a value. When they appraise new construction projects they have to work from plans and specs. The appraiser will be able to give you an accurate assessment of what affect your proposed improvements will have on your building. When you receive the appraisal report, you can see how much more your building will be worth after the work is completed.

You can then compare the increased value to the quoted costs for doing the work. If you plan to have contractors perform the work, they will be happy to give you a free quote for the price of the job. Make sure it is a firm quote and not an esti-mate. By comparing the quotes with the appraisal report you will quickly be able to determine the feasibility of the project.

If your equity gain will be marginal or unsatisfactory, abort the project. All you will have lost is a little time and the cost of the appraisal. If the figures show a hefty gain and you can afford to do the job, do it. By getting a before-and-after appraisal, you have eliminated much of the unknown. You know how much the job will cost and how much it will increase the value of your property. With this information you are able to make an informed decision.

By following this type of progression you take much of the gamble out of capital improvements. If on the other hand you jump into an improvement without enough information, you may lose your shirt. Learning to play the rental game is not particu-larly perilous, if you take your time and watch your step.

Attracting the Best Tenants-Fast!

Property managers are faced with filling vacant apartments from time to time. With some buildings, filling vacancies can seem like a full-time job. Vacant rental units translate into lost revenue. If you allow units to remain empty for long, the income performance of the property sinks into the red. You would think that a responsibility of such magnitude would command the attention and respect of any property manager, but this is not always the case.

For some managers, filling vacancies is the most dreaded aspect of their job. The length of time and the amount of paperwork involved with finding and moving in a new tenant can seem overwhelming. This is especially true for part-time rental managers. Unmotivated managers can come up with countless excuses for not getting a vacant unit occupied, but none of them pay the rent. To make money with rental property, you must keep it rented.

Professional management companies strive to fill empty apartments fast, sometimes too fast. Most management services derive extra income from renting a vacant apartment. By charging a rent-up fee, these businesses have a monetary motivation to find a tenant. Unfortunately, in their haste to put a warm body in an empty rental unit, some companies do not screen the rental applicants thoroughly. If a property is being managed by such a firm, the property owner may lose money twice with every bad tenant.

First, they lose money by paying a rent-up fee for a tenant they don't want and won't keep. Second, they lose money in damages or legal fees incurred while dealing with the unwanted tenant. What do you, the property manager stand to lose?

You could lose your reputation and possibly the contract to manage the property. It is critical to make solid decisions when screening and selecting tenants.

Once you are motivated to fill vacancies, you will need help. You will need something to pull tenants to the building you are representing. In addition, your methods should be aimed at pulling quality tenants. Creative marketing and advertising can fill both of these bills. If you learn to use these tools effectively, you will find that filling vacancies does not have to be the worst part of property management.

What Does Marketing Mean to You?

What does marketing mean to you? Marketing is the act of making goods or services desirable to a customer. In your case, it is the act of setting the stage to attract quality tenants to a rental property. When creating marketing plan for rental property there are many elements to consider. There are some elements you can improve and others that you can't.

If the building you are trying to rent pulls tenants of a lesser quality, you can change that with property improvements and marketing. In effect, improving the property, to make it more desirable, can be considered a form of marketing for the landlord. Your personal presentation of the property's features and benefits is marketing. Every time you describe the property to a prospect on the telephone, you are marketing the building. Many of your day-to-day activities fall into the marketing category.

Many people don't consider their actions as marketing. If they did, they would be more effective property managers. In the rental business you are selling time in vacant apartments. You must consider yourself a salesman if you are to reach the goals possible in property management. These sales skills will be used for much more than simply filling vacancies. They can be used effec-

> **✔ FAST FACT**
>
> If the building you are trying to fill is not in a desirable location, you cannot reasonably move tenants into the building quickly. However, you can overcome the objections to the location with creative marketing. This can speed up the rental process and make you a hero to the property owner.

> **✔ FAST FACT**
>
> In the rental business you are selling time in vacant apartments. You must consider yourself a salesman if you are to reach the goals possible in property management. These sales skills will be used for much more than simply filling vacancies.

tively when dealing with existing tenants, bankers, appraisers, and a host of other occasions.

If you stand back and look at your actions, you will probably see ways to improve your performance. The simple act of choosing the proper words can have an impact on your success. When you are dealing with prospective tenants, you are competing for their business. Other property managers and landlords are working to take tenants away from you. It is not as graphic as two landlords each grabbing one of the tenant's arms and pulling, but the competition is there. It is in classified advertising, signs, telemarketing, and phone manners. If you do not assert yourself to secure a good tenant when you find one, some other landlord or manager will fill a vacancy with your tenant.

> ▶ *PRO POINTER*
>
> Marketing can get expensive. With the rising costs of marketing, you must make the most of every dollar spent. Simply spending money in marketing attempts is not enough. You must design a marketing plan before you can get the most for your marketing dollar. After you have a solid plan, you must execute it with good timing. When the plan is in effect, you must not waste prospects generated from your marketing endeavors.

A Marketing Plan

Drafting a marketing plan does not have to involve fancy graphs and elaborate schemes. For the average manager or landlord, a pad of paper and a pen is all that will be needed in the way of supplies. A computer is helpful, but not necessary. The meat of a strong marketing plan is the research that goes into it.

> ✔ *FAST FACT*
>
> The meat of a strong marketing plan is the research that goes into it.

When you are laying out a strategy to capture quality tenants, you must look below the surface. While most landlords are placing classified advertising that they thought of at the last minute, you should be planning for vacancies. After all, you are a professional property manager. You know that at some point you are going to have to find new tenants. By starting early with your planning, you can make the most of your marketing.

Decide on what type of tenants your clients want, and then devise a method to attract them. For example, if you want college students, consider advertising in campus papers and putting notices on college bulletin boards. While students have been given a reputation for being bad tenants, you cannot believe everything you hear.

If you are geared up to handle students, you can make more money than you might think. Income property rented to students has an annual turnover rate. This offers the opportunity to raise rents each year. When leases are written to protect the property owner and you monitor the students closely, you can control the situation. Not all students destroy apartments for recreation. By screening the students you can look for the qualities you want in a tenant.

If you learn to master the proper handling of students, your money tree can sprout new growth. Since students tend to move each year, you can increase rents to reflect market rates each year. This is one advantage of having a yearly turnover. By bringing the rental fee up to match the market rate annually, you are likely to make more money than you would with stable tenants, who don't move for years at a time. This is just one example of how going outside the normal thinking pattern can increase your profitability.

Demographics

The foundation of a marketing plan will be research. By digging into the demographics of an area, you can plot your marketing course. Demographics can tell you almost anything you would wish to know about a community's people. You can determine income levels, the average number of children in each family, and other valuable information. By gathering this data, you can target your marketing to specific types of tenants.

You can obtain demographic information from a number of sources. Some of these sources include the following:

Sources of Demographic Information
- Local libraries
- Phone directories
- Cross-reference directories
- Mailing lists that can be rented by demographics
- The local housing authority
- Real estate agents

- Public tax offices
- Census reports

Collect as much data as you can to structure your marketing plan. The time invested will not be wasted. The faster you can fill vacancies for maximum money, the more money you are going to make as a property manager.

Building a Marketing Plan

When you know the type of tenants you want and have completed your research into your area's needs, you are ready to formulate a marketing plan. Start by writing down all the factors that you know will be wanted in a tenant. Check your demographics to see if the qualities you want in a tenant exist in the current market. It would be ridiculous to target your marketing to retired couples if the area doesn't have a significant population of retirees.

Now that you have established the type of tenant you want and know that they are available in the current market, all you have to do is figure out how to attract them. As part of your research you should take a close look at your competition. For example, how many bedrooms do competitive rental units have? Do the competing landlords offer incentives to people who become new tenants? Compare your building to the competition. How does your property stack up against the other guy's building?

The next step to consider is how you will let people know you have rental units available. You must evaluate your advertising budget and determine what will be the most effective way to reach your intended audience. Your advertising may be as simple as placing notices on community bulletin boards. If you are operating a high-volume rental business, you might use direct mail to reach your new tenants. Direct mail allows for very specific targeting of the market. There will be more on advertising later in this chapter.

> ▶ *PRO POINTER*
>
> Look for aspects of your property that will set it apart from the competition to maximize profits. Maybe your building offers free parking and the competition doesn't. Perhaps you allow pets and the others don't. Look for anything that will prevent prospective tenants from comparing apples to apples. You want your prospect to compare apples to oranges. If you set your building apart, you can justify a higher rent.

The last step of your marketing plan will involve the details of how you will handle prospects when they respond to your advertising. You should devise a checklist or script to use when you receive phone inquiries from your ads. This element of your plan is crucial. Phone inquiries are usually your first form of contact with prospective tenants. In a matter of seconds, an opinion can be formed that may affect the remainder of your dealings with the prospect. You must be well prepared to handle incoming calls. If you fail to accomplish this goal, much of your advertising money will have been wasted.

> ✔ **FAST FACT**
>
> Remember that as a professional property manager, the money that you spend on advertising is usually your money. Property owners rarely pay you on a cost basis for advertising. It is expected that you pay for the advertising and get paid a rent-up fee once you sign a suitable tenant to a lease.

After your phone work is done, you will be ready to move into the field. When you go out to show rental units, there should be a plan of attack. Your marketing plan should include how you will show your properties and the questions you will ask your prospects. In effect, your marketing plan should cover every step along your way to obtaining new tenants.

Executing Your Marketing Plan

When you have a plan you are happy with, you are ready to execute it when the time is right. Timing is a decisive factor in the success of your marketing plan. How will you know when the time is right? You will learn from reading, research, and most of all, from experience. As you go through the highs and lows of the rental management business, experience is a strong teacher.

> ▶ **PRO POINTER**
>
> Timing is a decisive factor in the success of your marketing plan. How will you know when the time is right? You will learn from reading, research, and most of all, from experience.

Management companies and landlords with large rental holdings keep their marketing plans operating almost continually. They use the repetition style of marketing. By keeping their names in front of the public on a regular basis, they become household names. When an individual is ready to rent housing, the person turns to the name that has been seen over the last several months. This type of marketing is effective for big-time operators, but it is too expensive for the average landlord. This can be an advantage to you as a professional manager. If you have a large number of units to rent on a regular basis, your company name will become known as a source of rentals.

One of the biggest mistakes you can make is waiting until you need a tenant to try and find one. If you know you will have a vacancy in thirty days, start your search for a new tenant immediately. If you wait until the unit is empty and refurbished, it may very well sit empty for a month, or more. Since good tenants give at least a thirty-day notice of their intent to vacate, you should work to find tenants a month before you need them.

The downside of this preliminary marketing is showing apartments that are still occupied by the incumbent tenant. It can be uncomfortable for you and the prospective tenant to poke around in someone else's home. Also, the rental unit may not show as well as it would if it were empty and clean. On the other hand, it may show better with furniture and personal belongings in it.

You will have to be the judge of which circumstances will increase your chances of securing a new tenant. If you decide you will want to show rental units before they are vacated, make sure that there are provisions in the lease to gain access for the showings. Most tenants will not object to your showing their unit, as long as you give them adequate notice.

> ✔ **FAST FACT**
>
> Empty rental units can give the feeling of a cold, hostile environment when they are shown to prospective tenants.

Prospecting Pointers

A good marketing plan, mixed with inducing advertising, should produce an abundance of prospects. You will have invested time and money to generate these prospects. It is important that you get a good return on your investment. To ensure a high rate of success, you must follow some sales steps in getting the prospects committed to your rental property.

Your first opportunity to utilize sales skills will generally come when a prospective tenant calls with questions about your advertised property. This phone call is where most landlords lose their prospects. If you lose your potential tenants in the initial conversations, you have lost time and money. Here are just a few of the ways that you lose:

- You have lost the time you spent developing your marketing plan.
- You have lost the time you spent on your advertising campaign.

- Your time devoted to placing ads and answering the telephone has been wasted.

- The money spent on your marketing efforts is also unsalvageable.

- You are losing money from the unoccupied rental unit.

- All in all, losing prospects is very expensive.

By implementing some sales approaches in your phone conversations you can save time and make the most of your marketing money. After the barrage of phone calls, you will have to show your rental units to the interested parties. This is a vulnerable time for inexperienced property managers. Mistakes made during the showing will quickly alienate the prospects and cause your units to remain empty.

▶ *PRO POINTER*

Advertising is expensive when it is done wrong and a bargain when handled properly. As a manager, you must learn to harness the power of seductive advertising.

Adopting sales skills will dramatically increase your success as a property manager. As in golf, a good follow-through is needed to seal your deal in renting apartments.

Advertising

Advertising is responsible for generating prospects to fill vacant rental units. If people don't know you have units available for rent, they cannot rent them. While advertising can make your business thrive, it can also strangle your cash flow until it dwindles to nothing more than a puddle. Advertising is expensive when it is done wrong and a bargain when handled properly. As a manager, you must learn to harness the power of seductive advertising.

What Is Seductive Advertising?

When I talk of seductive advertising, I am not talking about ads with sexy people in them. I am talking about advertising that peaks an incurable interest in the consumer. The seduction comes from the combination of descriptive words and selective inducements. The way that you structure your ad can make a tremendous difference in the phone calls it generates. To get a feel for how two different ads, for the same rental unit, can produce different results, compare the two samples ads below.

Sample Ad Number One

FOR RENT: Three bedroom condo with one and one-half baths. Large living room with view and fireplace. Modern kitchen with all appliances furnished. Exercise room and sun room on the upper level. Great location with many amenities. No pets. Lease, references and security deposit required. $1,550.00 per month. Call 555-1919 for details.

Sample Ad Number Two

FOR RENT: Available now for your inspection, this natural wood, chalet-style condo is perfect for living, loving, relaxing, working, and all-out enjoyment. A raised stone hearth surrounds a warm fireplace in the center of the huge great room. As you cuddle by the fire, you can recline and enjoy the exposed beams and vaulted ceiling. If you like the outdoors, open the mini-blinds on the fixed glass panels and let the lush sights of nature fill your home with beauty. When it's time to cook, you will appreciate the wrap-around kitchen with its time-saver appliances. An island sink accents this contemporary kitchen, abounding with cabinets and charm. Three spacious bedrooms will accommodate all your furniture and desires. The master suite offers access to its own powder room and a full bath serves the remainder of the home. As you walk up the open stairway to the balcony, you can enter the fitness center or the sun room. After a workout in your private gym, relax in the whirlpool, under the skylights of the sun room. This homey hideaway is conveniently located to work, shopping, and schools. Responsible pets will be considered. If you act now, you can capture the elegance of this stunning home for the next year with only your deposit and signature. This executive condo can be yours for the modest monthly rent of $1,550.00. Responsible tenants with references may arrange a private showing by calling Bob at 555-1919.

Evaluating Sample Ad Number One

Sample ad number one is an ad that will attract some attention and will no doubt generate phone calls. The ad mentions most of the most important features of the home, but it fails to demonstrate the benefits of the rental unit. The reader of the ad will have enough general information to make a decision as to whether he should call for further details. The advertisement is relatively short and therefore, relatively inexpensive to run in the paper. This sample ad is adequate, but not as good as it could be.

Even though this sample lacks strong pulling power, it is a better ad than some property managers place. When advertisers look at the cost of advertising, they keep the ad as short as possible. This is a mistake. After years of sales and marketing experience, I have found that descriptive ads not only generate more calls, they produce a higher quality prospect. Descriptive advertising costs more to place, but the results far exceed those of mediocre ads. Now let's look at how the second sample ad is an improvement over the first ad.

Evaluating Sample Ad Number Two

The first obvious difference between sample ad number two and sample ad number one is the length of the advertisement. Even if the second ad is no better in its content than the first ad, its length will catch a reader's eye. When a perusing prospect is reading the classified column, the prospect will be drawn to a large ad. Since most ads are short, long ads stand out from the crowd.

Now, let's examine each line of the second ad and see how it compares to the first ad:

- The first ad jumps straight to a description of the property.
- There is no introduction and a cold feeling exists in the ad.
- The second ad opens with a friendly introduction and sets the pace for the ad. It tells readers they are in control; the unit is available for their inspection. This adds a personal dimension to the ad.
- The opening is followed by descriptive text that makes the reader feel the style and appearance of the condo.
- In the first ad, the reader knows the unit is a condo, but he has no idea of what type of condo is being offered for rent.
- The many suggestions of potential uses for the condo fuel the reader's imagination.
- All of a sudden, prospective tenants can envision themselves in the condo, doing what they like best. The first ad tells the prospect that the condo has a fireplace, but the second ad suggests a pleasing scenario to accentuate the fireplace.
- The exposed beams and vaulted ceiling were never mentioned in the first ad. These special touches could be the spark needed to make the reader call you.
- In the first ad, the reader was told the unit had a view, but it didn't indicate what the view consisted of. A view of a parking lot or smoke stacks is hardly comparable with the view of a natural forest.

- Most housing seekers expect a modern kitchen and appliances to be included in their rental. The first ad's description of these features does little to motivate the reader. However, the second ad expands on the kitchen's assets and mentions key words like cabinets, charm, island sink, time-saver appliances, and a contemporary kitchen. Doesn't a contemporary kitchen sound more appealing than a modern kitchen? Time-saver appliances may be the same as any other modern appliances, but the term instills a level of excellence for the kitchen.

- The sentence about the bedrooms in the second ad allows the reader to fill in the blank. It tells the reader furniture will fit in the room, but it also opens the door to his imagination for the fulfillment of desires.

- The reference of a master suite is an added touch that tells the prospect this unit is designed for quality living.

- Letting prospects know that there is a powder room adjacent to the master suite may be all it takes to make your phone ring.

- In the description of the stairway and the balcony, in the second ad, the reader gets a feeling of an open-living concept. The combination of open living and natural views go together well.

- The first ad casually mentions an exercise room. Exercise is not a pleasant thought for many people, but fitness conjures an entirely different emotion. By changing the wording in the second ad, the reader is impressed with the upstairs facilities of the rental property.

- By describing the whirlpool and skylights in the second ad, the reader is more informed about the demeanor of the sun room. Prospects can see that this is a house designed for successful individuals.

- Both ads mention the location of the condo as being good, but the second ad indicates there is privacy surrounding the condo.

- The first ad eliminates many good tenants by refusing all pets.

- The second ad gives the landlord a choice in whether or not to accept pets. The hint that pets may be accepted will open the door to an entirely different market.

- Unlike the hard, cold words of the first ad, the second ad gets the point across about a lease and deposit in a soft manner.

- The simple use of the word responsible in the description of tenants will weed out some of the unsavory crowd.

- In the closing of the second ad, the reference to a private showing puts the rental property on a higher level. It indicates this property is perfect for professionals.

- By including a first name in the second ad, Bob has added an important element in the rental of his condo. When the reader calls, they will be calling Bob, not some unknown phone number. This may seem like a silly difference, but people will be less apprehensive if they know the name of the person they are calling. By removing apprehension, Bob has assured more calls and reduced the risks of the callers having their protective shields up during the initial contact.

Advantages

I made many comparisons between sample ad number one and sample ad number two as we evaluated the second ad. To go beyond those comparisons, let's consider the advantages of using the second ad, instead of the first one. These ads were written for a condominium, but they are representative of the types of ads you could use for any rental property. Whether you are trying to rent a detached home, an apartment, or even a room, the same advertising strategies apply.

The first comment many landlords will make about the two ads is the difference in the costs to run each of them. Certainly the second ad will cost more to run than the first, in terms of out-of-pocket cash. But, wise landlords and many professional property managers look beyond the obvious. While the first ad is less expensive to run, if it doesn't get the job done, it was a waste of money. The cost for the second ad will be inconsequential if it produces a high-quality tenant. You must get around the mental block of looking at the ad cost. It is imperative that you consider the results of each ad when deciding which type of ad will be the most beneficial to you.

I am confident the first style of ad will produce enough inquiries for you to fill your vacant rental, but will they be the best

▶ **PRO POINTER**

It is not uncommon for prospective tenants to call on an ad for one property and then rent some other property from the property manager who placed the ad that pulled the call. Just because a prospective tenant is not interested in the advertised property doesn't mean that the tenant will not lease another property that you have available.

tenants for your building? By using the tactics employed in the second ad, you can aim your ad at specific types of tenants. For example, sample ad number two was fairly generic, but it lends itself to a professional group, with stable tendencies. The first sample ad is not targeted to any particular type of person. There is a strong likelihood that you would receive a better tenant from the second ad than from the first. You can carry this type of targeting much further.

Targeting Your Advertisements

By using selective phrases, you can target your advertisements to reach a small segment of the rental population. Key words in your ads will stress the type of tenant you are looking for, without being obvious or discriminating. The way that you describe your property will turn some people away and other people on. With creative advertising, you can control the type of response you receive. In addition to the wording of your ad, the places that you advertise will influence the type of tenant who applies for residency. Let's look at some of the various ways you can target your advertising to reach a desired tenant.

How You Advertise

How you advertise your rental business will dictate the type of customers you work with. If you know the type of tenant you want, finding a suitable tenant will be as easy as targeting your marketing. If you prefer renting to individuals with college degrees, you can rent a mailing list and use direct mail to aim all of your advertising at prospects with degrees. If you like the idea of having a plumber in the house, a mailing list can provide you with the names and addresses of all the licensed plumbers in your area.

When you don't want to go to the expense of direct mail, you can word your newspaper advertisements to attract the attention of specific groups. If you want families with children, boast about the

✔ FAST FACT

Word-of-mouth advertising is the best type of advertising available. It is inexpensive and produces results in the recruitment of similar tenants. If you like the type of tenants you presently have, make them aware of upcoming vacancies. Your existing tenants may spread the word among their friends and co-workers to find your next tenant.

school systems, playgrounds, and entertainment near your rental units. If you prefer to avoid juvenile tenants, stress the adult and professional nature of your rentals. By weaving your ad with key words, you can influence the type of tenant you will be dealing with.

Where You Advertise

Where you advertise can be directly related to the type of prospective tenants your ads will pull. An ad in the local paper may produce varied results, but an ad in a company newsletter will target your market. Placing a notice on a bulletin board in the community grocery store is unpredictable. Putting the same notice on a bulletin board in specialized clubs or organizations is much more likely to generate the type of leads you are looking for.

The quality of the publication or location where you insert your advertisements will have a bearing on the type of tenants that respond to the ad. Putting fliers under the windshield wipers of cars in the shopping center, if this practice is not prohibited, may produce calls, but the nature of the prospects will be unknown. Circulating the same fliers among a selected neighborhood can produce enviable results. The point is, how you target your market will have a direct result on the type of tenants you find.

> ▶ *PRO POINTER*
>
> Don't leave fliers or other means of solicitation on private property where the property is posted with instructions not to solicit on the property. Many parking lots prohibit solicitation. The same is true for some private communities.

Choosing a Type of Advertising

Just as the locations of advertisements dictate the type of tenants you will pull, the style of advertising selected may also influence your results. Direct mail advertisements should produce a quality tenant, if you have the right mailing list. Public notices and fliers produce responses that are impossible to predict. Signs provide better qualified leads, but they may not be the type of tenant you are looking for.

When prospects call from a sign on a property, they know the location and the physical appearance of the property. This means two possible objections have been overcome before your phone rings. Location is always a determining factor in any prospect's decision to lease a property. Signs produce potential tenants that are willing to live in the area of your property.

For managers dealing in volume, radio advertising can be effective. When you utilize the air waves, you can aim your ads at known demographics. Any good radio station will provide you with the demographics of their listeners. By picking your stations and times carefully, you can control the type of tenant that is most apt to call about your advertisements.

Newspaper advertisements are probably the most common form of advertising used by property managers. These print ads produce the highest volume of inquiries. When the average person is ready to rent a place to live, they turn to the classified ads in the newspaper. Newspaper advertising is usually less expensive than other effective means of advertising. Another advantage to newspaper ads is the

> ✔ **FAST FACT**
>
> Recent changes in law make tele-marketing far trickier to perform properly than what was once allowed. Before you conduct any telemarketing activity, talk with your attorney to learn how to stay on the right side of the law.

lack of time required of the landlord in carrying out an ad campaign. With prints ads, once the concept is conceived, a phone call is all it takes to get the ad working.

Telemarketing can be considered a form of advertising. When you place calls at random, to solicit tenants, you are in effect advertising your rental units. Very few property managers include telemarketing in their marketing plan. Telemarketing requires a special type of approach to be successful. Some large companies rely on telemarketing for a percentage of their new rentals, but the average manger will never use this potentially effective marketing tool.

There are other types of advertising available to property managers, but these cover the majority of the types frequently used. For most landlords, print ads in local newspapers will be the extent of their advertising scheme. Let's look at each of these types of advertising and see how they may be applied to your needs.

Direct Mail

Direct mail is the best way to reach a specialized market. If you are managing high-end, executive suites, direct mail is an excellent choice. By renting a mailing list, you can mail your advertisement directly to specific professions or income levels. When you rent a mailing list, you can have it selected based on almost any criteria you set.

If you want to fill your vacancy with a doctor, you can rent a list consisting only of doctors. You can usually obtain their business address or their home address. Direct mail is hard to beat when you have a desire for specialized tenants.

Direct mail can get your advertising into the homes of thousands of rental prospects. You could direct your advertising assault on other apartment buildings. While you may be prohibited from soliciting tenants in other buildings with fliers, the advertisements mailed to the tenants will be delivered. Existing tenants are already renters. If you can give them a reason to move, you can fill your empty apartments with someone else's dissatisfied tenants.

✔ *FAST FACT*

Direct mail can get your advertising into the homes of thousands of rental prospects. You could direct your advertising assault on other apartment buildings. While you may be prohibited from soliciting tenants in other buildings with fliers, the advertisements mailed to the tenants will be delivered. Existing tenants are already renters. If you can give them a reason to move, you can fill your empty apartments with someone else's dissatisfied tenants.

By using direct mail you can keep your advertising secrets somewhat confidential. If you have a gimmick that works, you will not be advertising in a way to allow every other landlord and manager to steal your idea. When you want to test a marketing idea, direct mail can give you fast, accurate responses. If you can afford to implement direct mail, you should enjoy having desirable tenants to choose from.

The drawback to direct mail is its cost. If you are only renting a few units each year, the cost of direct mail is prohibitive. Quality name lists are not cheap and neither is postage. Even if you obtain a bulk rate permit, your postage costs can be staggering. Then there is the cost of typesetting and printing. Having your mailer folded is another expense. If your mailer will be sent in an envelope, stuffing the envelopes will take time or money. Unless you are dealing in a high-volume rental business, direct mail will probably not be cost effective.

✔ *FAST FACT*

The drawback to direct mail is its cost. If you are only renting a few units each year, the cost of direct mail is prohibitive. Quality name lists are not cheap and neither is postage.

Fliers

Distributing fliers around the community will attract attention, but not all of it will be the kind of attention you are hoping for. For example, if you stick fliers under the windshield wipers of every car parked at the shopping mall, you may get a notice from the mall requiring you to clean up the discarded fliers. When people see a notice on their car that they are not interested in, many of them drop the flier in the parking lot. If enough people do this, it makes quite a mess. The shopping mall may require you to clean the litter from their parking lot or they may clean it up and send you a bill for the clean-up.

The advantage to fliers is their low cost. They are inexpensive to have printed and require only time to circulate. Fliers are not one of the more classy methods of advertising. If you use fliers, you may not find the type of tenants you hope for. Except in unique circumstances, fliers should not be used for renting your vacant units.

Signs

Placing a sign in the window of a vacant property can be a very effective tool in renting the unit. People see the sign and by the time they call you, they are interested in the building and the location. This is the good part of using signs.

There is a bad side to the use of signs. When you place a sign on a property, you are inviting vandalism. The undesirable elements of the community may use your vacant property for shelter, parties, or other more destructive events. A sign in the window of a vacant apartment can draw more trouble than tenants. The use of signs must be evaluated on an individual basis. If you can use a sign without fear of property damage, the sign can produce good results.

Radio

Radio advertising is too expensive for the landlord with only occasional vacancies. Unless you are running a busy management company, radio advertising will not be affordable. If you are in a position to use radio ads, they can work very well.

By carefully selecting the time and stations that your ad will run on, you can target your market. Using the station's demographics, you can write a script to suit the listeners. If your ad runs during the rush hour, thousands of people will hear about your rental property. If you decide to advertise on the radio, budget enough money to keep your ad running frequently. Repetition is important to the success of radio ads.

Print Ads

Classified print ads are what most landlords use to fill vacancies. When you are looking to generate a high volume of calls with a limited budget, newspaper ads are the best choice. Newspaper ads are also quick to perfect and to put to work. With a phone call to the paper, you can be receiving tenant inquiries the next day. The simplicity and economy of this type of advertising makes it the most popular for many property managers.

Print ads allow you to tell the public as much, or as little, as you like about your rental unit. A prospective tenant can read the ad over and over again at his leisure. He can compare it to the other ads surrounding it. All of these are good reasons to use print ads. Most managers invest their advertising budget in classified ads, but display ads have their place too.

Display ads are much more expensive than an in-column classified ad, but they can produce much faster and better results. If you buy a classified ad, your ad may get lost among all the other ads. A well designed display ad will stand out and attract attention. Normally, a classified ad will be all that is needed to fill your vacancy. If you are willing to invest a little more money, a display ad should generate more calls.

When you place a classified ad, be descriptive. Long descriptive ads result in better qualified prospects. They also reduce curiosity calls. For example, if you don't include the rental amount in your ad, many of your callers will not be interested once they know the cost of the accommodations. These curiosity calls tie up your phone and rob you of valuable time. The more you put in the ad, the less wasted time you will have with unsuitable prospects.

Display ads should be open and concise. Too many advertisers cram these ads full of words and clip art. A simple display ad, with a strong border and open space in the ad, will be easier to read and will attract more attention. Look through the paper and see what types of ads catch your eye. By studying other people's ads, you can learn to make your ads more effective.

Incentives

When all else fails, buy your tenants with incentives. In tight economies and competitive markets, incentives are sometimes needed to encourage tenants to sign up with you. The incentive may be as simple as providing a free microwave oven with every apartment rented. At the other end of the scale, you might give your new tenant tickets for two to an exotic vacation.

The value of the incentive should be determined by the value of the tenant. If you are losing a thousand dollars a month on a vacant apartment, giving away a hundred-dollar microwave oven to fill the vacancy is a bargain. When it comes to incentives, you can use your imagination.

If money is tight, waiving the requirement of a security deposit may fill your apartment. If a prospect is looking at five apartments that are all about the same, the savings you offer by waiving the deposit will entice the tenant to rent your unit. I don't recommend waiving deposits, but in tough times, it can keep mortgage payments current for the property owner.

Offering one month of free occupancy is another way to attract people watching their budget. This method is used often and has lost much of its pulling power. With so many landlords offering a free month's rent, you will just be a part of the crowd. But, there is a way to set yourself apart without spending more money.

Assume you are willing to offer a free month's rent. Also assume a month's rent is $1,400.00. In this scenario all of your competitors are offering a free month's rent with every lease signed. Why not change your offer to a romantic week-end for two at a flashy resort? If this doesn't suit, how about two tickets to the destination of the tenants choice with a value of up to $1,400.00. Most people will not take the $1,400.00 saved from the free rent to take a vacation, but if you are offering a free vacation, they may jump on it.

In today's rental market, one of the most effective incentives is the allowance of pets in the rental unit. I know that most landlords cringe at the idea of allowing pets, but pets can be your ticket to more money and less vacant apartments. People with pets consider the critters part of the family. They would no more give up their pet than they would their children. If you are one of the few advertisers allowing pets, you can corner the market on some top-notch tenants.

> ✔ **FAST FACT**
>
> If you are one of the few advertisers allowing pets, you can corner the market on some top-notch tenants.

Tenants with pets are often more responsible than tenants without pets. By properly screening the tenant and the pet, you can come to terms that will appeal to you and the tenant. You can require an additional deposit for protection against any damage done by the pet. The lease can include strong language to control the circumstances of the pet. With enough desire, you can find amicable terms to accept pets.

Tenants with pets are less likely to move as often as tenants without pets. The lack of rental property allowing pets helps to ensure that your pet owners will not move. In addition to a pet deposit, you can probably charge a higher rent and still keep your units full, when you allow pets. If you decide to allow pets, I am sure you will find filling vacancies will be much easier and faster.

The Knockout

When you combine a strong marketing plan with effective advertising, you can deliver a knockout punch to your competition. The one-two punch of marketing and advertising can make you more successful than you know. It will be well worth your time and effort to learn all you can about sales, marketing, and advertising. When you master these skills, you should be able to minimize your vacancy rate and maximize the rate of return on your rental investments.

CHAPTER EIGHT

Tenant Strategies and Procedures

As a property manger, tenants are your business. Without tenants, you are not going to stay in the rental business for long. Successful property managers know the value of good tenants and will go to any reasonable length to keep them. It is the investors and property owners who are more infatuated with their spreadsheets than their tenants who wind up in the bankruptcy court. If watching your pennies will make your dollars grow, keeping good tenants will build a pleasing spreadsheet. Tenants are the cornerstone of your business. If you fail to recognize the importance of even the most common tenant, you will find yourself in financial trouble before you know it.

To accomplish the goal of maintaining desirable residents, you must exert some personal effort. In a landlord-tenant relationship, it is the little things that add up. This is also true for property mangers. If you ignore a good tenant's legitimate request to repair a leaking faucet, you are starting a frustration in the tenant that can lead to losing the tenant.

Desirable Tenants

Word-of-mouth advertising and referrals are the best ways to acquire desirable tenants. Your present residents can be an excellent source of new tenants. If you have been keeping your residents happy, they will be glad to help you fill vacancies. If you let the present dwellers know you need a new tenant, they may turn one up before you can. When people are at work or meeting socially, housing is a common topic of conversation. If someone is complaining about their present living conditions, your tenant scout may be able to plug your building. With the right timing and this kind of referral, your vacancy may be filled expeditiously, with a remarkable inhabitant.

Military Base Bulletin Boards

If your community is home to a military base, you might capture a respectable tenant from the base's bulletin board or referral system. Military personnel are generally well disciplined and responsible. By placing your rental units on the referral system at the base, you may never have to advertise elsewhere to find acceptable tenants. Most bases assist their incoming personnel in finding suitable housing. If you are on their list, you can take advantage of the frequent personnel changes at military installations.

Referrals

When your rental property is convenient to large corporations, you can capitalize on the corporate shuffle. As executives come and go you can cash in on their housing needs. Major corporations offer all types of support to their valued employees. One of the common services offered is help in finding a home. By contacting the large companies in your area, you can get on their referral list.

Being on the referral list of a major corporation can eliminate your need to advertise for tenants. A side benefit is the financial qualifications of your lessee. If the prospective tenant is a mobile executive, the prospect should be financially secure. As a property manager, your concerns for collecting rent should be put to ease when you rent to corporate executives through a referral service.

The Local Housing Authority

Most cities have an agency devoted to dealing with the housing needs of the local population. These agencies can be an almost endless source of tenants, if your property meets the minimum requirements of the agency. The local housing authority can be of great help to you. It can provide invaluable information to help you establish a reasonable rental rate. The agency can give you historical data to dissect for building your marketing plan. A trip to the housing authority is worth your time. You will never know what benefits you may derive from the agency unless you investigate its many services.

Real Estate Brokers

Real estate brokers can be your best friend if you are looking for short-term tenants. Brokers deal with people buying and selling houses. During these transactions, it is not uncommon for the principals to need temporary housing. If you have an established rapport with several brokers, you may never have to advertise for tenants.

Taking in short-term tenants has its advantages. You can keep your rental fees at a current level, due to the frequent turn over. Most short-term tenants know they will have to pay a higher rent for their temporary tenancy. This allows you to collect a higher rent and enjoy a more attractive net income.

Benefit from Keeping Good Tenants

By now, your mind should be swirling with a multitude of methods for finding good tenants. Well, finding good tenants is only part of the battle. Often times the most difficult part of property management is keeping good tenants. It does very little good to find good tenants, if you cannot keep them. Advertising is effective in finding good tenants, but it can get expensive. The less you have to advertise for residents, the more money you will retain at the end of the year.

Most of the suggestions given here for finding tenants do not require an extensive outlay of cash. In whatever method you use to attract good people, keeping them happy will reduce your vacancy rate and your advertising expenses.

▶ *PRO POINTER*

By reducing the time and money spent on filling vacancies, you will enjoy higher profits from your income property.

Initial Contact

A property manager's relationship with a tenant begins with the initial contact between the two parties. This contact is normally made by telephone. If you are short or rude on the phone, prospective tenants may not have a continued interest in your property. Make a habit of being pleasant and friendly in all your contact with tenants. Make an effort to remember the prospect's name. People like to be called by name and will appreciate your effort in taking an interest in addressing them accordingly.

First impressions are made in a matter of seconds. You may not get a second chance to alter the initial opinion recorded in a prospective tenant's mind. If the tenant calls and there are dogs barking and children screaming in the background, you may not make a professional impression on the caller. If you are conducting your business from home, attempt to control the atmosphere to maintain a professional image.

Showing Property

If you have a successful phone conversation with prospects, they will want you to show them the rental unit. Keep in mind that many good tenants have full-time jobs. It may be very difficult for the prospect to take time off from work. Be prepared to show your units in the evening and on week-ends. This is when your customer is available. If you insist on showing the property during normal business hours, you may lose the ideal tenant.

✔ **FAST FACT**

Keep in mind that many good tenants have full-time jobs. It may be very difficult for the prospect to take time off from work. Be prepared to show your units in the evening and on week-ends. This is when your customer is available. If you insist on showing the property during normal business hours, you may lose the ideal tenant.

Attempt to cater to the prospect's needs for a convenient showing. Avoid showing property when you will have to rush through the showing. If the inspection is going well, you should stick with it and close the deal. Going out to show an apartment when you must leave the showing after twenty minutes to make a lodge meeting is not a good idea. Don't force the tenant to conform to your time table. Remember, the tenant is the customer and you are the vendor who is working for the property owner.

When you arrive for the showing, dress appropriately and be friendly. If you give tenants the feeling that they are inconveniencing you, they will probably not stay long. Start a conversation using information you extracted in your phone interview. Talk about subjects that the prospect has an interest in. If the tenant is a golfer, talk about golf. If you don't know anything about golf, ask questions. People love it

▶ **PRO POINTER**

Tenants want more than a comfortable place to live. They want a property manger and landlord that they can get along with. If you can build a basis for uncomplicated conversation, you are on your way to securing the tenant.

when they can give advice on a subject they know well. By insinuating that you are considering taking up golf, you could be closing the deal through casual conversation.

Tenants want more than a comfortable place to live. They want a property manger and landlord that they can get along with. If you can build a basis for uncomplicated conversation, you are on your way to securing the tenant. Tenants also appreciate a manger who has an interest in their lives. By showing such an interest, you are setting yourself apart from many property managers. Inexperienced managers open the door and let the tenant roam at will. They rarely talk about anything other than the terms of the rental. While this approach will bag some prospects, your success will be much higher with a friendly, but effective, sales approach.

> ▶ *PRO POINTER*
>
> Treating the tenant to a cup of coffee or a snack at a nearby restaurant is a good idea for assuring a signature on your lease. Escort the tenant to a relaxing gathering place and cut your deal in comfort.

Making the Deal

Once the tenant wants to rent one of your units, be professional in the presentation of your paperwork. Don't shove papers at tenants and expect them to sign the agreements without reading the text. Treating the tenant to a cup of coffee or a snack at a nearby restaurant is a good idea for assuring a signature on your lease. Escort the tenant to a relaxing gathering place and cut your deal in comfort.

Having all of your paperwork in order will put a tenant at ease. If you present your forms in a business-like manner, tenants will not feel like you are pulling a fast one on them. Use professionally printed forms and agreements. Cheap photocopies do not induce a feeling of comfort. They make you look like a fly-by-night operator. If you have attractive forms, on good quality paper, the tenant will be less likely to resist signing them. Go through all of your rental policies with the tenant. Make sure there are no misunderstandings before committing yourself to a lease. When all is well, sign the deal.

> ▶ *PRO POINTER*
>
> Use professionally printed forms and agreements. Cheap photocopies do not induce a feeling of comfort. They make you look like a fly-by-night operator. If you have attractive forms, on good quality paper, the tenant will be less likely to resist signing them. Go through all of your rental policies with the tenant. Make sure there are no misunderstandings before committing yourself to a lease. When all is well, sign the deal.

After the Lease Is Signed

After the lease is signed, your work at keeping the tenant begins. You successfully acquired a desirable resident, now it is up to you to ensure that the tenant will stay with you. This part of your job never ends. When the lease was signed, your job of finding a suitable tenant was over. Keeping that tenant is not so easy. You must make a conscious effort to maintain a favorable relationship, for as long as you can. Being paid the rent-up fee for securing the tenant is good, getting a regular check for keeping the tenant will be even better.

This responsibility extends from the move-in process to the move-out process. Even after tenants leave you, if they leave on good terms, they have value to you. The tenants can recommend your building to friends and co-workers. You may be able to use them as a reference to remove apprehensions from new prospective tenants.

Communication

Communication plays an important role in successful property management. When communications between is poor, the relationship will suffer. Bad communication creates confusion. Confusion creates controversy. Once you are in an adversarial role with a tenant, the relationship may be damaged beyond repair. You can avoid most conflicts with clear communications. To look at how you can benefit from concise communication skills, let's examine some examples of how they will help you.

✔ **FAST FACT**

Bad communication creates confusion. Confusion creates controversy. Once you are in an adversarial role with a tenant, the relationship may be damaged beyond repair. You can avoid most conflicts with clear communications.

Rental Policy

You should establish a standard rental policy for all of your tenants. The rules for all of your tenants should be the same when they are within the same property. Obviously, different property owners will have varying rules that they will want followed. As the

✔ **FAST FACT**

The rules for all of your tenants should be the same when they are within the same property. Obviously, different property owners will have varying rules that they will want followed. As the property manager, you work for the property owner and must enforce their rules.

property manager, you work for the property owner and must enforce their rules. Your tenants will talk to each other. If they find you have different rules for each tenant, problems can arise. Once you have made your rental rules or have had them established by the property owner, put them in writing. When you have all of your rental policies prepared, staple them together or put them in a binder. Make duplicate copies of your original policy to give to each new tenant. Have all prospective tenants read and agree to your policy prior to signing a lease.

Leases

Leases should be prepared by an attorney. The lease should be written in terms any tenant can understand. Do not fill the lease with a maze of legal jargon. Have the lease dictate the terms of your agreement with the tenant in an informative and enforceable manner. If you have to go to court with your tenant, the lease will be your most effective weapon.

> ▶ *PRO POINTER*
>
> Once you have made your rental rules or have had them established by the property owner, put them in writing.

✔ *FAST FACT*

It is a good idea to have tenants sign copies of rental policies. If you have signed rental policies when questions come up, you can show tenants where they accepted the policies before signing a lease. Having this type of documentation can stop many arguments before they happen.

✔ *FAST FACT*

An attorney should include language in a lease to include all of the terms of the rental policy. You could have your attorney duplicate the rental policy in the lease, or he could refer to your policy manual as an attachment to the lease. In any event, include all pertinent facts, rules, and related language in your lease.

A Move-In List

By having your tenants complete a move-in list you eliminate the possibility of some misunderstandings in the future. Tenants should complete move-in forms and sign them. Their signatures will indicate the acceptance of conditions for the premises at the time occupancy is taken. The list will also document the condition of the rental unit for future reference.

When it is time for the tenant to leave, you can use the move-in list to assess damage caused by the tenant. If the walls of the rental unit look like they where shot with a shotgun from all the pictures the tenant hung, you can prove they were not in that condition when the tenant moved in. By being able to prove before and after conditions, you are in a much stronger position to win any battle over damage deposits.

When you go over a move-in list with tenants, explain why and how it will be used. If tenants know you will have a record to prove any damages that they are responsible for, they should be better tenants. The way you present yourself in this meeting is pivotal.

If you tell tenants you insist on a signed move-in list to protect you and the property owner from destructive tenants, new tenants may feel insulted. When you explain the use of the move-in list, expand upon how it protects both of you. Tell tenants that by providing a comprehensive move-in list, they will not be held responsible for existing damage. Explain how that without the list, existing damage may not be noticed until a tenant terminates tenancy. By telling tenants how the move-in list works to their advantage, tenants should be eager to cooperate. This is only one example of how your presentations to tenants can affect your relationship with them.

Past-Due Rent

When rental payments are past due, you must take action. Too many landlords wait in hopes that the tenant's check will arrive in the next mail delivery. This is not the proper way to run your business or deal with your tenants. If the rent is due on the first of the month, it should be in your hands by no later than the tenth of the month. If it is not, you must approach the tenant to learn the reason for the lack of payment.

Inexperienced and unsuccessful landlords and property managers usually take one of two courses of action when their rent is not delivered on time. They either do nothing or they accost the tenant with threats and rude language. Neither of these tenant tactics is the correct method for solving your problem. If you just wait, your cash flow is affected and the situation can build into an ugly scene. If you run to the tenant like a crazed maniac, you will damage your relationship and may wind up feeling like a fool. For all you know, there may be a very reasonable excuse for the tardy rent.

When rent is overdue, you should contact the tenant in a calm and professional manner. Depending upon your normal means of communicating with a tenant, your contact may be by phone, mail, or a personal visit. Let the tenant know you have not received the rent and ask for an explanation of the circumstances. Some of the reasons and excuses that you may be given for not yet receiving a rent payment could include any of the following:

- You may find that the tenant mailed the rent and it was misplaced in the postal service.

- You might be told that the tenant had been working out of town and overlooked the rent payment.

- Your tenant may have been on vacation and forgotten to mail a rent check.

- Maybe there has been a serious illness in the tenant's family that has distracted the person from paying bills.

- It is possible a tenant is out of work and doesn't have the money.

The list of excuses could go on and on.

If a tenant makes no response to your request for payment and an explanation, get ready to take legal action. If the tenant has a good reason for being late with the rent, you may want to work with the individual. If it has been a simple oversight, you will collect your rent and go on about your business. If the tenant has fallen on hard times and can't pay the rent, you must make a decision. You must decide whether to work with the tenant or to evict the resident for non-payment. Answering this question is likely to require a conference with the property owner. Most owner's like to make their own decisions on these types of matters.

When the tenant has been a good tenant, with a steady payment history, you should consider working out a deal to avoid eviction. If this is not the first time you have had problems with a tenant, you may wish to use this breech of the lease to remove the tenant. In considering the possibility of accepting a partial payment or waiting for payment, remember the cost and time involved in finding a good tenant. Check with the property owner and get a written statement of instructions to follow in solving the problem.

When it comes to money, document every step you take. If a tenant gives a partial payment, draft an agreement detailing the terms for accepting the small payment. If you decide to give tenants an extra month to get back on their feet, draw up a written agreement describing the details. Always retain your rights to pursue any legal means available to you for the collection of unpaid monies. Also make it clear that because you are allowing an extra grace period, you are not releasing the

► **PRO POINTER**

If you have to evict a tenant and find a new one, you are going to lose rental income. If the tenant can solve the financial problems quickly, you and the property owner will be money ahead. Only you and the property owner will be able to decide what course of action you wish to take. In general, if you can work with good tenants to keep them, you will be better off in the long run.

tenant from the obligation of paying for the delinquent rent. Your attorney will be able to advise you on how to retain all of your rights to financial collections and evictions.

Routine Maintenance

All rental property will need routine maintenance from time to time. This is an area of property management where many managers go astray. All too often managers will put off repairs until the last possible minute. This is detrimental to the property and to your relationship with tenants. When tenants request legitimate repairs or adjustments in rental units, respond quickly to the request.

When a tenant calls, arrange a time to get into the rental unit to evaluate the problem. Keep your scheduled appointment and show the tenant you care. Thank the tenant for bringing the deficiency to your attention. Depending upon the nature of the problem, the tenant may have saved you money by calling to report the problem.

✔ **FAST FACT**

I have seen more disputes develop from ignored maintenance than any other single cause, except for money.

I have seen more disputes develop from ignored maintenance than any other single cause, except for money. When these confrontations arise, it is usually with good tenants. Bad tenants don't care about your property. Because they don't care, they will not advise you of problems hurting your investment. But, good tenants, who respect you, will take an interest in your building. When they find a problem that is detrimental to your property, they will call you. If you fail to respond, they lose confidence in you. After all, it is your building to manage; you should be concerned for its upkeep. When the tenants feel they are more concerned than you are, they become frustrated. This frustration can build to a massive eruption. Let's look at an example of how your lack of interest in maintenance needs can cause hard feelings between you and your tenants.

Let's say one of your tenants calls to report a kitchen faucet with a steady drip. When they call, they get your answering service and leave a message. You procrastinate on returning their call, because you don't like dealing with tenants. They continue to call and you finally return their call. After telling you about the problem, the tenant asks when you would like to come into their home to correct the leak. You tell them you will be by the next day, at noon.

The tenant comes home from work to meet you. You get involved in other activities and don't keep your appointment. You don't even call to let the tenant know you will not be coming by. When you don't show up, the tenant calls, but only gets your answering machine. The tenant gives up and goes back to work. After a few days of playing phone tag, you schedule a new time to fix their leak. This time you do show up, but you don't have the proper tools to do the job. This is another day of time off from work wasted for the tenant. The longer it takes for you to fix the leak, the worse your relation becomes with the tenant.

While you are putting off doing the inevitable, you are upsetting a good tenant and wasting water and money. There is no excuse for not responding promptly to tenant complaints. If the complaint is not justified, deal with it. If it is a legitimate complaint, correct it. Don't ignore the tenant. They are calling to help you. Your attitude and actions in these cases can swing the tenant relationship in either direction. If you show an interest and fix the problem, the tenant will be happy and continue to respect you. If you don't, the tenant may build up resentment towards you and decide to move into another building.

I have known landlords who put off replacing burned out light bulbs in their hallways for over two weeks. This was in large multi-family buildings, in a city known for its criminal element. The tenants did not like coming home to dark hallways. When the landlord bought the building, all the tenants were prompt in paying their rent and were overall good tenants. After numerous requests to replace the light bulbs went unanswered, the tenants called the code enforcement office. It was not until the code officer contacted the landlord that the light bulbs were replaced.

This type of negligence in maintenance and the poor handling of tenants ultimately cost the landlord his buildings and his credit. His inadequacy as a property manager caused him to lose his good tenants. When filling the vacancies, he used bad judgment and got bad tenants. In less than two years, he lost all of his rental properties and was forced to file bankruptcy. This type of disaster can strike you, if you don't learn and practice good tenant tactics. While the person in this example was the property owner, similar trouble will occur for property managers who operate improperly.

General Suggestions

There are some basic procedures that will always apply to your property management business. Here are some key points to keep in mind:

- Treat tenants like respectable citizens.
- Remember that your tenants are the people who make it possible for you to remain in the rental business.

- Tenants will pick up on your feelings and actions. If they do not feel appreciated, they will not stick around for long.

- Don't ignore tenant complaints. The longer you stall tenants, the more enraged they become.

- Don't hide from tenants. Hiding behind an answering machine is one of the worst things you can do when dealing with your tenants.

- Don't be afraid to stand your ground when you are in the right

- When you make a mistake, be willing to take responsibility for your actions. If appropriate, apologize to your tenants.

- When you have good tenants, surprise them with a token of your appreciation. Place a bouquet of flowers in the apartment for their scheduled move-in date. When your tenants arrive, they will be thrilled to see the flowers.

- Be sensitive to your tenant's needs. If you have an elderly couple on the third floor, the steps may be an obstacle for them. If you have a unit coming available on the first floor, offer the rental to the elderly couple before you advertise it. They may not want to relocate, but they will appreciate your consideration and offer.

- Keep your building and grounds clean and well groomed. When you show the tenants you respect your property, they will be more likely to respect it too.

- A neat building will attract and hold a better quality tenant than a neglected dwelling.

- Provide good lighting in and around your property. Sufficient lighting will reduce vandalism and improve the comfort level of your tenants.

- If you must take aggressive action against a tenant, do so in a business-like manner.

- Never get into a shouting match with your tenants.

- Renewing leases with existing tenants can save you time and money. If you can convince your existing tenants to renew their leases, you will not have to fill vacancies. This, of course, saves time and money. Keep track of when your tenants' leases are due for renewal. Before the due date, schedule a meeting with the residents. If you have done a good job managing the property, getting them to renew their lease should be easy.

The Summary

The summary for this chapter is simple; strive to get and keep good tenants. As simple as this may sound, expect to spend extra effort to reach your goal. Whenever possible, don't settle for less than the best. By following the suggestions here, you should have some of the most content tenants in the neighborhood.

Collecting and Raising Rents the Right Way

Collecting rent is what the property management business is all about. Whether you buy rental property or manager property for others, your main motivation is the income that will be provided by the rent that you collect. Rent collection is one of the primary objectives of every landlord and property manager. It is also one aspect of owning and managing rental property that many people hate. They love having the rent money, but they despise collecting it. If you are going to be successful in the rental business, you must be successful at collecting rent.

✔ **FAST FACT**

Successful property managers have learned to motivate their tenants to pay their rent on time. The managers have also learned to see problems developing in their early stages. When you can catch a problem soon enough, you can often solve it before it becomes a burden.

Collecting Rent

Since people enter the rental business to collect rent, why do so many of them dislike the act of collecting their rent checks? How do you feel about collecting rental income? There are countless reasons for why landlords don't look forward to collecting their rent. When rent checks arrive in the mail, the landlords are happy. When they must exert effort to collect past-due rent, many landlords are weak. They don't want to confront their tenants. In some cases they are afraid to approach their tenants. To survive in the rental game you must get around these fears and dislikes. You must take control and collect the money due you. This is a key reason why you can succeed as a property manager. As long as you are willing to do the dirty work in the rental business, many landlords will pay you to do it.

If you don't like chasing after past-due rent you must develop a plan to avoid being put in that situation. Many elements contribute to the success of managers who are not forced to go after their rent. Successful property managers have learned to motivate their tenants to pay their rent on time. The managers have also learned to see problems developing in their early stages. When you can catch a problem soon enough, you can often solve it before it becomes a burden.

By implementing procedural techniques, you can reduce the frequency with which you must hunt down tenants for your rent. With knowledge and experience, you can use salesmanship to win the battle over late rent. When you are up against a tough tenant, there are ways to strengthen your position while weakening the tenant's. Thorough screening of tenants is only one way to reduce the likelihood of delinquent rent. This chapter is filled with tips and techniques to help you overcome the hurdle of collecting your rental income. If you master these skills, you will not have to worry about your dislike for chasing rent checks, they will come to you.

Methods That Work

As a property manager, you will have to find the methods that work best for you in collecting rent. Not all of the following ideas will suit your temperament or circumstances, but many of them can be incorporated into your rental business. These suggestions are proven performers, used by all types of landlords and property managers. Some of the tips are not well known while others are common knowledge among property managers. With the proper organization and use, these methods will make your life easier and your bank balance fatter.

The Lease Is the Backbone

The lease is the backbone of your rental business. The lease dictates the terms and conditions of your agreement with a tenant. Many of the suggestions here will only be effective if they are properly

> ▶ *PRO POINTER*

When you are ready to draft a lease, include notes on all the procedures you intend to use in your collection of rental income. Have your attorney review your notes and draw up a formal lease. Once you are operating with the right lease, your job of collecting the rent will be much easier.

addressed in your lease. Before you sign up new tenants, be sure your lease protects you and your clients and gives you the needed control over tenants.

Communication

Concise communication will solve more rent-related problems than any other single maneuver. When the communication channel is open between you and your tenant, you may never have a problem collecting your rent. When communication breaks down, trouble begins to swell. When you lease a rental unit, go over the terms of the lease and rental policy with the tenant. Make sure the tenant understands the terms and conditions. By getting all the cards on the table early, you can avoid many future hostilities.

Don't avoid a subject because it makes you uncomfortable to talk about it. If you are going to have a clash with a tenant, have it before you sign the lease.

You are in business to make money. The tenant knows this, and you know it. Explain to the tenant that you depend on prompt rental payments to meet your obligations. Further tell the tenant that if rent is delinquent it can put all of the other tenants, as well as yourself, in jeopardy. If you impress upon the tenant that you need prompt rent payments to keep the building running smoothly, the tenant may be less likely to run late with the rent.

Many tenants assume all landlords are rich. They believe you don't need the money, except for your golf game or new luxury car. Their opinion of property managers is not much different. If you show the tenant that you are just an average person, working for a living, the tenant will be more apt to pay rent on time. Make it clear to the tenant that you cannot tolerate tardy

▶ **PRO POINTER**

If a tenant doesn't like your terms for rent collection, find a different tenant. Putting a bad tenant in a building is one of the worst acts you can commit as a property manager.

✔ **FAST FACT**

If tenants have intentions of not paying their rent, you might scare them off with a hard-line stance. If this is the case, you have saved yourself time, money, and grief. Don't be afraid to spook a tenant, but don't come off looking like a jerk. If you present your rental policy in a diplomatic manner, good tenants will play by the rules and bad tenants will deserve what they get. Keep the communication lines open at all times. If you stop talking with your tenants, you are headed for trouble.

rent payments. Explain that your credit, your future, and your family are at stake. If you let the tenant know how serious you are about collecting the rent promptly, the chances of the tenant being willing to cooperate should improve.

Screening Tenants

The first step in making rental collections easy is doing a complete screening of all prospective tenants. You cannot look over a rental application and decide to rent to the applicant. You must check references, credit ratings, job stability, and all other pertinent facts. If you place many tenants, you will do well to join a credit reporting bureau. As a rental business, you can join a credit agency for a set annual fee. Then you will pay a nominal fee for each credit report you request. The cost of these services is a bargain. Weeding out one bad tenant will more than pay for a year's worth of service from the agency.

> ✔ *FAST FACT*
>
> As a rental business, you can join a credit agency for a set annual fee. Then you will pay a nominal fee for each credit report you request. The cost of these services is a bargain. Weeding out one bad tenant will more than pay for a year's worth of service from the agency.

Rental Intervals

It is up to the property owner to set rental intervals. Most landlords choose to collect their rent on a monthly basis. Monthly rent is the industry standard, but it is not the only way to do business. An owner can set the interval to be anytime that is acceptable to all parties. A landlord could ask you to could collect rent on a daily basis, but this is much too time consuming. Many landlords set their rental intervals on a weekly basis. They have some good reasons for doing this. Property managers don't generally like this approach, due to the additional work in collecting and accounting for rent so often.

> ✔ *FAST FACT*
>
> Many landlords set their rental intervals on a weekly basis. They have some good reasons for doing this. Property managers don't generally like this approach, due to the additional work in collecting and accounting for rent so often.

Pros and Cons of Weekly Rent Collection

- When rent is due each week, a tenant has less opportunity to fall behind on large sums of rent money before you can take action. You are dealing with a week's rent being past due instead of a month's rent.

- This type of rental collection is labor intensive, but effective.
- You have more paperwork to process.
- More time is involved with the collection process, but you reduce the amount of money you are likely to lose from a bad tenant.
- There is more money to be made in a year when you collect rent weekly. This is the main reason why investors like weekly collection.

Let's compare how you will come out collecting rent on a weekly basis, as opposed to on a monthly basis. For our example, assume you have set a monthly rent of $900.00. When you collect twelve rent checks, one for each month, you have a total of $10,800.00. Most people consider it to be four weeks in a month. This is a false belief. If there were only four weeks in a month, there would only be forty-eight weeks in a year. By charging a weekly rent, you collect for four additional weeks. This means that for every rental unit you have, you collect an additional $900.00 a year. With a six-unit building, this amounts to $5,400.00 a year in increased revenue. With a large number of rental units the additional income is quite impressive.

Since most people look at a monthly rental amount and divide it by four to arrive at a weekly amount, they will have no qualms about paying your weekly fee. In their mind, they will multiply your weekly charge by four when comparing it to other properties offering monthly rents. This makes you appear competitive when you are actually charging more. This is a trick many old-school landlords use to increase their net income.

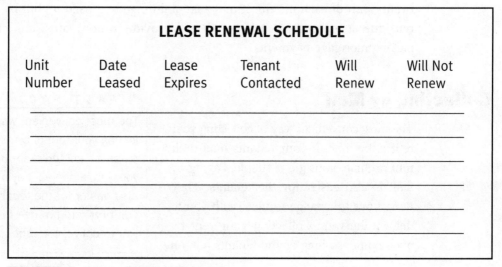

LEASE RENEWAL SCHEDULE

Unit Number	Date Leased	Lease Expires	Tenant Contacted	Will Renew	Will Not Renew

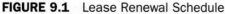

FIGURE 9.1 Lease Renewal Schedule

Picking a Due Date

Just as property owners can choose any rent interval they like, the owners can also pick a due date that suits their needs. Of course, tenants will have to agree to the date, but that shouldn't be a problem. Standard procedures call for a tenant's rent to be due on the first day of each month. Then many landlords allow a grace period of five to ten days beyond the due date. With this arrangement you may not see the rent until the tenth of the month. If the owner has a mortgage payment due on the first of the month, waiting until the tenth of the month for your rent can put some stress on the owner. There is a way to avoid this.

Rent is traditionally due on the first of the month, but there is no reason why a property owner can't break tradition. Tenants are accustomed to paying rent on the first of the month, but they will be willing to work to other schedules, if they are motivated. Imagine if you set a rental due date as the twenty-fifth of the month. What would this do for your property owner?

If a tenant's rent is due on the twenty-fifth of September, you should have the rent in plenty of time for the owner to pay the October mortgage payment. Even if you allow the tenant a grace period you will still have your money five days earlier than if the rent was due on the first of the month. When a tenant is first moving into a building you may have to pro-rate the first month's rent.

Tenants usually wish to move into a new building on the first of the month, since their old residence was most likely on a first-of-the-month rental cycle. All you have to do is pro-rate the rent from the twenty-fifth of the previous month to the time the tenant takes possession. Thereafter the tenant's rent will be due on the twenty-fifth of each month. It may take a little getting used to, but by having your rent due at the end of each month will provide a more consistent cash flow for making mortgage payments.

Collecting by Mail

The most convenient way of collecting your rent is by mail. If your tenants mail their rent on time, your job is simple. Paying by mail is also easier for the tenants. They don't have to arrange to meet with you to deliver the rent. Collecting your rent by mail is fine, so long as the tenants pay on

✔ **FAST FACT**

The most convenient way of collecting your rent is by mail. If your tenants mail their rent on time, your job is simple. Paying by mail is also easier for the tenants. They don't have to arrange to meet with you to deliver the rent.

time. Many landlords give their tenants pre-addressed, stamped envelopes to mail their rent in. This makes it a little easier for the tenant to put a check in the mail. You would do well to consider this tactic as a property manager.

Collecting in Person

Collecting the rent in person is an effective way to improve your percentage of on-time rent. When you are standing in front of a tenant it is much harder for the tenant to deny paying you. When you routinely collect the rent in person, you avoid the excuse of checks being lost in the mail. Personal collection takes time away from your other work. It is an added overhead of your rental business. You can't be generating new income when you are going door to door to collect rent. The fact that you are forfeiting the opportunity to make more money by collecting money already owed to you is a loss or overhead expense.

One good aspect of collecting the rent in person is your regular contact with the tenants in your building. You see them frequently and have a chance to develop a relationship. When handled properly you can parlay these meetings into your advantage. By keeping the tenants happy you avoid vacancies. Often all it takes to keep a tenant happy is a personal interest in their job, children, living conditions, or favorite sport.

> ✔ **FAST FACT**
>
> By spending a few extras minutes to talk with your tenants when collecting the rent you are able to be a person, not a cold, greedy property manager. This type of personal interaction is invaluable to the tenant-landlord relationship.

When you pick up the rent personally you get to see the building on a routine basis. Going from unit to unit will allow the opportunity to spot-check the apartments for damage or abuse. While you are in the building you can inspect common areas for any items that may need attention. If a smoke detector is missing, you will know about it before the code enforcement office puts you on notice. There are many benefits to collecting your rents in person.

You should spend enough time with the tenant to maintain good relations, but don't get trapped into spending half your day with a single tenant. Some tenants will

> ▶ **PRO POINTER**
>
> There are also some drawbacks to face-to-face rental collections. There will be tenants who love to gossip and tie you up for hours. You cannot afford to waste your time.

be chronic complainers. Most of these tenants would never go to the trouble of writing a letter of complaint, but when you are standing in their doorway, they will go on and on about whatever is bothering them.

Having the Rent Delivered

Some property managers insist that the tenants personally deliver their rent to the rental office. If you run your business from your home, I doubt you will enjoy having a string of tenants lining up in front of your door. Most managers don't want their tenants to know their home addresses. If you have an office outside of your home you might want tenants to deliver their rent, but I wouldn't. When tenants come to your office, you have no control over when they will be coming. This can disrupt your normal business day.

Tenants will not be anxious to personally deliver their rent unless the rental office is located in the rental building or complex. If tenants have to drive across town to deliver their rent, they are more likely to put the task off until they are on that side of town. This can delay your rent collection.

> ▶ *PRO POINTER*
>
> I believe collecting by mail is the most desirable way to collect your rent. If mail collection is not effective, I would go to the tenants to collect my rent. There are few occasions when I would want a tenant to bring the rent to my office.

> ✔ *FAST FACT*
>
> Some property managers give their tenants coupon books to pay their rent with. Since people are used to coupon books for their car and installment loans, having a coupon book for their rent makes sense. The added expense of having coupon books printed is minimal when compared to the cost of other forms of rent collection. Whether you mail out monthly statements or issue coupon books, your rent will be more likely to arrive on time when these methods are used.

Sending Monthly Statements

Should you send tenants monthly statements to remind them to make their rent payment? Well, it couldn't hurt. You should not have to send monthly statements to your tenants. When tenants sign a lease, they know your rental terms. They know when the rent is due. If they are responsible tenants, you shouldn't have to send them monthly reminders to meet their obligations. While you should not have to send out statements, your rent collection may be more successful if you do.

It is effective to use both coupon books and monthly statements. Some people will put the coupon book in a desk drawer and forget about it. If they receive a statement in the mail, their memory will be jogged. Enclosing a self-addressed, stamped envelope with your statements will prove to expedite the mailing of rent checks. If all tenants have to do is stick a check in the provided envelope and mail it, they will do so promptly. If they must go to the post office to buy a stamp, your rent payment may be delayed. The easier you make it for your tenants to pay their rent, the better off you will be.

Offering Discounts

Should you offer rental discounts to tenants who pay their rent on time? Many landlords believe you should. I disagree. I don't disagree with a discount policy, but I don't believe you should reward people for doing what they are supposed to do. In my discount program, tenants receive a discount if they pay their rent early, but not if it is only paid when due. I believe that by offering a discount for rent paid on the due date encourages late rent payments.

Tenants believe that once they miss their discount it doesn't matter when they pay the rent. This defeats your intentions behind a discount program. With my method the mental attitude is different. Tenants that pay their rent on time pays full price, but is not charged a late fee. The tenants who pay early avoid late fees and benefits from a five-percent discount. Tenants who pay late are charged a late fee and are put into the collection grinder. By maintaining a strong position and treating all tenants the same, this method has worked well for me. If you start making exceptions, you erode your policy and lose control.

Grace Periods

A majority of property managers allow their tenants a grace period on their rent. Some hard-nosed managers are standing on the doorstep of a past-due tenant when the clock ticks one minute past midnight. I believe grace periods should be allowed, but under controlled circumstances. I can see no reason to allow a ten-day grace period. Five days is plenty of time to compensate for a holiday or slow mail service.

Some tenants will assume their rent is not due until the end of the grace period and will assume that if the rent is later than the grace period that you will give them a warning. If you don't enforce the rules of your lease with authority, you will lose control. Tenants will learn that you are a softy and they will bleed you to the end. You may not have any intention of evicting a tenant who is late with the rent for the first time, but you should start the paperwork for eviction to protect yourself.

Late Fees

Tenants expect your lease to have a clause relating to late fees. Anyone who has had credit is aware of late fees. They are a common element in installment loans and leases. Are late fees effective? They help, but they are not a cure-all. Hard-line bad tenants will not care whether you charge late fees or not, they are not going to pay them anyway. Good tenants will not resist the presence of late fees because they will be paying their rent on time. Late fees will help borderline tenants to pay the rent when it's due.

If your lease calls for late fees, collect them. If you fail to charge the late fees, tenants will soon ignore them. When you make paper threats that are not followed up on, they are worthless. There is no point putting it in the lease if you are not going to enforce the rule.

> ✔ **FAST FACT**
>
> The longer your grace period, the longer you go without cash or the ability to take action. It is very important to keep a tight rein on your rental collection. If you allow a ten-day grace period it is easy to overlook past-due rent. Manipulating tenants will use the grace period to extend the use of their money. If they know they won't be in default until the end of the grace period, the chances are they will not pay the rent until the end of the grace period, if you are lucky.

> ✔ **FAST FACT**
>
> Every evicted tenant begins the trouble with a first time. When rent is late the first time, get your paperwork in order. If you wait, by the time you realize eviction is inevitable you will have lost substantial income. Starting the paperwork doesn't mean you must evict the tenant, but it gives you the option.

Friendly Reminders

Do friendly reminders work? They work for tenants who have overlooked the rental due date. Even good tenants can be going through a rough period in their life and forget to pay the rent. For them, it will not be intentional to rob you of your rent money. They will have just let the rent payment slip their mind. For these tenants friendly reminders are effective.

It doesn't cost much to send out reminders and they can bring your rent in earlier. But, if you are going to use friendly reminders, mail them as soon as the due date has passed. Don't wait until the end of the grace period. By the end of the grace period you should be sending out legal notices, not friendly reminders.

Calling Tenants

Many management companies employee collection specialists for the sole purpose of calling tenants and collecting rents. A phone call can replace the mailing of a friendly reminder. It is more difficult for a tenant to ignore a phone call than a friendly reminder in the mail. Calling to remind tenants their rent is due is effective, but be prepared for excuses.

When you make collection calls you will get more excuses than you could imagine. A few of the excuses will be legitimate, but most will be ludicrous. It will be

▶ **PRO POINTER**

If you plan to use telephone calls to collect past-due rent, make provisions for doing so in the rental lease. Have language in the lease that allows you to make phone calls between certain hours to inquire about past-due rent payments. Have your attorney create the legal language to avoid problems down the road.

up to you to decide when your tenants need temporary relief from their rental responsibilities, but don't be too generous. Even if you feel bad for your tenant, protect yourself. Start the required paperwork to allow you all legal options in removing the tenant if events turn bad.

Personal Visits

If you are willing to make a personal visit to past-due tenants your collection percentages will improve. Friendly reminders are fine and phone calls work, but it is hard to beat a face-to-face meeting. When you are looking tenants in the eye it is hard for most of them to lie to you. Your physical

✔ **FAST FACT**

I must say that I am not a supporter of personal visits to collect rent. The potential problems associated with these visits push the risk management of business beyond my comfort level.

presence can be all it takes to have the tenant produce a rent check. With this said, I must say that I am not a supporter of personal visits to collect rent. The potential problems associated with these visits push the risk management of business beyond my comfort level.

Don't use these meeting to make macho threats. Your tenant has rights and you had better know them and not violate them. If you verbally abuse the tenant you may find yourself under arrest. Be diplomatic in this meeting. Show concern for the tenants and their reasons for not paying their rent. If you can't collect with kindness, rely on the legal system. Our judicial system may leave a lot to be desired, but it is your only reasonable option when you cannot collect through amicable means.

Standing Firm

When you are collecting your rents, don't turn into a jellyfish. You, or your client, have a contractual agreement with tenants. If the tenants breech their agreements, there is no reason for you to stray from the printed word. Follow the terms of the lease to the letter. If you step backwards the tenant may bowl you over. It is imperative for you to retain control.

Cash, Check, or Charge?

In what form will you collect your rent? Will you accept cash, checks, or charge cards? Most landlords collect their rent in the form of personal checks. This is an accepted practice and is the most common method of rent collection. While personal checks are the most common form or rental payment, they are not the only option. Your rent may come as a money order or bank check. Progressive property managers accept major credit cards for rental payments. Cash is also legal tender, but it provides potential for problems.

Personal checks are good for many reasons. They can be replaced if they are lost or stolen. Your tenant can stop payment on the missing check and issue a new one. Personal checks can be sent through the mail without fear. Checks provide physical proof of rental payments. This can come in handy in legal disputes and tax audits. The only bad side of personal checks is the fact that they can bounce. Since personal

✔ **FAST FACT**

The rental lease should spell out the acceptable forms for rental payments.

checks are not collected funds, there is a risk that the check will not be honored by the bank.

Money orders are as good as cash, maybe better. When you have a money order in hand, you know you have your rent money. Unlike personal checks, money orders don't bounce. Money orders provide the opportunity for proof of your rental collections. By making a photo-copy of the money order you can prove the date the rent was paid and the amount paid. For tenants without checking accounts, money orders are a good way to collect your rent.

Bank checks work on a similar principal to money orders. They are typically collected funds that protect you from overdrawn bank accounts. The bank check can be copied to provide physical proof and documentation of your rental transaction.

> ✔ **FAST FACT**
>
> Bank checks and money orders are two of the best ways to ensure your rent payment has been made with viable funds.

Credit cards seem to be here to stay. You can buy dinner and charge it. Clothes can be charged on credit cards. Why not make it three out of three. People need food, clothing, and shelter. If they can charge their food and clothes, it stands to reason they should be able to charge their rent. Many management firms will accept plastic to pay the rent. As the owner of a rental business you can probably arrange to accept credit cards, too.

> ▶ **PRO POINTER**
>
> When tenants pay rent with credit cards you know the rent money is good. Once you call for authorization, the money is as good as in your bank account. By accepting credit cards you can remove many of the excuses for past-due rent.

Should you accept credit cards? Credit cards provide you with two big advantages. When tenants pay rent with credit cards you know the rent money is good. Once you call for authorization, the money is as good as in your bank account. By accepting credit cards you can remove many of the excuses for past-due rent. When the tenant is pleading poverty you can offer to charge the rent to a credit card. By being able to charge their rent, tenants are not as likely to make you wait for your payment.

Be advised that the use of credit cards is not without its price. As a credit-card vendor you will be charged a fee for the privilege. Normally this fee is a set percentage. Before you sign up for credit card services, read the agreement. If in doubt, have your attorney review the documents. The fees charged are usually fair and are a small price to pay for collecting your rent on time.

It is bad business to accept cash for rental payments. This is a fact for many reasons. When a tenant pays with cash it is hard to document the payment. If you accept cash, fill out a receipt for the money. Include the date, a description of what the payment is for, and have the tenant sign the receipt. You cannot reasonably refuse cash, it is legal tender, but you should discourage cash payments.

If it is known that you collect your rent in cash, you could become the victim of crime. This is especially true if you go door-to-door when collecting your rent. Some seedy character may wait until you have picked up all the money and then relieve you of it. How the crook gets the money can be left to your imagination. He may hit you over the head, shoot you, cut you, or use some more creative method. Cash collections are not a good idea.

Bad Check Charges

When your lease contains the proper language you can penalize tenants for bouncing their rent checks. When a tenant gives you a bad check it can cost you money. If you bounce checks because of the tenant's bad check, you will be charged a fee from your bank. Bad checks can put a crunch on your cash flow. By the time the tenant makes good on the bad check, the mortgage payment for the building may be late. If your lease calls for a steep penalty fee on all bad checks, the tenant may think twice before giving you worthless paper.

Past-Due Promises

Past-due promises don't pay your bills. When the rent is late your tenants will always have an excuse. As a past-due rent collector you will collect many more promises than checks. The problem is, you can't spend promises. Novice managers and landlords lose a lot of money by depending on past-due promises. If you are going to accept promises, at least put a time limit on them. Never accept a promise that says, "I'll send the rent as soon as I can." This type of promise will force you into the poorhouse.

✔ *FAST FACT*

Novice managers and landlords lose a lot of money by depending on past-due promises. If you are going to accept promises, at least put a time limit on them. Never accept a promise that says, "I'll send the rent as soon as I can." This type of promise will force you into the poorhouse.

Pin the promises down. If a tenant claims she will send you a check within the next week, ask for a specific date to expect the payment. When the payment doesn't arrive, take assertive action to collect on the broken promise. If the tenant promises to pay you in two weeks, ask her to sign a promissory note for the delinquent payment. The note will help you if you go to court and if the tenant is lying, the note may call her hand. Past-due promises are rarely kept.

Separating Lies from Excuses

It can be perplexing to separate lies from excuses. There are times when even your best tenants will need help. If they have a bad bout with an illness, they may need some time to catch up on their rent. When a tenant gives you a reason for being late with the rent, you must decide what to do. Does the tenant have a legitimate excuse, or is the tenant lying to you? It is not as difficult to sift through the excuses and lies as you may think.

If a tenant is telling the truth the individual should be willing to cooperate with you. The earlier advice about asking for a promissory note is a good example.

When a tenant says that he has been laid off from his job, but will be going back to work in two weeks, do you believe him? If you have a long rental history with the tenant you may feel confident he is telling the truth. If you have doubts, ask him if you can call his employer to confirm the date set for the tenant to return to work. If he allows you to call the employer, you will know he has a reasonable excuse for being late with the rent. If he hedges and avoids giving you his employer's name or number, he is probably lying.

✔ **FAST FACT**

If tenants intend to pay you, they will not mind signing a note for money owed to you. On the other hand, if tenants are lying, they will not want their signature on a written agreement of payment. Research can go along way in telling excuses from lies.

▶ **PRO POINTER**

As a landlord or property manager, you must be aware of the laws pertaining to your business and avoid harassing your tenants for late rent. It can get very frustrating when you know a tenant is hiding behind an answering machine, but your legal actions are limited. You cannot go to the tenant's apartment in the middle of the night to accost him for the rent. There are many laws protecting tenants. If you don't educate yourself in these legal matters you will be the one on the wrong side of the judge.

With these types of methods you can quickly identify troublesome tenants. When you are unable to get satisfactory answers to your questions you should start legal proceedings. The longer you put off the legal process, the longer you will have to go without income.

Keep Solid Records

Good records are instrumental to any business. They are especially valuable when you may become engaged in a legal battle. When you run your rental business, document your actions. Make photocopies of rental payments. Keep a phone diary of the dates you call your tenants. Even if they are not home, write down the date and time that you attempted to contact them. Use return-receipt mail when you are mailing legal notices and save the signed receipts. The more you document during your dealings, the better off you will be in court.

Starting a Paper Trail

When tenants are in default of your lease, you must start a paper trail. There will be reams of paperwork between the non-payment of rent and eviction. If you don't handle the process correctly, you could lose the battle on a technicality. Laws vary from location to location, but they all dictate specific requirements for you to perfect your legal options.

✔ FAST FACT

If you are new to the property management business, seek the advice of a good lawyer. Have the lawyer handle your first case involving a bad tenant. If you pay attention to the schedule of events you may be able to take care of your own legal notices, filings, and responsibilities in the future. Don't attempt to play lawyer. When it comes to drafting legal documents, hire an attorney. If you insist on preparing your own documents, at least have them reviewed and approved by an attorney.

Partial Payments

Be careful in accepting partial payments. In some circumstances the acceptance of a partial payment can weaken your legal position. Your attorney can instruct you in ways to accept partial payments without deteriorating your legal stance. If you decide to take partial payments, make sure you are not making a bad situation worse.

Increasing Rental Income

Increasing rental income is always a primary interest for successful investors. As an owner of income property, the more income you receive, the more successful you are. Many rental expenses remain the same during the ownership of a building. If costs remain unchanged, increased income will put more profit in your pocket. Obviously, if you increase your rental income, you should increase your profit. Many investors learn a hard lesson from this concept.

Novice investors buy a building, immediately raise the rents, and project their future profits. Do you think their profit projections prevail? More often than not, their projections take a dive into deep red ink. Cold greed rarely produces a profit. These same investors could have seen significant income increases and reduced vacancies with an organized business plan. Do you know when and how to successfully raise rents?

The average investor has no idea of the potential repercussions from the simplest act. Investors typically know money and investments better than they know people. These investment skills are important, but without people skills, you can be engulfed in trouble, fast. A well-rounded investor will have numerous skills. Some of these skills include:

- Sales ability
- Public relation skills
- Knowledge of legal matters
- An in-depth knowledge of current market trends
- Have a knowledge of the banking industry
- Have a working knowledge of building and fire codes
- Be connected to a strong network of real estate professionals

The types of professionals who typically enhance an investor's profit potential can include the following:

- Investment brokers
- Attorneys
- Certified public accounts
- Maintenance services
- Mortgage brokers

- Private lenders
- Remodeling contractors
- Insurance agents and others

Many of these contacts offer an investor angles for increasing the bottom line of a financial statement. After all, making money is what income property is all about. What follows is advice on the numerous ways to increase rental income, without negative side-effects.

> ✔ **FAST FACT**
>
> Indiscriminately increasing rents can result in a loss of income. Your spreadsheet may show a seven percent increase as a profit, but if your tenants revolt and move; your increase results in an income loss.

Change-of-Ownership Rental Increases

The first opportunity real estate investors have to raise rents is when they take possession of a new property. There is a tendency among inexperienced landlords to immediately raise the rents with a change of ownership. This is an opportune time to increase the rental income, but the timing and method of these increases is critical to your success. It is not enough to randomly pick an increased rental figure and send a notice to the tenants. Frequently, the result will be a mass exodus and a significant negative cash flow.

A large negative cash flow is the last thing you want when taking over a new building. At the best, you lose money, at the worst, you lose the property. You may have noticed that the current rents are below present market rents when you evaluated the purchase of a building. This knowledge is valuable, but doesn't justify an immediate rental increase. For all you know, the prior landlord raised the rents before placing the property on the open real estate market.

If the tenants have had an increase in their rent within the last six months, your increase could force them to move. Anytime you have a vacant rental unit, you lose money. There is the expense of cleaning the unit, advertising for tenants, and your

> ✔ **FAST FACT**
>
> Property managers can use many of the same tactics that investors and landlords use when they manage their own buildings. Understanding the procedures employed by property owners will help you as a property manager. Even if you are not an owner of income property, learn to think like one.

time in interviewing tenants. If your time is valuable, the time spent showing apartments can cost you major money

A Letter of Introduction

When you first acquire a building, send the tenants a letter of introduction. Professional property managers should send tenants a letter of introduction when the manager takes over the management of a building. Explain that their home has been placed in your hands and you hope to develop a good relationship with each of them. A comment expressing your acknowledgement of their importance to your building's operation will go a long way. Don't treat the tenants like rental slaves. Explain how their presence is important to you and the rest of the tenants.

▶ **PRO POINTER**

The first meeting with your new tenants will reveal much about them and your recently acquired investment or building to manage. This should be a non-confrontational meeting, with the intent of gathering vital information. Since the tenants know you are coming, they will try to make their apartments as neat as possible. They should be on their best behavior and a little intimidated. All of this works in your favor.

Stress your interest in meeting with them to hear their likes and dislikes about their living quarters. Tell the tenants how you view them as a partner in your rental business. Without tenants, your business will wind up in the bankruptcy courts. In your letter, schedule a time to meet with each tenant. The residents will be nervous about rental increases and changes in the tenancy rules. Be aware of this expected fear and approach them with a consoling demeanor.

Read the Room

When you enter an apartment, check it out closely. The condition of the apartment can tell you much about the tenant. Here are some things to look for:

- If the apartment is a mess, you know the occupants may not be the type of tenant you want.
- Are there any unpleasant odors?
- Is there evidence of property abuse?
- What is the thermostat set at?

- Check out the furniture and personal property.
- Does the tenant appear to be a transient or a settled, mature individual?
- The more you notice from reading the room, the better your chances are of making solid decisions.

Within the first few minutes, tenants will probably inquire about any intended rental increases. Don't skirt this issue, address it in a non-committal way. Explain how you have just purchased the building or have just taken over the management of the building and are not aware of the current market rents for the area. Tell the tenants that you will be assessing the property, the tenants, and the market conditions, before making any decision regarding rental increases.

Change the subject by asking them for feedback on their living conditions. Take notes as the tenant talks. When the tenants see you making notes about their comments, they will begin to respect you. By exhibiting an interest, you will be paving the way to raising the rents successfully.

Initial Meeting

After your initial meeting with the tenants, you will have a good idea of the tenants you classify as desirable. Review the notes taken during your meeting with the residents. Ask yourself some questions and do some research to determine what the best course of action is. Here are some examples of what to consider:

- Note the expense involved with making the corrections needed to satisfy the tenants.

✔ **FAST FACT**

Allow tenants to ask you questions when inspecting rental properties. In most cases, there won't be many questions to answer. Tenants will be reserved and unlikely to pose questions about your plans or abilities. The mere fact you are willing to hear them out will make an impact. Your purpose in this meeting is to gather data and gain control. If the tenant does complain, listen and take notes.

▶ **PRO POINTER**

When a resident is distressed about a leaking faucet, fix it. The wasted water is costing money and adding to the tenant's frustration. Ignoring minor repairs usually costs a landlord more money than correcting the problem promptly. Aside from higher utility costs and building deterioration, ignoring these problems may cost you a tenant.

- Carefully examine the existing leases or rental agreements.
- When do the agreements expire and how does the recent sale affect the leases?
- Are there provisions in the lease for the new owner to cancel the existing leases?
- Are the present rents at the same amount found in the lease?
- Draw as much information from the existing leases as possible for your planning purposes.
- Start a file on each tenant and put all applicable notes in the file.
- Contact the local housing authority and request all available data pertaining to historical rental information for the last three years.

Making Sense of the Data

Making sense of the data that you collect is the key to setting the right rental rate. Use only the information pertaining to properties in the same general location of your building. Break the information down according to the number of bedrooms in each unit. Ideally, comparisons should be made with buildings housing a similar number of apartments. A two-bedroom apartment in a duplex should bring higher rent than the same apartment found in a twelve-unit complex. Note who is responsible for utility expenses. If the tenant pays for utilities, their rent will probably be lower. Find the most comparable information available to determine your rental income ceiling.

When this stage of you evaluation is complete, turn to the local newspaper. Look through the classified advertisements for price and availability of rental property. Again, keep your comparisons fair and comparable. Use only examples from similar apartments, in the same basic area. Are pets allowed, and if so, is additional rent charged for the privilege? What amenities are included in the rent for comparable properties? The more information you compile, the better your chances are of getting the most out of your property.

With your research complete, you can draw an accurate conclusion on your present rental income status. Are your rents below the current market amounts? How does your property compare with other buildings for parking, utilities, and condition? Assuming your building is equal to the ones studied, you can evaluate your maximum rental increase. If you are at or above market rates, there is still a chance you can increase your monthly rental charges.

They Won't Want to Move

If you found the tenants to be happy in your meeting, they will not want to move. If the surrounding apartments are charging $850, per month, can you charge $875? If your tenants are presently paying $850, per month, you probably can. It will not be worth the cost and inconvenience for the tenant to move. Would you go through the hassles of moving to save $25 per month? If you decide to raise the rents, don't send a letter to all the tenants notifying them of the increase. Instead, arrange to meet with them again.

This meeting is an excellent opportunity to have the tenants execute a new lease and to acknowledge any changes in policy. When property is transferred, there are frequently changes in the rental rules. They may pertain to parking, storage, or any number of other items. These changes should be in writing, acknowledged, and accepted by the tenant's signature.

Take a detailed outline of your rental comparison findings with you. When you advise tenants of the increase, they may say that it is unwarranted. If this happens, show them your research findings. When they see moving will save no more than $25 per month, their attitude may change. You can help expedite this change by

▶ *PRO POINTER*

When meeting with the tenants to raise rents, meet with them separately. Start with the least desirable tenant. This tenant will be your testing ground.

pointing out the costs and inconvenience of moving. If you have justification to retain the tenant's security deposit, you have even more leverage. Don't abuse this power and come off looking like a villain.

Monitor tenant reactions as you work your way from the least desirable to the most desirable tenant. If you are catching heavy flak from all the tenants, back off on the rental increase. If you feel your attempt to raise the rent is too risky, assure the tenants you will not raise the rents at this time. But, don't miss this opportunity to increase your cash flow. By following this approach, you will almost always be able to see some increase in your income.

Breaking Out of the Pack

In order to obtain maximum monthly rents, you must set yourself apart from the competition. What will your building allow you to offer prospective tenants? Here are some characteristics to consider:

- Do your apartments have more bedrooms or bathrooms than other units on the market?

- Are the rooms in your units larger than average?

- Total square footage is a consideration when setting rental income figures.

- Larger apartments should be worth a little more than their smaller competition.

- The number of bedrooms has a great deal of influence on value. An additional bedroom puts your unit in a whole different category and allows for substantially higher rent.

- If you can offer more than one bathroom, you should expect a higher rent.

These factors are routine and recognized by most investors. In many cases, you have little control over these features of a property. The building either has the qualities or it doesn't. When maximizing your rental income, explore all of the possibilities. Don't overlook the obvious, but never fail to look below the surface. It is the hidden value of a building that offers the highest rate of return.

▶ *PRO POINTER*

Here are some examples of dormant opportunities. Do buildings in your area allow pets? Do you allow pets? If you don't, you should consider changing your policy. People with pets are frequently more responsible and less likely to move. This is especially true of older tenants. Pets are generally discouraged in apartment buildings and rental homes. This is an opening for the aggressive entrepreneur to capitalize on.

Pets

Imagine your ease in finding quality tenants if you are one of the few landlords willing to allow pets. People often consider their pets part of the family. They don't want to part with their cuddly companions and will go to extremes to provide housing for them. As a landlord, you can profit from this love of animals. Creating a pet policy will increase your income and decrease your vacancy rate.

Take some time to make a comprehensive policy regarding pets. Some factors to consider include the following:

- Require an additional security deposit when pets are admitted.

- The amount of this deposit should be determined by the type of pet and the possible damage that could be caused by the animal.

- In addition to the deposit, charge an additional monthly fee for tenants with pets. This can be justified due to increased risk of loss on your part.
- The amount of additional deposits will vary with geographic locations, but $25 to $50 per month shouldn't be unreasonable.

Consider what this new policy does for you. The additional deposit protects you from property damage. Allowing pets expands your base of qualified tenants and reduces your downtime between vacancies. Pet people don't move as often, so you reduce your vacancy rate.

Water Beds

Water beds are another frowned upon object in the minds of most landlords. When the competing advertisements say, "no water beds allowed," yours should state, "water beds welcome." Why should you incur the risk of flooded apartments when other landlords refuse to? Because, you can make more money and not increase your risk. You can require the tenant to enter into a written agreement for the privilege to use a water bed. Additionally, you can require the tenant to provide insurance coverage for any damage done by a water bed. These liability policies are available and you can be protected in any reasonable amount you deem necessary.

Storage

Storage is another source of additional income. If your building has facilities for storage, you can charge extra for it. I am not talking about chicken-wire enclosures in the basement. Those types of storage areas are more of a fire hazard than an asset. If your building has provisions for lockable, secure storage, it is valuable. Does the property have garages on it? Are you charging additional rent for the garage space? If you aren't, you should be. Also consider a change in use for the garage. Look for the highest and best use of all your assets. Perhaps the garage should be converted into storage lockers.

Parking

In some cities, parking is a problem for residents. If this is true in your location, you may be able to charge extra for your parking space. If this is feasible, compare the rents in other buildings and their parking arrangements. After comparing your building to the competition, adjusts your fees accordantly. When your property doesn't have sufficient parking space, look at your options. Can you fill in a section of the lot and create space? Could you convert some of the lawn into a parking area? Use your creative ability to increase your income when parking pays.

Coin-Operated Laundries

What else can you do to increase your building's income? Are your apartments equipped with private laundry facilities? Do you offer a laundry room for tenants to share? Are you presently using coin-operated laundry equipment? In buildings without private laundry hook-ups, coin-operated machines in a common laundry room can add thousands to your rental income. Installing the plumbing and electrical connections for a laundry room is not going to break your bank. This add-on investment should pay for itself in short order.

If your building doesn't have a basement, consider remodeling a small section of the building. Adding a laundry room to the exterior of the building is another way to overcome space problems. Project your planned earnings from the machines and evaluate your personal situation. If the installation cost isn't too great, the laundry should be a money maker.

By now, your mind should be spinning with ideas to increase your rental income. I'm sure there are other ways to increase your building's income, but these are some of the best. Be creative, and use your entrepreneurial skills to add to the list. Different locations and buildings offer various opportunities. Work on it until you find the procedure best suited for your individual situation. In your search for the best methods to increase income, remember, reducing expenses can be more effective than increasing income.

> ✔ *FAST FACT*
>
> Keys to a prosperous laundry room include good lighting and security. Clean conditions and regular maintenance on the machines are compulsory for a profitable laundry operation. These laundry rooms can be placed in the basement of many buildings. If there is no plumbing at floor level, a relatively inexpensive, pump system can be installed. This system uses a holding tank and a float-controlled effluent pump. When the washing machines discharge into the holding basin, the excess water is pumped up to the building's main plumbing drain.

My Top 20 Tenant Problems and How to Solve Them

Tenant problems range from small inconveniences to major trouble. Experienced property managers often defuse tense situations before they get out of hand. With every year of experience that you gain as a manager, you will be building your list of war stories. As you network with other rental professionals, you will hear about their experiences. By learning from your own experience and listening to the stories that other professionals are telling, you can develop skills to minimize problems with tenants.

There are some basic procedures that apply to many tenant situations. While some circumstances require special action, following the fundamentals will keep you out of, and get you out of, a lot of trouble with tenants. A few of the key fundamentals are listed below:

- Make all of your agreements in writing.
- Keep rules the same for all tenants within the same building.
- Respond to tenant requests, even if you have to reject their requests.
- Communicate clearly and often with tenants.
- Stay in control at all times, but treat tenants with respect.
- Don't lose your temper.
- Never smoke in buildings that you manage.
- Return phone calls as promptly as you can.

- Avoid getting too friendly with tenants; keep your relationship on a business level.

These suggestions are just a few examples of how to work with tenants. You will develop many tactics on your own as you gain more experience.

Problem after Problem

Tenants can hit a property manager with problem after problem. It is not uncommon for most of the problems to come from the same tenants over and over again. What can you do to reduce the problems that you have to deal with on a daily basis? There are a number of ways to work out differences with tenants. Many times the approach you take will depend on the tenant and the type of problem that you are dealing with. As we move through this chapter, I am going to share my top 20 tenant problems and solutions with you. The order of the problems is not methodical. I will be listing them as I remember them. If you are ready, I will take you on a tour of decades of property management experience as both a landlord and a property manager.

Unauthorized Residents

Unauthorized residents frequently show up in multi-family buildings and apartment complexes. These are people who have not been screened or approved to live on the premises. Registered residents move these people in without telling you. Why? Sometimes it is to save money, if you charge extra for roommates. Tenants sometimes don't think to have their live-in friend register as a tenant. This can be an honest oversight.

> ▶ *PRO POINTER*
>
> Unauthorized residents have the potentially to present you and the property owner with serious problems. Since the residents are not signatories on a lease, they are not bound by your rules and regulations. Don't allow unauthorized residents in your buildings.

Unauthorized residents have the potentially to present you and the property owner with serious problems. Since the residents are not signatories on a lease, they are not bound by your rules and regulations. Don't allow unauthorized residents in your buildings. Keep track of vehicles to see if there are any unlisted vehicles spending a lot of time around your building. This can be a tip to unregistered residents.

TENANCY CHANGE ORDER

This tenancy change order addendum shall become an integral part of the lease/rental agreement dated _____, 20_____, between _____, tenant and _____, landlord, for the dwelling located at_____.

This tenancy change order addendum shall serve to change the original terms of tenancy as dictated by the above-mentioned lease/rental agreement. Tenant and landlord agree to the following changes and amendments to the existing lease/rental agreement for the property located at _____

_____.

Changes in Tenancy

_____

_____

_____

_____

_____

The above-detailed changes are the only changes agreed to and in force. Other than for the above changes, the original lease/rental agreement is in full force. By signing below, both landlord and tenant agree to the detailed changes in the existing written agreement between them.

_____   _____
Landlord   Date   Tenant   Date

FIGURE 10.1 Tenancy Change Order

Garbage Disposers

Apartments that have garbage disposers in the kitchen can be problematic. Many tenants don't know the proper procedure for using a food grinder. I can't count the number of times that I have had to snake kitchen drain lines when garbage disposers were abused. This is especially true in older buildings, where the kitchen drains are piped with galvanized steel pipe.

While garbage disposers are an amenity, they can also be a liability in service calls to plumbing contractors. It may be worth considering the removal of all garbage disposers. If you leave them, at least educate your tenants in the proper use of the device.

Extension Cords

The use of cheap extension cords can create a fire hazard. It is not uncommon for tenants to string substandard extension cords all over rental property to operate their modern appliances and electronic equipment. This can be a sizable risk in older buildings. Modern construction normally offers adequate electrical outlets. Old buildings usually have old wiring. The strain that can be put on the electrical system when extension cords and power strips are used can create a fire risk. It can also burn out fuses and trip circuit breakers.

Inspect apartments periodically and look for unsafe use of extension cords and electrical devices. If you discover this type of situation, serve notice to the tenant to correct the problem immediately.

Unreported Leaks

Unreported plumbing leaks can do a lot of damage. You would think that tenants would notify you if they had water coming through their ceiling, but not all of them do. They sometimes don't want to be a bother. I have seen floors rotted out from toilet leaks, ceilings that have fallen from leaks in apartments above them, and so forth. Ask your tenants to please report any suspicious conditions in and around

▶ *PRO POINTER*

Consider working out a deal with property owners to reward tenants who report maintenance or security problems with their buildings. The tenants live in the building. They see and hear things that property managers and landlords don't. Giving a tenant a gift certificate for a free dinner on the town is a bargain if it saves you money in building repairs.

their rental units. Catching problems quickly can save the property owner a lot of money.

Non-Payment

The non-payment of rent is certainly high on the list of problems for property managers. There are many reasons why tenants can't, or don't, pay rent. This problem has been discussed earlier. Your best defense for this problem is a strict lease, good communication with your tenants, and a willingness to chase after rent money when it is not paid. You will need thick skin, but you won't last long in the rental business if you can't collect the rent that is due to you.

Late Payments

Late payments for rent hurt cash flow. The same techniques used for non-payment of rent can apply to late payments. When you have a lease drawn up by an attorney, make it painful for tenants who pay them rent after the due date. Charge steep late fees. Have language included in the lease that allows you to evict tenants who are late paying their rent three times in a single year, or something along these lines.

Bounced Checks

Bounced checks are not much better than non-payment of rent. The advantage that you have with a bounced check is that you have more evidence to go to court with and you are more likely to reach a quicker, successful collection of your money. Your lease can have strong language in it to deal with bounced check. In addition to this, talk with your tenants who bounce checks and try to work the problem out amicably. If this doesn't work, go to court and seek relief from a judge.

> ▶ *PRO POINTER*
>
> When you have an attorney create a lease for you, make sure that the lease addresses as many situations as you can think of. Don't leave anything to the imagination. Set rules and establish remedies for those who violate the rules. This is your best cure for problem tenants.

Poor Upkeep

The poor upkeep of a rental unit can be costly for the property owner. A lease should address the responsibility of tenants to maintain their homes in an acceptable fashion. The lease should allow for periodic inspections of the rental unit. Make these inspections. See if the tenants are keeping the rental unit up to the standards required by their lease. If they are not, serve them with a notice and follow the language in your lease to resolve the issue.

Parking Lot Problems

Parking lot problems come in many forms. Let me give you a few examples of how tenants can cause problems in parking areas:

- Tenants who work on their vehicles in your parking lot can leak fluids that may cause you problems with local officials. Imagine having an oil spill in your parking lot.
- If you limit the number of vehicles each rental unit is allowed to have, tenants who buy additional vehicles can eliminate parking for some of your tenants who are playing by the rules.
- Where will tenants park boats, ATVs, and campers?
- Do you want tenants washing their cars in your lot and spraying the cars of other tenants with water? I doubt if your other tenants will appreciate it.

These are just some of the types of parking lot problems that you could encounter. As with all potential problems, try to address them in your lease. Once tenants sign your lease and rental policy, you have much more power to enforce rules and regulations.

Pets

Pets that are not known about can be a financial disaster for a property owner. If pets are allowed in a building, most leases will dictate the types of pets that are approved. Many tenants acquire pets after becoming residents. They may not tell you that they have added Fluffy or Spot to their family. This can be bad.

Pets that use your carpet as their bathroom create a costly problem. Not only will you have to replace the carpet, but you will also have to replace the pad under the carpet. Cats can scratch window sills and shred window treatments. Dogs can chew baseboard trim and scratch interior doors. The damage can run into thousands of dollars.

If you are going to allow pets, collect enough of a damage deposit to protect yourself. Make sure that all pets in the building are approved by you for occupancy. Your lease and routine inspections of rental units are the best solutions to the pet problem.

Trash in Common Areas

I don't understand why, but some tenants like to leave their bags of trash in common areas. You can provide trash receptacles at multiple locations, and some tenants will choose to leave their rotting garbage in the hallways. Not only is the smell disgusting, the garbage creates a health and safety issue. This cannot be tolerated and must be settled quickly. Your lease should have provisions for this type of problem. Make sure that it does. Serve notice on the guilty tenant immediately and enforce the terms of your lease quickly.

▶ *PRO POINTER*

When you find garbage bags in you common areas, how will you know who put them there? Garbage left in common areas is not considered private property. Open the bags and look for envelopes addressed to your tenants. This can be pretty strong proof of who put the garbage in the common area.

Vandalism

Vandalism can be a problem in any building. Sometimes it is the tenants, or their children, who are responsible for the vandalism. Then there are people off the street who use your building as a playground for their vandalism. This can be a difficult problem to solve.

You can reduce interior vandalism by installing security doors and only giving access keys or cards to tenants. Closed-circuit cameras are another way to catch the offenders on tape. If you use cameras, try to hide them. Visible cameras may deter some illegal activity, but the cameras may become the focus of vandalism or theft.

Cameras can be hidden by building small boxed areas in a corner where walls meet a ceiling. Put a heat-register grill on the box. This will appear to be a vent duct. The camera can watch the surveillance area through the grill.

Loud Music

Loud music is a common complaint in rental buildings. Once again, the language in your lease should address this matter. Solving this one is usually as simple as calling a tenant and asking them to turn down the tunes. You might have to serve them with a formal notice and push the issue with the terms of your lease. The problem will normally be fairly easy to solve.

Constant Phone Calls

Constant phone calls from problem tenants can make you think about changing professions. There are some tenants who simply like to talk. Their property manager is as good as anyone to talk with when they are lonely or bored. Not only is this annoying for you, it gets expensive. Time that you could be spending making money is spent babysitting talkative tenants.

While you must respond to reasonable requests from tenants, you can limit the phone calls. Have your lease state that phone calls are to be made for emergencies only. All other requests and correspondence must be in writing. Explain that this is to memorialize their request and to establish a record for the property owner. With a little creative language, your lawyer can make it reasonable for you to avoid chatty tenants on the telephone.

> ▶ **PRO POINTER**
>
> If you are responsible for emergency repairs and similar short-notice needs in the buildings that you manage, invest in a pager and cell phone. When you sign on as a property manager, you lose your freedom of punching out at the time clock.

Illegal Activities

Tenants sometimes conduct illegal activities in homes and apartments that they rent. You might be surprised at what some tenants will do in rental property that you are managing. As a manager and broker, I have seen a lot of illicit activity when showing properties. My experiences have included discovering basements filled with marijuana under grow lights, prostitution outlets in apartments, and drug labs in kitchens. This is not even counting the drug dealers and fences for stolen property that was stored onsite, and similar criminals. You have to keep the criminal element out of your buildings. If you run into illegal activities, notify the local authorities. Call the police and let them do their job.

Domestic Disputes

Domestic disputes are not uncommon in rental properties. Sometimes the parties to the dispute live together in a rental unit. Other situations have a disgruntled party who does not reside in the building coming to a tenant's apartment and making a scene in the hallway. This cannot be allowed to happen. Tenants will feel threatened. You can experience vacancies if you tolerate yelling and screaming in your halls and rental units. When there is a domestic disturbance reported to you, call the police and let them put an end to the problem.

Home-Based Businesses

Home-based businesses are allowed by some property owners. This practice is fine for some types of businesses. For example, a self-employed writer or graphic designer might do business at all hours of the day and night without bothering neighboring tenants. But, if the nature of the business creates heavy traffic through the building, tenants are likely to object to having so many strangers in their building. If you plan to allow home-based businesses in your buildings, set the guidelines for them in your lease. Your attorney can assist you in the terminology to use in the lease.

Commercial Tenants

Commercial tenants can cause you far more problems than residential tenants. Many commercial rental spaces are leased with equipment in place. Examples could include restaurants, storefronts, and similar buildings. When you let tenants have access to equipment that you, or your client, own, there is the risk of damage or theft. Control this situation with a substantial deposit that will offset your potential losses if a bad tenant decides to leave in the middle of the night with your equipment.

> ▶ *PRO POINTER*
>
> Talking with tenants will often resolve problems. There are times, however, when talking to tenants can put you at some level of risk for a lawsuit. Don't take your job casually. Treat tenants with respect and avoid topics that could result in legal action.

When Tenants Move

When tenants move, you must do a move-out inspection. This is when you discover all of the damage caused by a tenant. If you have done your paperwork properly, you will have a move-in checklist on file that the tenant signed to acknowledge the condition of the rental unit at the time occupancy was granted. Without this form, you could have a problem. Tenants who have not completed and signed move-in forms may claim that current damage to your rental units existed from the beginning of their residency. Don't get put in this position. Do your paperwork when you lease a rental unit and keep the signed move-in list on file. It's hard for tenants to dispute what they put in writing previously.

Abandoned Property

You may have to deal with abandoned personal property when tenants move out. This is especially true when tenants leave without notice. It's not pleasant to find a trashed apartment that is full of junk furniture, clothes, and other worthless belongings. When this happens, the mess must be cleaned up. It's unlikely that you will find the guilty tenant anytime soon. Make sure that your lease authorizes you to clean out the rental property and dispose of the abandoned belongings. Without legal authorization to dispose of the property, you could find yourself in a bad way once you have trashed the junk. Cover your bases well.

Prosper

Go forward and prosper as a property manager. It is a good profession when you have the right attitude and personality. You will have to learn a lot along the way as you work in the rental business. Reading this book is a good step in the right direction, but don't stop here. Seek training where you can find it. Read more books. Educate yourself. Taking on the management of rental properties for others is a lot of responsibility. It is not an easy job. Don't underestimate it. Prepare yourself and profit. Good luck!

Evicting Problem Tenants

Evicting problem tenants is rarely pleasant. It is a costly, time-consuming act that doesn't help you make many friends. But it is part of a property manager's job. The eviction process is one of the most miserable experiences you are likely to have in the rental business. The costs involved with moving a problem tenant out of a building can be staggering. To get a tenant out of a property can easily take months. During the period of time that you are going through eviction proceedings you will probably not be able to collect rent from the hostile tenant. Attorneys and the fees associated with eviction are expensive. This all adds up to a financial disaster for you and the property owner.

When you are forced to evict a tenant, rental income from the resident is non-existent and you are spending big bucks to remove the tenant legally. It doesn't get much worse than this in your day-to-day responsibilities as a property manager. Can eviction be avoided? Eviction cannot always be avoided, but there are ways to reduce the odds of going through the disgusting experience.

✔ **FAST FACT**

Many novice property managers think evicting a problem tenant is no big deal, until they attempt to do it. Once you find yourself in the middle of eviction proceedings you begin to understand the formidable task you have undertaken.

What Is Eviction?

What is eviction? By definition, eviction is the act of removing a tenant by legal procedures. Eviction is only one small word, but it carries mammoth consequences. Inexperienced landlords do not know what they are risking when they threaten to evict a tenant. Many novice property managers think evicting a problem tenant is no big deal, until they attempt to do it. Once you find yourself in the middle of eviction proceedings you begin to understand the formidable task you have undertaken.

Unfortunately, by the time most landlords realize their mistake, it is too late to reverse the procedure. It is not until their course of action is all but carved in stone that these landlords appreciate how much time and money is being lost by their actions. This is one reason why landlords retain the services of property managers.

Once you have experienced the pain of evicting a tenant you will probably do everything within your power to avoid ever doing it again. If you have never evicted anyone, you are lucky. If you have first-hand knowledge of the eviction process, you understand why I call eviction the ugliest word in property management. When you manage rental property you must be prepared to evict tenants.

> ▶ **PRO POINTER**
>
> When you enter into an agreement with a property owner to manage a rental property, make sure that the owner will pay all legal fees involved with conducting evictions. Don't assume the cost of evictions as a part of your standard fee for property management.

What Does It Take to Evict a Tenant?

What does it take to evict a tenant? Eviction requires money, time, and an organized approach. Do you need a lawyer to evict a tenant? There is no rule that says you must engage an attorney to evict someone, but it is a wise investment. Evictions can get down and dirty. Having legal representation is advantageous for all landlords, and it is especially beneficial if you are not experienced in conducting evictions. Unless you handle numerous evictions, on a regular basis, you should retain an attorney to assist in your eviction actions. As a property manager, your client should be responsible for legal fees associated with your eviction of a tenant.

How long does it take to remove a bad tenant? The eviction process can take several months. It is not unreasonable to assume you will be dealing with some aspect of the eviction process for four months, or more. Why does it take so long to remove a problem tenant? The process is time consuming because of the steps required to remove the tenant legally. There are notices to be delivered, hearings to be had, and legal action to be taken. All of these factors add up to make the process long and arduous. Let's take a look at some of the specific requirements involved in the eviction process.

Legalities

The legalities for eviction vary from location to location. The information you are about to read is not legal advice and the procedures for conducting a legal eviction in your jurisdiction may vary. Before you commence any eviction action, become well informed of the laws in your area. I advise you to consult an attorney before putting yourself into jeopardy with any actions they may compromise your position.

The Last Step

The last step before starting eviction proceedings is usually the issuance of a final notice. Evictions are normally required to remove tenants who are not paying their rent, but the eviction could be the result of tenants who have not adhered to the terms of their lease. In either case, you could issue a final warning to a tenant before beginning the eviction ritual.

These warnings normally give the tenant a prescribed period of time to comply with the terms of their lease. If the tenant does not comply within the given time, more formal steps will have to be taken. This will be the beginning of your eviction process.

▶ **PRO POINTER**

Remember, in most evictions, the tenant will not be paying rent while you are in the process of removing him from your building.

Eviction Papers

The first step in an eviction is the filing of eviction papers. Eviction papers are usually filed with the county court. When you file the papers, you will be given a court date. The court date could be a few weeks into the future, but it could be much more distant. Depending on your court system, the first court date could be more than a month away. Remember, in most evictions, the tenant will not be paying rent while you are in the process of removing him from your building.

Going to Court

When your court date arrives, you must sit around the court and wait for your case to be heard. Expect to lose a full day from your business when you must attend court. If you are lucky, the tenant will not appear in court. When the tenant does not show up, the judge will generally order an eviction. This is not an unusual scenario. Tenants frequently fail to appear at their eviction hearing.

> ▶ *PRO POINTER*
>
> Expect to lose a full day from your business when you must attend court. If you are lucky, the tenant will not appear in court. When the tenant does not show up, the judge will generally order an eviction.

If a tenant does appear, you could be in for more delays and problems. Depending upon the grounds for your eviction, the court could rule in favor of the tenant. If you have all of your paperwork in order and have obeyed the laws in your actions, you should win. However, winning is not always what you might think it is. The judge could throw you a curve.

Court-Ordered Continuations

Court-ordered continuations are not uncommon. If tenants can impress the court with their reasons for being evicted, the judge may be granted a continuance. This stay allows tenants time to resolve their conflict with you. If the tenants are behind in their rent, the continuance provides time for them to pay the past-due rent.

Court-ordered continuations are normally given when tenants claim a hardship case. Not having any place to relocate to could be considered a hardship, especially if children are involved. If tenants can prove they are behind in their rent because of illness or unemployment, the judge may go easy on them. If the court issues a stay, it may be for a couple of weeks or a month. So far, you are just getting started and the tenants have bled you and the property owner for two months of free housing. Your client has invested money in the legal action and you have lost time from work. See how this can get frustrating and expensive?

Going Back to Court

If a tenant does not comply with the terms of a court-ordered decree, within the continued time, and most of them won't, you will be going back to court. When you go to court for the second time and prove that the tenant ignored the court's requirements, the judge should order the tenant's eviction. If you are suing the tenant for money, the court may also enter a judgment against the tenant. While this is what you hope happens, you cannot count on it.

Court-Ordered Extension

In your second court appearance the tenant may be awarded another continuance. To manage this, the tenant will have to prove hardship, but some tenants know as much about eviction laws as lawyers do. Don't be surprised if you leave your second day in court with a bad taste in your mouth.

Being Awarded a Judgment

If you are fortunate enough to be awarded a judgment against a tenant, don't count your money until it is in your hand. When the court enters a judgment against a tenant, it proves that the tenant owes you a determined amount of money. The judge will set terms for the judgment amount to be paid to you, but you don't have the money yet.

If the tenant does not have enough money to pay the judgment, you must continue with legal actions to collect the money. When a tenant doesn't have much cash or valuable assets, you may never recover your cash. Your expenses in pursuing the money may exceed the value of the judgment.

> **✔ FAST FACT**
>
> Getting a judgment against a tenant is not a guarantee of payment. The judgment means that the court system has ruled in your favor, but getting the cash can still be an uphill battle and it may be one that you will not win. I have seen many judgments awarded where the money never materialized.

Delivering Eviction Orders to the Sheriff's Office

Once you have an eviction order from the court, you must deliver it to the county Sheriff's office. When you deliver the papers to the Sheriff, a time will be scheduled for the eviction. The date for the eviction could be two weeks, or more, into the future. Remember, you, or your client, are paying legal expenses during this time, but you are probably not collecting rent from the tenant.

Hurry Up and Wait

Once the Sheriff has an eviction order, all you can do is hurry up and wait. By now your stress level is peaking and your blood pressure may be off the scale. When this whole mess started you had no idea of how long it would take and how much time and money it would cost you. You are in the right and the tenant is in the wrong. You are winning the battle, by legal standards, but the tenant is living rent-free in your apartment. How is this fair?

> ✔ **FAST FACT**
>
> Do all that you can to prevent the need for evictions. The cost and lost time associated with an eviction proceeding destroys the financial reports on an income property.

The Sheriff Serves a Tenant

When the Sheriff serves a tenant with an eviction notice, the tenant may leave voluntarily. But, this is not always the case. If a tenant refuses to leave, you will have to spend more money. It has been my experience that by this stage of the game the tenant usually moves out in the middle of the night. Professional deadbeats know how long they can squat on your property, without paying rent, before they have to leave. What happens if when tenants don't move out under their own power?

Paying for a Moving Company

When your problem tenants refuse to move, you will be paying for a moving company to move them. The Sheriff will make arrangements for a moving company to extract the individual's belongings, but you may have to pay for the moving company. This can get expensive, fast. When the moving company arrives, the Sheriff will supervise the removal of the tenant's possessions. If necessary, the Sheriff will remove the tenant with physical force. Evictions rarely get to this stage, but when they do, it adds considerable expense to an already expensive proposition.

Regaining Your Property

Once the Sheriff has cleared your property of the problem tenant, you will regain access to the property. Regaining your property was the purpose for the eviction. However, once you have regained control of your rental unit, it will probably be in shambles. The tenant may have destroyed it, just to get revenge on you. If the unit has been trashed, you will lose substantial money in preparing it to rent to a new tenant. You might initiate new legal action against the tenant for the damages, but don't count on recovering your losses. There are numerous cost associated with evictions. Some of the costs include the following:

- The cost of an eviction will vary greatly, depending upon the circumstances.
- If tenants know how to work the system, they might stay in your unit, rent-free, for four months, or more. You lose four months rent.
- You lose a few days of pay because of your court appearances.
- You lose more time from work in meeting with your attorney.
- Even more time is lost from work to file and deliver documents.
- There are court fees.
- Filing fees are an expense.
- Attorney fees add up quickly.
- When you add it all up, a difficult eviction could cost thousands of dollars.

With so much money at stake, it is well worth your effort to try to avoid evictions. The money is only part of it; the stress involved in a tough eviction can engulf you. Now that you know approximately how an eviction goes, let's examine ways for you to avoid gaining personal experience with evictions.

What Are the Causes for Eviction?

The primary cause for eviction is the non-payment of rent by a tenant. When you have a tenant who is not paying rent, eviction is the only sure cure. Another cause for eviction is the violation of the terms of a lease agreement. If a tenant has brought two large dogs into your building, when your lease does not allow pets, you may have to evict the tenant. Any breach of your lease agreement could be cause for eviction.

▶ *PRO POINTER*

How can you avoid evicting a tenant? Well, sometimes you can't avoid eviction proceedings, but many times you can. If I had to choose a single method to reduce my eviction rate, it would be communication. Clear, open communication is an excellent way to solve most landlord-tenant disputes.

How Can You Avoid Evicting a Tenant?

How can you avoid evicting a tenant? Well, sometimes you can't avoid eviction proceedings, but many times you can. If I had to choose a single method to reduce my eviction rate, it would be communication. Clear, open communication is an excellent way to solve most landlord-tenant disputes. There are many ways to reduce the number of evictions you are forced to endure. Let's take a look at some of the best ways to reduce your losses by avoiding evictions.

Communication

Communication is one of the best defenses you have against evictions. Unless you are dealing with a hard-core, professional squatter, communication will resolve most problems. While communication will not generate cash for a pauper, it can lead to acceptable terms that are better than the results of an eviction.

Many tenants quit paying their rent because of a disagreement with their landlord or property manager. While this action is not acceptable, it may be correctable. If you fail to respond to a reasonable request from a tenant, you must expect some action by the tenant. Since most tenants are not aware of the proper manner to pay their rent into escrow, until the conflict is resolved, they simply don't pay the rent. If you take fast legal actions against the tenant, you are in the middle of an eviction that might have been avoided. Simply talking with the tenant may solve the problem and get your rent checks flowing again. Never underestimate the power of open communication.

> ✔ **FAST FACT**
>
> Eviction can take a long time. Cutting the right deal with a troublesome tenant can have the tenant out of your building in a flash. Face the facts; you, or your client, are going to lose substantial money in obtaining an eviction order. You could pay the tenant to leave your building and come out money ahead. This strategy might be well worth running past the property owner before beginning eviction proceedings.

Making Concessions

While it may go against your grain to make concessions, sometimes giving in is less expensive than fighting an eviction war. I am not suggesting that you roll over and play dead. It is important for you to handle each situation with care. Your other tenants will be observing the outcome of the conflict. If you cave in for one tenant, others will try the same tactics.

MUTUAL TERMINATION AGREEMENT

For good and valuable consideration,_____,

landlord and _____, tenant agree to

terminate the lease/rental agreement presently in force and dated

_____. Said lease/rental agreement for the property located at

_____, shall become null and void,

once consideration as been given and terms and conditions are complied

with, as described below, and this document is executed by all parties.

Terms of Consideration

_____

_____

_____

_____

_____

In this mutual termination, both landlord and tenant agree to the

disposition of deposits and financial responsibilities in the following

manner: _____

_____

_____

_____

_____.

_____   _____

Landlord   Date   Tenant   Date

FIGURE 11.1 Mutual Termination Agreement

By making concessions you can eliminate the tenant quickly. Eviction can take a long time. Cutting the right deal with a troublesome tenant can have the tenant out of your building in a flash. Face the facts; you are going to lose substantial money in obtaining an eviction order. You could pay the tenant to leave your building and come out money ahead.

Tactics to Avoid

There are certain tactics to avoid when you have problem tenants. Here are some of them:

- Do not verbally abuse tenants. You could be arrested and sued for this type of abuse.
- Never enter a tenant's rental unit without the proper notification and permission.
- Don't get cute and change the locks on the tenant's doors; this is childish and improper.
- Don't even think of impounding any of the tenant's property to hold hostage for your rent.
- Don't get lazy with your paperwork. When you get to court, your paperwork is what will win the case for you.

Avoiding Evictions

Examples are often easier to understand than the words of wisdom are. I am about to give you some examples of how you might avoid evictions. Most of these examples are true case histories of my past experiences. I believe that these examples will make it much easier for you to understand how to work with evictions.

Example One

Imagine owning a single-family rental. The house is old, but in good shape. The only drawback to the quality of tenants you are able to obtain is the property's location. The house is situated on the fringe of a bad area. You bought the house cheap and are hoping that neighborhood revitalization will increase the home's valve. In the meantime, you are using your long-range investment as a rental property.

Being relatively new to the rental business, you rent the house to two young men. They are carpenters, without much credit history. You are wise enough to know this is a questionable decision on your part, but you hope for the best.

Time passes and the carpenters find themselves out of work and unable to pay their rent. As a reasonable landlord, you arrange a meeting to discuss the situation. In talking with the carpenters, you decide to allow them to trade their labor in renovating the house for rent, until they can find stable employment. This seems like a good plan and you leave happy.

When you go over after about a month to inspect the progress on the renovations, you are shocked. Your rental home's kitchen was never gorgeous, but now it doesn't exist. The men have completely gutted the kitchen. A further inspection of the home reveals more damage. The carpenters began the renovations, as discussed, but they have the house in shambles. While you are standing in the living room, you begin to itch. When you look down, your legs are covered in fleas. The house is invested with biting inhabitants.

Discarded personal possessions are scattered around the house, but there is no sign of human life. The carpenters have obviously moved on to better accommodations. You are left with no rent, a destroyed and flea-infested house. This story is based on true facts surrounding one of my first rental properties. I obviously made many mistakes in my early judgments. This was a case where I should have never rented the property to the unqualified tenants in the first place. After I did rent the property and they couldn't pay the rent, I should have forced them to move. But, instead, I made a deal that cost me thousands of dollars to reconcile. I don't favor evictions, but there are times when it is the only acceptable course of action.

Example Two

In this example you are the landlord of a nearly new, single-family home. Your tenant has been an average tenant with a decent payment history. All of a sudden, the tenant's rent checks begin to be returned for insufficient funds. At first, you just re-deposit the checks and don't make a big issue of the problem. As time goes on, the rent checks start arriving late, past the grace period. Not wanting to let a bad situation escalate, you try calling the tenant.

When you tire of talking to the tenant's answering machine, you contact your lawyer. By this time the rent checks have stopped coming altogether. The attorney writes a letter to the tenant advising him to pay up or get out. When there is no response from the tenant, your attorney proceeds with the appropriate legal steps.

When the court date arrives, the tenant doesn't show up. You are awarded an eviction order and a judgment against the tenant. While you are waiting for the Sheriff to serve the eviction order, you ride by the house. All the window treatments are gone and so is the tenant. You are left without your rent and a judgment against a person you cannot find. What could you have done differently?

In this case there is little room for criticism. You could have acted more quickly in starting legal action, but you did not procrastinate for an unreasonable time. You tried to communicate with the tenant by phone and by mail, but received no return communication. You engaged an attorney to ensure the matter was handled through the proper legal channels. In this case, there wasn't much you could have done differently.

This misfortune happened to me with the second rental property I owned. It is a wonder I continued to stay with the rental business. But, as I became more experienced, I became better qualified to discourage the downside of being a property manager.

Example Three

As the landlord, you are faced with a tenant who has stopped paying his rent. Up until the rent quit coming, it had always been paid promptly. You attempt to call the tenant, but there is no answer. After a ride-by inspection of your rental unit, it appears to still be occupied, but there is no evidence of the tenant's car. What do you do? You could begin eviction procedures, but we already know how expensive evictions are. Here are some tips on how to resolve your problem.

Post a notice on the tenant's door. The notice should advise the tenant of his default on the terms of the lease. The notice should also instruct the tenant to call you, immediately, to avoid legal ramifications. Refer back to your file for the tenant's rental application. The tenant should have provided names and phone numbers for people you should call in case of an emergency. If the tenant doesn't respond to your notice within twenty-four hours, call the names on the rental application. For all you know, the tenant may have been involved in a serious accident.

If the contact people cannot provide information on the whereabouts of your tenant, call his employer. Don't say anything to anyone about the tenant's late rent. When you call, tell the people you are concerned because you cannot locate the tenant. The tenant's employer should be willing to verify if the tenant is still employed and reporting for work.

After conducting your missing-person investigation, you should be armed with new information. If the tenant is going to work regularly, you know he is still in the area. If phone calls, posted notices, and certified mail to not produce results in making contact with the tenant, begin eviction proceedings.

If the tenant does respond to your request and calls you, arrange a face-to-face meeting to discuss his financial problems. Maybe the tenant has a family member who has taken ill. This could be a legitimate reason for being late with the rent. If the tenant has a good track record with you, arranging different terms may be effective in collecting your money.

Have the tenant sign a promissory note for the money he owes you. Talk with him and arrange a payment schedule he can live with, until he is back on his feet. Document all of your dealings with the tenant. Your written documentation may be needed later. Follow-up on the tenant's story to prove its validity.

Set a time limit on your new terms. If you agree to extend the special payment arrangements for sixty days, put it in writing and have the tenant sign the agreement for the new terms. Don't allow the tenant to fall behind in the new terms. If he can't maintain his commitment to your new deal, ask him to leave. If he refuses, go for an eviction order.

Example Four

In this example you have a tenant who is unable to pay his rent. He has run out of money. Your best efforts to resolve the problem have failed. You have asked the tenant to leave, but he says he can't, because he doesn't have any money. Will you file for an eviction order?

This problem requires some thought. The tenant is not angry with you; he just can't pay his rent. He is willing to move to an apartment with lower rent, but he cannot afford to move. You understand the tenant's plight, but you need your rental income. On the surface it appears you have no choice, except to evict the tenant. What do you think you should do?

Talk to the tenant and see how much money he needs to get out of your unit. You may be surprised at how little it will take for this person to vacate the property. Assume, for the sake of this example that the tenant would be happy to move, if he only had $1,500.00. Now granted, $1,500 dollars is a lot of money, but consider your options.

If you evict this tenant, the process may cost you five grand, not to mention the hassle. If you loan him the $1,500.00, you get rid of him quickly. Sure, the chances are good he will never repay the loan, but you are still $3,500.00 ahead of the game. This type of concession makes sense.

A word of caution, don't be foolish enough to just give the tenant $1,500.00. Have him sign a note for the loan. If he never repays you, you have a bad debt to write off. Instead of giving the tenant the money, work with him to make his moving arrangements. Make sure that by parting with your money, you are getting rid of the tenant. The last thing you want to do is give the guy the money and still be stuck with him for a tenant.

The Side Effects of Eviction

Up until this point, we have talked about eviction on one level. We have looked at the direct effects of what going through an eviction are like. Now, we are going to study the side effects of eviction.

Finding Replacement Tenants

When you evict one tenant, you must find a replacement tenant to take the place of the evicted tenant. You can never be sure if the replacement tenant will be better than the person you just evicted. There is significant cost involved in the eviction, but there can also be a high price to pay in finding a replacement tenant.

You will most likely have to advertise for new tenants and ads can be expensive. You will have to prepare the rental unit for new occupancy. This is never without its cost. Then, you will invest hours of your time in handling phone inquiries and showings of the vacancy. There will be all the necessary paperwork to prepare. When you total your expenses for finding a replacement tenant, they can scare you. It will be in your best interest to find a workable solution to your tenant problems, without relying on eviction procedures.

Your Reputation

If you build a reputation as an eviction expert, tenants will shy away from your building. When rumors circulate, they often neglect to present the facts properly. You may be tagged as a person who indiscriminately throws defenseless tenants out into the cold streets. Maintaining a good reputation as a fair landlord is important to the longevity of your rental business.

No Winners

There are no winners in an eviction. As the landlord, you lose time and money. The same is true of professional property managers. Tenants lose their homes and dignity. Unless you are dealing with the lowest life forms, you should be able to find a better solution to your problems than eviction.

In Summary

As you have seen by now, eviction is not an act to be taken lightly. The cost of eviction takes its toll, both financially and mentally. Do everything you can to avoid eviction procedures. By approaching your problems with an open, and sometimes creative, mind, you can find a way to solve them.

Many landlords are plagued with evictions. These landlords, for the most part, are victims of their own poor management. If you follow the rules of the game, you will eliminate many of the causes that lead to eviction. In all my years in the rental business, I have only ever had to resort to eviction procedures twice. Considering the large number of properties I have owned and managed, you might make it through your career without ever having to deal with an eviction.

Taxes and Insurance

Taxes and insurance are important to the successful operation of rental properties. If you have been doing property management for long, you have experienced the impact that these issues can have on your profitability. If you are new to the rental business, first-hand experience is an expensive way to learn about these items.

Insurance Needs

What are your insurance needs? How much insurance is enough? How can you cut your best deal on the most advantageous insurance? These three questions have a great deal of bearing on how successful you will be as a property manager.

Not having the right insurance can put you out of business overnight. Poor insurance coverage can force you into bankruptcy. Not having enough insurance can be as bad as not being insured at all. Having too much insurance, or the wrong kind of insurance, can erode your net income. Learning to find the most affordable rates will take some research, but it will pay for itself.

Landlords need more and different types of insurance from what a property management firm needs. For example, a landlord will normally insure the property that is being offered for rent. A property manager does not have to insure the properties that are being managed. However, it can fall within the scope of a management company to stay on top of required or needed insurance for property owners. With this in mind, we will begin with your needs as a property manager and then touch on the various types of insurance that property owners are most likely to be interested in.

Business Insurance

Business insurance is a good idea for any type of business. Not all businesses require the same types of insurance. Some insurance is not considered mandatory, but it can be a good idea to have it. For example, nearly all good businesses will carry liability insurance, but the company may not carry key-man insurance. Talk with your attorney and your insurance provider to explore the various types of insurance that you should invest in. To understand more about this, let's talk about some of the types of insurance that you should consider.

Liability Insurance

Liability insurance is generally considered essential to any business. Without general liability insurance, you are inviting disaster. This insurance covers you when any numbers of events occur. For example, if someone enters your office and falls due to slippery flooring, you will be looking to your liability insurance for assistance.

Errors and Omissions Insurance

Errors and Omissions insurance is often referred to as E & O insurance. Who hasn't made an honest mistake from time to time? If you make a mistake in a written agreement, an advertisement, or a verbal statement, you may have to depend on E & O insurance to get you out of a mess. This is a common type of insurance for real estate brokers and property mangers to maintain.

Worker's Compensation Insurance

Worker's compensation insurance is required when you have employees who are not close relatives who are willing to waive their coverage. If you employ anyone who is not directly related to you, expect to pay a premium on Worker's compensation insurance.

> ✔ **FAST FACT**
>
> Failure to carry worker's compensation insurance when you have employees can turn into an expensive nightmare. Don't attempt to cheat the system on this matter. It is far easier to make regular premium payments throughout the year than it is to come up with a large sum of money at the end of the year.

Inland Marine Policies

Inland marine policies are used to protect property that you my have in your vehicle. Most car insurance covers a small amount of content theft, but if you carry expensive computers, cameras, or other items with you, consider buying an inland marine policy to protect your belongings.

Office Contents

Office contents should be insured for loss. Even if you don't own the property where your office if located, you can still obtain insurance for the contents of your office. Given the high cost of equipment found in a modern office, having good insurance coverage on the items is essential.

Other Types of Insurance

Other types of insurance to consider include life insurance, disability insurance, key-man insurance, and so forth. Seek advice from experienced, licensed professionals when planning your insurance needs.

> ▶ *PRO POINTER*
>
> Insurance premiums make some business owners cringe. While the cost of insurance is substantial, having losses without insurance can be much more costly. Don't cut corners on insurance. Protect yourself, your business, and your assets.

Property Owners

Property owners should insure their investments. As a property manager, you should have some working knowledge of the types of insurance commonly held by property owners. When you own your own income properties, you will want to insure your assets properly. What follows are some types of insurance for property owners to consider.

Fire Insurance

Do you need fire insurance? Yes; property owners should carry fire insurance coverage on their property. If your property is financed, your lender probably requires fire insurance to be kept in force on the property. The lender will want to be named as the first insured and will want coverage in an amount sufficient to pay off the loan, if the building is destroyed by fire.

The amount of coverage required by the lender is rarely enough to cover a property owner's financial interest in a property. You should not insure a $200,000.00 building for $300,000.00, but you should insure it for its appraised value. If you

carry only enough coverage to satisfy the
lender, in the event of destruction, you
may lose a minimum of twenty-percent of
the property's appraised value. Your loss
could be much more, depending upon
your equity position.

Insure your building for replacement
cost value. Some fire policies leave you
holding the bag in the case of a partially
destroyed building. Make sure that your
policy will pay current, going rates to
repair or replace your loss.

> ▶ **PRO POINTER**
>
> When you are deciding on how
> much coverage to buy, consider
> the land value of your property.
> Deduct the land value from the
> appraised value of the complete
> property. By fire insurance stan-
> dards, your land cannot be
> destroyed. You will be wasting your
> money to insure the land.

Extended Coverage

When you are setting up your fire insurance, look into the advantages of extended
coverage. Most insurance companies will offer a long list of coverage for any imagin-
able loss. By adding this type of coverage, the cost of the premiums may be greatly
reduced. Some companies refer to their extended coverage as package policies. What
are some of the types of coverage you might look for in extended coverage? Well,
there are quite a few, let's take a look at some of them:

- Windstorm coverage can insure your building from damage caused by windstorms. Do you need this coverage? To answer this question, consider how
  often windstorms wreak havoc on properties in your area. Most landlords
  can do without this coverage, but you may need it.

- Covering your property with insurance to protect against vandalism is a good
  idea, no matter where the building is located. You never know when some
  deranged mind is going to take pleasure in trashing your building. Hostile ex-
  tenants are sometimes involved in revenge against landlords and property
  managers. Protect yourself from vandalism with the proper coverage. The
  cost should not break the bank.

- How about explosion coverage, do you need it? I believe you do. Many property owners prefer to gamble on the fact their building will not blow up, but
  I'm not one of them. If your building explodes, there is going to be major
  problems. Not counting the damage to your building, there may be personal
  injuries and untold property damage to cars and other buildings. Gas leaks,

defective relief valves of water heaters, gas cans for lawn mowers, and a number of other possibilities exist for explosions. I don't see how you can avoid having explosion insurance.

- Lightning may never strike the same place twice, but if it strikes your building once, and you are not insured for it, you will learn an expensive lesson. Buy lightning insurance.

- Unless your building is made of glass, hail insurance probably isn't necessary. It may come as a part of a package, and no insurance is bad to have, but hail coverage would not be high on my priority list.

- What are the odds that your building will be involved in rioting and looting? If you have a duplex out in the country, you shouldn't need riot insurance. If you have a building in the inner city of a major metropolitan area, you might be wise to invest in riot insurance.

- Insure your building against damage caused by broken pipes. Even in a new building, you can never be certain when the plumbing system may turn into a sprinkler system. Water can cause severe damage. I recommend you invest in the peace of mind afforded by insurance for damage caused due to broken pipes.

- If your building is in Oklahoma, I doubt that you will need protection from falling trees. If your property is in Maine, falling trees could present a problem. Take a look at your property. If it is in danger of falling trees, consider the coverage, if not, forget about it.

- Freeze-up coverage is a viable consideration for buildings subjected to cold weather. Like with falling trees, your location will dictate the likelihood of freeze-ups.

The list of extended coverage is a long one. For the most part, common sense will tell you if you need a particular type of coverage. Some of the other coverage that you may find available are: smoke damage, falling objects, collapse, landslides, flooding plumbing fixtures, and so on.

Theft Insurance

Theft insurance is usually a good investment. There never seems to be a shortage of crime. However, if you don't have anything of much value at, or in, your rental property or office, you may not need theft insurance. Your tenants should have tenants' insurance to cover their possessions. If all you have on the premises is appliances, I wouldn't worry about paying premiums for theft insurance. On the other hand, if you keep equipment, supplies, and other valuables on site, buy theft insurance.

Glass Breakage

Insurance to cover glass breakage could come in many forms. It might be addressed in vandalism insurance. Glass breakage is a consideration in many other types of insurance. Talk with your insurance agent to determine your specific needs for various types of glass breakage, but give serious consideration to purchasing insurance to protect your glass. This may not be so important in a small building, in a good location, but big buildings, in rough neighborhoods can lose a lot of glass.

Mechanical Systems

It is possible to obtain insurance on your mechanical systems. This coverage can be purchased to cover various aspects of your mechanical equipment. With some policies, you will be covered for the full replacement value of your heating system, if it dies. Other policies might offer a loss-of-rents benefit as part of their mechanical coverage. Typically, inspections of your equipment will be made before this type of coverage is offered.

Remember, insurance companies play the odds. If they offer inexpensive insurance, they don't expect to pay claims. If the rates are high, they have been burned by claims they had to pay. Evaluate your risks, your worst-case out-of-pocket expenses, and decide for yourself if you want to pay to insure your mechanical systems.

Flood Insurance

Flood insurance is expensive. If your property is located in a designated flood zone or flood plain, you may have to pay for flood insurance to appease your lender. Standard insurances policies do not cover flood damage; you must have flood insurance to protect against this disaster.

You may have trouble finding a company that offers flood insurance, but they are out there. Obviously, if your property is not located anywhere near the one-hundred-year flood plain, you shouldn't need flood insurance. A good mortgage survey will typically indicate if a property is in danger of flooding. Assess your situation and make your own call, but if you are in an area subject to flooding, check out policies that cover flooding.

Earthquake Insurance

Earthquake insurance can be compared to flood insurance. Substitute the word earthquake for flood, and follow the advice given above.

Outside Improvements

If your property has outside improvements, like swimming pools, fences, or parking lots, you may need additional insurance. The cost of insuring these outside improvements may prove to be prohibitive. Check with your insurance agent and determine if the premiums are worth their price.

Mortgage Insurance

Mortgage insurance against the payment due on a mortgage used to be popular. Today, the cost of this insurance prohibits most people from obtaining it. Basically, this insurance will pay off the mortgage of your property in the event of your death. Most people find a decreasing-term life insurance policy to be just as effective and not as expensive.

Title Insurance

Title insurance is sometimes referred to as mortgage insurance, but it is not. Title insurance insures the title you possess for your property. Title insurance is a one-time expense and it is not very costly. I would never buy real estate without title insurance.

Title insurance provides some guarantee to your ownership of a property. While title insurance cannot guarantee you will not lose the property, it does promise to reimburse you for your loss. This insurance protects against unknown heirs or other people with a legal right to the property you think you own. If a long lost heir turns up to claim his rightful property, you may have to hand over your building to the rightful owner. If you have title insurance, you will receive financial remuneration for your loss. If you don't have title insurance, you must simply give away your property and cut your losses.

Title insurance is required by lenders in many states. Even if title insurance is not required by your lender, insist on having the insurance. The possible repercussions of not having title insurance are scary.

Auto Insurance

In my opinion, anyone driving a car should carry auto insurance. If you are not concerned about the cost of repairing or replacing your car, be concerned about the lawsuits that may steal your property. If you are sued for an accident and lose, the winner may be awarded a judgment against all of your assets. This, of course, would include your rental holdings. Don't risk it; get good auto insurance.

Other Auto Insurance

If you allow an employee to drive one of your vehicles, you need non-owned auto insurance. This insurance protects you from losses revolving around the results of your employee driving your vehicle. Just because you are not driving your vehicle doesn't mean you can not be sued for damages caused by your car. Check this coverage out if you allow outsiders to drive your vehicle.

Loss of Rents Insurance

I feel every investor should consider purchasing loss of rents insurance. If your building was to be rendered uninhabitable, how long could you make the mortgage payments? If a fire sweeps through your apartments, the tenants will not be likely to pay their rents for the period of time they are displaced. How will you meet your hard expenses, like your debt service? Loss of rents insurance can bail you out in these circumstances.

These policies are designed to assist you when you cannot collect rents for your units for extenuating circumstances. Talk to your agent and see if you can justify the premiums for loss of rents insurance. If you can, go for it. Loss of rents insurance provides comfort and peace of mind.

Water Bed Insurance

I have saved water bed insurance for last because I believe tenants with water beds should be required to pay this insurance. As a landlord, you should be able to obtain insurance to protect you from damages incurred from leaking water beds. However, most savvy landlords stipulate in their leases that tenants with water beds must pay for water bed insurance to protect the landlord's property. Use you own judgment, but give some thought to having the tenants with water beds pay these premiums for you. After all, if the tenants didn't own water beds, you wouldn't need the insurance.

Identify Your Needs

When it comes to insurance, the first step you must take is identifying your needs. This process will tell you which forms of insurance can be scratched from your list. For example, if you own an apartment building in the middle of a desert, you don't need flood insurance. You have been given enough fuel to fire your imagination. Look over the example of insurances discussed and determine what your needs are.

> ▶ *PRO POINTER*
>
> Take a hard look at package deals for insurance. Extended coverage or package deals can be a great value, as far as insurance deals go. By lumping your coverage into a package, you may be able to reduce your overall costs.

Shop Around

When it comes to finding the best price available for suitable insurance, you must shop around. Prices fluctuate greatly between different insurance companies. A company that gives you a dynamite quote on liability insurance may gouge you on fire insurance. The other problem with insurance is that the premiums usually go up every year. Once you are established with a company, they seem to take you for granted. At each anniversary date, they see an opportunity to strip you of your money.

I despise insurance payments as much

> ✔ *FAST FACT*
>
> Deductible amounts can make a huge difference in the price you pay for insurance. Depending upon your cash reserves and financial standing, policies with high deductibles can be your best bet. Insurance is always a gamble. The insurance companies are gambling you will not make a claim. You are gambling that you will. By choosing a policy with a high deductible, you can have coverage for situations you can't handle financially, without having premiums that burden you.

as the next person, maybe more so, but I keep paying them. You have to. As disgusting as they are, you need insurance, and premiums are the price you pay for some type of peace of mind. This is not to say that having insurance will save you, but it can't hurt.

Tax Matters

Taxes may be the second ugliest word in owning income properties, preceded only by eviction. I have never met anyone who enjoyed paying taxes. Many investors enter the rental business in search of tax shelters. This was much more so before the change in the tax laws back in 1986. Today, tax advantages can be quite limited for landlords, but they do still exist. Tax matters are similar to legal matters. You should consult experts within the field before making decisions on either. I recommend that you talk with a certified public accountant to establish the best tax strategy for you.

Property Taxes

If you own real estate, you are well aware of the existence of property taxes. For most property owners, property taxes are responsible for a big piece of the pie when it comes to expenses. For landlords, there is no getting around property taxes. They are a cost of doing business. When you are projecting your profits and possible losses, don't forget to allow for property taxes.

Doing Your Own Income Taxes

Do you prepare your own income taxes? If you have more than a couple of rental properties, you are probably losing money

> ✔ **FAST FACT**
>
> It has been my experience that a good accountants do not cost you money, they save you money.

by doing your own taxes. Tax angles are complicated, that's why Certified Public Accountants (CPAs) make so much money. If the job was easy, nobody would bother with passing their exams to become CPAs. It has been my experience that a good accountants do not cost you money, they save you money. I have done my own taxes and I have hired experts to prepare my returns for me. As a thriving landlord, I don't believe you can afford not to hire a professional to find the tax advantages you are entitled to.

Keeping Good Records

Regardless of who does your taxes, keeping good records is a key function in beating the tax bite. Well-organized records are also comforting during an IRS audit; I know, I've been there. For the record, my files stood the test of the audit. Most investors envision a tax audit as their worst nightmare. I felt this way until I went through my first audit. If you have good records, and haven't skewed the numbers, an audit is nothing to lose sleep over.

Seek top-quality advice when it comes to legal, tax, and insurance matters. These are areas of your new business that you cannot afford to scrimp on. Interview multiple experts until you find the ones who you are comfortable with. Having the right experts on your team improves your odds of success.

CHAPTER THIRTEEN

Financing

Bankers are essential to the successful operation of most businesses. The property management business is no different. Whether you are remodeling an existing building, buying a new one, or seeking operating capital for your management business, the chances are good you will seek financial assistance. When you look to a lender for help, you must present a persuading proposal. Simply walking in and requesting a loan for ambiguous reasons rarely works.

Seasoned lenders look for key elements in loan requests. If the right information is available to bankers they are more likely to grant your loan. Providing inadequate information is a major cause of loan rejections. The style in which you present your proposal can influence a banker's decision. Your personal attitude and demeanor can have much to do with the success or failure of your loan request.

Bankers know numbers and like to see them laid out well. In most cases you will want your proposal to be concise and easy to understand. At times you may wish to cloud the spreadsheet with complicated information. While it is usually best to provide a clearly drawn plan, there are times when confusing the loan officer with complicated formulas and big numbers can work to your advantage.

To maximize your borrowing power you must learn to manipulate your lender. This will take some time. You must learn what your lender reacts to and how the keeper of the cash reacts. Once you know the right buttons to push, getting your loan approved can be easy. The manipulation could be as simple as knowing what types of loans different lenders like to make. While one bank may be generous with improvement loans, the bank may not want acquisition loans. It will be up to you to get inside your banker's head and find the path to success.

When you know how to create a winning spreadsheet, you increase your odds of acceptance for loan requests. The process of building a salable proposal is not difficult, but you must know how it's done. This chapter is going to teach you how to package and present information to improve your chances of being approved for a loan.

Should You Borrow Where You Bank?

Should you attempt to borrow money from the bank where you keep your money? Logic would say you should, but your present bank may not be as liberal as others. In the old days people tried to keep all their dealings with one financial institution. Today, many investors have found it is wiser to spread their business out among several banks. To answer the question of where to borrow money, you must ask questions and do research.

> ▶ *PRO POINTER*
>
> If you are looking to borrow money for your business, you will need a detailed business plan to share with your lenders. The loan officers are going to want to see how much money you need, what you plan to do with it, how it will improve your business, and how and when you will pay the loan off.

All banks will welcome your savings account, but they are not all so willing to loan you money. Just because you have your accounts with a particular bank does not mean that bank will be aggressive in its lending policy. Some banks like to loan money for automobiles and home improvement loans, but not for rental property. There are banks that will be happy to loan on rental property up to four-units in size, but they may not even consider a loan for larger buildings. Other banks prefer dealing in larger multi-family buildings. Construction and rehab loans are loved by some banks for their short terms and high rates of return. Other lenders are afraid of construction and rehab loans, due to the risks involved. Getting operating capital for your business can require a special lender. Finding the right lender for your type of loan is the first step towards getting your loan request approved.

The Right Lending Institution

Finding the right lender is critical to your success in finding suitable financing. There are banks, savings and loans, credit unions, and private investors to choose from.

These lenders are not the only ones available, but they are the ones most often used. Mortgage bankers and mortgage brokers also play a part in the list of most popular lenders. When you are planning for financing, you should investigate all the options available to you.

Not all lenders are the same. We have already discussed how different lenders prefer different types of loans, but there are other differences. Some lenders sell their loans in the secondary market. These lenders must meet pre-determined criteria in their loan packages. They can be inflexible to your needs. If your request does not fit the mold of a secondary-market loan, you will be denied. Banks that hold portfolio loans have the ability to make any type of loan they wish to. If you are seeking creative financing, portfolio lenders are what you are looking for.

Loan officers also come in different configurations. Many loan officers are on the payroll of the lending institution. They get a steady paycheck whether you get your loan or not. They may be nervous about losing their job by making bad loans. This type of loan officer is likely to be the hardest to deal with. Loan originators who are paid a commission will generally work harder to get your loan approved. They know that if you get your loan, they get a commission check. This monetary incentive motivates commissioned lenders to be more aggressive.

Mortgage brokers add a new dimension to the game. These commissioned brokers are not tied to a single source for placing your loan. Mortgage brokers work with a stable of lenders to place all types of loans. Since they are not restricted to a single source of money, they can often get a loan approved when others have failed. There are fees involved when using a mortgage broker, but they can be well worth the cost if they make your deal come together.

> ► **PRO POINTER**
>
> Loan originators who are paid a commission will generally work harder to get your loan approved. They know that if you get your loan, they get a commission check. This monetary incentive motivates commissioned lenders to be more aggressive.

> ✔ **FAST FACT**
>
> In recent years, online lenders have popped up on the Internet. Some of these money sources may be viable for your business. However, given the nature of long-distance dealing, check out the lenders very carefully before giving them too much information or money for loan origination.

With so many choices, how will you find the right lender for your loan? You can narrow the field by asking questions and doing some research. You must ask yourself the first questions. These questions pertain to the type of loan you want, the interest rate and points you are willing to pay, and the terms that will be acceptable to you. Once you know what you want, you will start asking the lenders questions to determine if they are the right lender for your loan request. Your research will be used to identify liberal lenders who are most apt to work with you.

Banks

Banks are normally the first place people think of when planning to borrow money. Banks are a logical, and often good, source of financing for various projects and purchases. A commercial bank may be able to accommodate all of your banking and borrowing needs. Most banks will issue financing for owner-occupied and non-owner-occupied buildings. Since many investors don't live in their rental properties it is important for their lenders to work with non-owner-occupied loans. If you are planning to borrow money for your day-to-day business operations, you will want to make sure that your lender will handle this type of financing.

Banks are capable of providing financing for acquisitions, construction, renovations, repairs, and re-financing. An aggressive bank will offer portfolio loans. With all their ability, banks may be your best source of financing. Banks have the tools to make your financing plans work, if they are willing to use them.

> **✔ FAST FACT**
>
> Not all banks are willing to exercise the full extent of their lending power. The reluctance of various banks can force you to expand your search parameters.

Credit Unions

If you belong to a credit union, you should check with them for your financing needs. Credit unions operate differently from most banks. A credit union may approve your loan request when a commercial bank would deny it. If you are seeking financing for buildings with more than four units, credit unions may not be willing to help you. Some credit unions will not even consider loaning money for commercial-grade rental properties. My experience has shown that credit unions do not typically deal in commercial-style loans. But the rates at credit unions can be very appealing, so it is worth checking to see if there is a way to work out your needs with a credit union.

Mortgage Bankers

Mortgage bankers specialize in mortgage loans. If you are buying a new property or re-financing an existing property, these lenders can be very helpful. The bulk of their business is comprised of these two types of loans. Generally they will not be your best source for rehab money, construction loans, or business loans, but they love long-term take-out loans.

Mortgage Brokers

Mortgage brokers are freelancers. They work with you to find financing at any of their numerous sources. They may find the money for your loan from an insurance company, a bank, a private investor, or some other source. Mortgage brokers are typically paid in the form of a commission. Once they secure and close your loan they derive income equal to a percentage of the loan. Some mortgage brokers charge an up-front fee and others charge a flat-rate fee, instead of a percentage of the loan amount.

Dealing with mortgage brokers can get complicated. Paying up-front fees is dangerous. You pay the fee without any guarantee of receiving loan approval. Most mortgage brokers don't have the authority to approve loans. They simply place them with a willing lender. The big advantage to mortgage brokers is their large stable of lenders. Since they work with so many lenders, they are often able to do in a day what it could take you weeks to do. Their variety of lenders also makes it possible for them to place loans that others would have to deny.

Private Investors

Private investors are responsible for much of the money used in real estate transactions. Normally their money is channeled through commercial financial institutions, but some investors will loan money directly to borrowers. The interest rates for private money are often higher, but the

> ✔ **FAST FACT**
>
> The interest rates for private money are often higher, but the flexibility for approval is also usually greater. There are additional risks involved when you deal with the private sector. Individuals are not regulated in the same way commercial lenders are. This can lead to a no-holds-barred loan agreement. If you are playing in a game with no rules, you can get hurt. Be careful when you borrow money on the street.

flexibility for approval is also usually greater. There are additional risks involved when you deal with the private sector. Individuals are not regulated in the same way commercial lenders are. This can lead to a no-holds-barred loan agreement. If you are playing in a game with no rules, you can get hurt. Be careful when you borrow money on the street.

Choosing a Loan Officer

After deciding which type of lending institution best suits your needs, you will have to find the best loan officer. As not all financial institutions are the same, neither are all loan officers equal. Some loan originators are super conservative, while others are aggressively liberal. Some will want complex strategic planning worked out for how the money will be used and repaid. Others will only want to see the bottom line of what you want and how it will be secured. Lenders paid on a commission basis should be more willing to stretch the ratios and bend the rules than a lender receiving a payroll check each week.

> ✔ **FAST FACT**
>
> Lenders paid on a commission basis should be more willing to stretch the ratios and bend the rules than a lender receiving a payroll check each week.

How will you know which loan officers are most likely to approve your loan? Check with your friends and fellow investors. Real estate brokers can often give you the names of friendly bankers. Start with lenders working on a commission basis. There is an easy way to distinguish these loan officers from the payroll type. Call the lender and explain that you want to make out an application for a loan. Ask if the lender will meet you at your home or office. Lenders who are willing to leave their offices to come to yours are probably on commission. When loan officers refuse to abandon their desks, they are most likely on the institution's payroll.

Many other factors influence loan officers in their decisions of loan requests. Inexperienced loan originators may not have the savvy to understand your loan proposal. If you have a detailed plan with extensive math and formulas, these young loan officers may say no, just because they don't understand your projection methods. On the other hand, new loan officers might go out of their way to get your loan approved to generate more customers.

Loan officers with years of tenure may be reluctant to approve any but the most desirable loans for a bank. With only

> ✔ **FAST FACT**
>
> There is no way to know what a loan officer is going to do until you know the loan officer.

a few years until retirement, these older loan officers will not want to lose their position by making high-risk loans. But, seasoned loan officers have the experience needed to read between the lines. They can often sense a good deal that may not look so good on paper. It will be up to you to evaluate each loan officer on their own merit. Find the ones you have confidence in and give them a try. Until you run some loan requests in front of various loan officers you will not be able to identify the best ones to work with.

A Loan Proposal

Once you have a good idea of which lending institution and loan officer you will be working with, you are ready to start putting your loan proposal together. Allow adequate time for this process. The work can take days to accomplish. Time required to structure a solid proposal will be directly related to the research needed and the manner in which you will present your proposal.

▶ *PRO POINTER*

Once you have a good idea of which lending institution and loan officer you will be working with, you are ready to start putting your loan proposal together. Allow adequate time for this process. The work can take days to accomplish.

If you have the power of a computer and suitable software, structuring a viable loan package will go a lot quicker. With the computer you can play the "what-if" game to hone the edge of your spreadsheet. Computers allow this type of testing to be done in a matter of minutes. If you are working manually, with a pen and paper, your time invested will be considerably more.

Your contacts in and around your business will have bearing on how quickly you can formulate a successful plan. If you have good working relationships with brokers and appraisers, your research will not take as long. If you know other investors who are willing to share information, you can expedite the process of running your numbers. Having a contact in the local housing authority can produce needed statistics in record time. All of these factors contribute to the time it will take to put your proposal together.

Defining Your Desires

Before you start drafting your plan, define your desires. Know exactly what you want and what you are willing to settle for. This part of the process can save you untold hours later. If you know your plan will not work if the loan's interest rate exceeds a certain percentage point, you can rule out many lenders with a quick phone call. If you are sure the only way your loan will fly is if it is a portfolio loan, you can narrow the field of lenders even more.

Don't just think of ideas and desires, write them down. When you are in the heat of negotiations you may forget important aspects of your plan if they are not in writing. After all of your desires and potential compromises have been determined, you are ready to move on to the next step. The next step is deciding what it will take to convince your lender to make the loan.

Think Like a Banker

Put yourself into a banker's shoes and learn to think like a banker. You obviously believe in your plan or you would not be pursuing it. By removing your personal emotions and thinking like a banker you can find flaws in your plans. Remain unbiased and scrutinize your plans. Ask yourself the questions you envision a banker would ask. Here are some typical questions to consider:

- How long will it take you to repay the loan?
- Will the loan increase your net cash flow?
- Will the purpose of your loan improve your financial position or damage it?
- What will you be using as security for the loan?
- What is the purpose of the loan?
- Name three ways in which the loan will make your business more profitable.

Continue with this line of questioning until you can not think of any other questions to ask.

Image that you are loaning your money to an investor for the same purpose as the one you want a loan for. Would you agree to loan the investor the money? If you answered no, why wouldn't you make the loan? Find as many flaws in your plan as possible. It is much better for you to find them than it is for the banker to find them.

Pulling Information Together

When you feel your reason for wanting to borrow money is bulletproof, start pulling your supporting information together. This information will come from a multitude of sources, some of which may include the following:

- Start with your personal financial statement. If this document is not strong enough, the rest of your efforts will be wasted.

- After preparing your financial statement, you will need to gather tax returns for at least the last two years.

- Account numbers for credit-card debts, interest rates on the loans, and the payoff amounts will be required to accompany your proposal.

✔ *FAST FACT*

If you walk in with a shaky plan, the banker will have a bad first impression of the deal. If you put a bad taste in the banker's mouth with your first proposal, it will be very hard to sell the loan request on an amended proposal.

- List all the details of any installment loans you presently have.

- The loan amounts and account numbers for all of your real estate loans should be included in your information package.

- If you have been divorced, a copy of your divorce decree will be helpful.

- In general, gather all the information available to make it easy for the loan officer to evaluate your loan request.

The remainder of your information gathering will be centered around the purpose for your loan. You will want to paint the prettiest picture you can for the loan officer. If you are borrowing money to add a coin-operated laundry to your building, compile data to prove the potential earnings you can expect from your investment. This information should include details on how the laundry will increase your cash flow and your property's value. The information may be obtained from appraisers, brokers, other investors, or any source of viable information. Even interviewing your tenant's could prove your point.

If you have twelve tenants, ask each of them how often they do laundry and if they would use a coin-operated laundry if you installed it in the building. Record the responses and run the numbers. If they are good, ask each tenant to write a brief letter documenting their response to your survey.

✔ *FAST FACT*

You will want to paint the prettiest picture you can for the loan officer. If you are borrowing money to add a coin-operated laundry to your building, compile data to prove the potential earnings you can expect from your investment. This information should include details on how the laundry will increase your cash flow and your property's value.

These letters will help to build a strong case when you sit down with the lender. If the loan officer can see that you have tenants willing to use your new facilities, the lender will be more inclined to give serious consideration to your loan request. By running the numbers you can show the loan officer the expected revenue. All of this type of documentation will make obtaining financing easier.

An Example

Here is an example of how you might create a plan to present to a lender for the improvement of a rental property. Let's say you want a loan to convert an unused attic into living space. This could require a large sum of money. To justify such a loan you will need strong evidence that the venture is worthwhile. For this type of loan you will need to complete a market study. You must know the demand for housing and the amount of money tenants are willing to pay for rental units. By investigating existing units, comparable to those you plan to create, you can determine what you are likely to receive in increased revenue.

Getting prices from contractors will give you the numbers needed to estimate the cost of your project. Looking through historical data will produce numbers you can use to project the operating expenses for the new units. When you have all of your numbers put together you can begin to see the overall picture. You will see what the project should cost and what it should mean to you in terms of cash flow and property value. Then you can further project the time needed to break-even on the investment. By doing all of this planning before you talk to a loan officer, you are building a strong case.

In some instances your research may prove to you that your plans are not as good as you thought. This saves you the embarrassment of taking a bad plan to a banker. If the numbers work, you are prepared to make an impressive presentation to the loan officer. If you convince the lender that the plan will work, the loan officer is inclined to lend you the needed money.

Packaging Your Proposal

How you package your loan request can influence a lender's decision. If you go in with papers sticking out of your briefcase and coffee stains on your spreadsheet, the

✔ **FAST FACT**

Bankers appreciate a well organized and complete loan package. It makes their job easier and makes you appear more professional.

banker will be impressed, but not favorably. In the banking world, neatness counts. Bankers appreciate a well organized and complete loan package. It makes their job easier and makes you appear more professional.

Have your documents laid out in chronological order. There is nothing worse than losing your place or searching for an elusive report in the middle of a loan application. Placing your papers in a presentation binder is a good way to keep them in order and to give a good impression. Have your exhibits labeled so that the loan officer can identify them quickly.

Preparing to Meet Your Lender

Preparing to meet your lender is the next step in making a successful loan application. You should know your proposal inside and out before meeting with a loan officer. If you must rummage through your papers to answer a lender's questions, it will appear that you are not well prepared to execute your plans. Commit your proposal to memory.

> ▶ *PRO POINTER*
>
> Whenever possible, have a friend or spouse act as a loan officer while you give your presentation. This role playing will expose flaws in your proposals. It will also acquaint you with the proposal and your presentation.

Work all of the bugs out of your proposal and presentation before you meet with a banker. When you sit down with your loan officer you should be calm, confident, and convincing. Your presentation will have a significant affect on the lender's opinion of your proposal. If you ramble back and forth and have trouble defining your needs, desires, and plans, the lender will not have confidence in you or your plan. Once you are prepared, call your lender and make an appointment for loan application.

Formal Loan Applications

Formal loan applications can take on many different looks. For some lenders the process entails piles of paperwork. Other lenders prefer to hear a verbal presentation, to see if they are inclined to move ahead to a written application. The process for formal loan application will depend on the lender you are dealing with. Normally, the process will involve an oral discussion, followed by a written application. It is during the face-to-face talk that you have the opportunity to convince your lender to say, "Yes".

If you have prepared well for your meeting, you can change the mind of even a doubting loan officer. There will be few situations when a concise plan, delivered in a confident manner, will not lean the loan officer in your direction. Loan officers are used to meeting people for all types of loans, under all kinds of circumstances. A majority of these loan applicants are not well prepared or organized. With the right presentation, the lender will pay close attention to your plans. As the lender mentally compares your presentation to the haphazard requests that routinely come in, your ideas will sound great.

Your paperwork and numbers have to substantiate what you tell a banker. If you have a winning spreadsheet to cement a successful talk, you all but have the loan. Let's look at some examples of different loan proposals. There will be two proposals, one will be better than the other. Put yourself in the loan officer's chair as you read each request. As you are reading, formulate an opinion of approval or denial for the loan. I think you will quickly see what a difference the concept and approach of your proposal can make to an attentive loan officer.

Example One-The Wrong Way

In this example, the investor, Joe, is applying for a loan to add a coin-operated laundry facility in the basement of his building. His building has twelve, two-bedroom rental units. The rental units do not have provisions for individual laundry equipment. Joe's tenants are presently required to take their dirty laundry to a Laundromat down the street. Let's see how Joe's loan request looks.

Joe wants to borrow $12,000.00 to install a laundry room in his building. The reason for installing the laundry room is to increase cash flow and the property's value. Joe has decided this improvement is worthwhile because his tenants must leave the site to do their laundry. He is convinced he will make more money after the facilities are installed.

When he asks you, the loan officer, for a loan, he tells you all about his plan, but only in the detail described above. He has quotes from contractors to prove the approximate cost of the improvements, but this is the only factual information, other than the description of his building that is provided. Are you willing to loan Joe $12,000.00? Do you need more information to make a sound decision? Well, if you loaned Joe the money based on these sketchy details, you probably wouldn't be a loan officer for long.

Joe has failed to provide enough information for you to make a clear evaluation of the loan. Joe is like many other landlords; he knows what he is thinking, but he doesn't do a good job of putting his thoughts together for the loan officer. This type of loan request will either be denied or will be countered with a request for additional information. Now let's see how Mike asked for the same amount of money for the same improvement.

Example One-The Right Way

Our second investor is Mike. His circumstances are identical to Joe's. He wants to do the same work on the same type of building, under the same conditions. The difference is in how he asks for the money he wishes to borrow. Here is Mike's loan request for your consideration.

Mike wants to borrow $12,000.00 to install a laundry room in his building. The reason for installing the laundry room is to increase cash flow and the property's value. Mike has decided this improvement is worthwhile because his tenants must leave the site to do their laundry. He is convinced he will make more money after the facilities are installed. When Mike goes over his proposal with you, the following facts are outlined:

- There are twelve apartments in the building. Two of the apartments are occupied by single men. Eight of the apartments house a husband, wife, and child. The last two apartments are occupied by husbands and wives. There are twenty-two adults and eight children living in the building. None of these people do laundry with personal equipment. They all go to the corner Laundromat to clean their clothes.

- There are affidavits included in the loan-request package from each responsible tenant requesting the installation of coin-operated laundry facilities to be installed in the building. Each resident has included an estimate of their weekly spending habits for cleaning their clothes. Based on the numbers provided by the tenants, they collectively spend around $80.00 per week at the Laundromat.

- Mike has indicated he wishes to install four washing machines and six dryers. Since it takes longer to dry clothes than it does to wash them, there is a need for more dryers than washers. With this number of units, one-third of all the tenants could do laundry at the same time. This is adequate to keep tenants from becoming frustrated because there are not enough machines. If the tenants were constantly waiting for a machine to become available, they would go to the Laundromat down the street.

- Mike has requested $12,000.00 to create his laundry room. This amount includes all expenses incurred to make an operational laundry, as described. According to the income amounts estimated from the tenants' affidavits, it will take just under three years to recover the cost of the investment. After the loan is repaid, Mike's cash flow will increase by approximately $4,000.00 per year.

- Mike is asking for a five-year loan. He wants the additional two years to allow for vacancies, operating expenses, maintenance, and repairs. He is certain the coin-operated machines will pay for themselves in less than the requested five years.

- Mike has included three quotes from reputable contractors for the costs to provide the laundry facilities. According to the contractor's quotes, the job can be done for $10,600.00. Mike is asking for a loan approval in the amount of $12,000.00 to guard against cost overruns, but does not expect to borrow more than the actual cost of the job.

- Mike points out that his building has twelve units and is considered a commercial income property. Since the value of this type of building is based largely on the income performance of the building, the increased cash flow will increase the property's value. According to the documented projections Mike as put together, the $12,000.00 investment will be recovered in the third or fourth year, but no later than the fifth year. After this time, all income from the laundry, except that used for operating expenses, maintenance, and repairs, will be profit.

Mike has all of his facts and figures neatly arranged and protected in a binder. He hands it to you for a decision. Do you think you will give Mike the loan for the laundry room? Mike has made his proposal clear and has supported it with documented facts. There is no reason why you should not give him the loan. Your file, as a loan officer, is well documented to verify your reasoning in approving the loan. You get a good loan and Mike gets the laundry room he wants.

The Comparison of Right And Wrong

In Joe's case, he did not provide much information. The information he did provide was not substantiated with facts and figures. There were no contingencies planned or shown for cost overruns, vacancies, or other unforeseen obstacles. He did not disclose how many washers and dryers he planned to install. He said he wanted to increase his cash flow and property value, but he didn't provide any projections for these factors. All in all, Joe did not present a winning proposal.

When Mike made his loan request, he was well prepared. He had statements from his tenants to support his feelings that a coin-operated laundry would be a successful investment. He had numbers to project his increased income. He allowed for unforeseen problems in the cost of the job and the time it might take to recover his investment. He knew how many machines he needed to get the job done, without going overboard. In general, Mike made a proposal that was too good to deny.

The Winning Pitch

Now you have seen what a difference a well prepared loan package can make. The more factual information you supply, the better your chances are of having your loan approved. With the right information, packaged and presented professionally, you greatly increase the odds of having your loan request approved.

CHAPTER FOURTEEN

Maintenance: Indoor and Outdoor

When you decide to manage rental property, you must assume responsibility for building maintenance needs. If you don't have any experience in the maintenance and repair of real estate, this responsibility can be a burden. There will be times when tenants call in the middle of the night to report a broken water pipe or some other emergency. When this happens, you must know what to do. It may mean calling a professional, or your maintenance person, to respond to the call. It may mean going out yourself to solve the problem. Before you are faced with an after-hours emergency, you should have a plan for handling such calls.

Even when there are no emergencies, there will be routine maintenance required to keep rental property in good repair. Ignoring routine maintenance will lead to more emergency calls and lost money. This regular maintenance may involve cleaning the heating system or cutting the lawn. In any case, these regular chores must be attended to. As a property manager, it is up to you to schedule, coordinate, and inspect all the work done on the properties that you manage.

Since many investors know money, but are not experienced in maintenance and repairs, the property maintenance aspect of your rental business could be the most difficult to deal with. Your clients may have trouble understanding why they should spend money before they have to. However, investing in routine maintenance can save a lot of money on repairs in the future.

If you rely on experience to teach you how to make repairs or even to arrange repairs and maintenance, your lessons can be costly. This chapter will cover the most common requirements for the maintenance and repair of rental properties. It will be up to you to decide if you will perform the work yourself or hire others to do the job for you. Most importantly, you will learn what to look for and what to expect from properties in need of repair or maintenance.

Principles and Procedures

Whether you are running a single-family house or a twelve-unit apartment building, many of the repair and maintenance procedures will be the same. Once you understand the principals involved, you can apply them to all of your residential rental units. Commercial properties may require additional or different procedures. This chapter is broken down into the areas where attention may be needed on various buildings. For example, there are sections on the outside of the property, the hallway, the basement, the roof, the interior of the rental unit, and so forth.

Upkeep

You must decide how you will arrange for the upkeep of rental property. Will you do the work yourself? Many landlords that are unable to perform technical work inside their buildings are quite capable of keeping up the exterior of their property. While you may not know how to solder copper pipes or clean a heating system, you are probably more than qualified to cut the grass at rental property you are in charge of. The question is should you do the work? This is a question you must answer for yourself, each investor and property manager may have a different answer.

Is It Cost Effective?

You must determine if it is cost effective for you to do the exterior maintenance work. It may be more beneficial for you to hire a company to take care of the maintenance for you. If you can be making deals while they are cutting the grass, you should be money ahead. Some investors and managers enjoy doing exterior work around their properties. It gives them a chance to take a break from the stress of fighting their day-to-day battles. Cutting the grass

> **▶ PRO POINTER**
>
> When you contract someone to do a job, you must tell them what to do, when to do it, and to some extent, how to do it. If you have no idea of what the subcontractor should do, you are at the mercy of the subcontractor. This is a bad position to be in.

can relax you while providing needed exercise. The final decision must be made based on your personal situation.

Will you hire subcontractors to take care of the work for you? If you are not going to do the work yourself, you can hire independent contractors to do it for you. But, are you qualified to supervise and coordinate subcontractors? When you contract someone to do a job, you must tell them what to do, when to do it, and to some extent, how to do it. If you have no idea of what the subcontractor should do, you are at the mercy of the subcontractor. This is a bad position to be in.

Hiring People

Before you begin hiring people to do a job, learn something about the work they will be doing. Read books and research the subject until you can talk intelligently about the work to be done. Showing a contractor that you have a basic understanding of a job will help you avoid rip-offs. Make all of your arrangements and agreements in writing. Having a written agreement with your subcontractors will reduce your risks of failure in the property management business. It is easy to become lazy at doing the required paperwork when working with contractors. But, you can run into financial disasters if you don't follow good business procedures in all your dealings.

If you don't protect yourself with written agreements, the property you are managing may have mechanic liens placed against it. If you have to defend your position in court, written agreements are the key to victory. No matter how well you know an individual, don't get sloppy on you paperwork.

Scheduling Routine Maintenance

How much do you know about scheduling routine maintenance? Knowing when to schedule regular maintenance is mandatory for a property manager. If you fail to keep a building running smoothly with routine maintenance, repair bills will get out of hand. If you don't know what to do or when to do it, seek help. The help can come from books, seminars, or consultations with contractors. For example, if you don't know how often to have a heating system cleaned and tuned up, ask a few heating contractors. Don't rely on the advice of just one contractor. Ask three contractors and compare their answers. By doing this type of research, you can avoid many major repairs with simple maintenance.

✔ **F A S T   F A C T**

Knowing when to schedule regular maintenance is mandatory for a property manager. If you fail to keep a building running smoothly with routine maintenance, repair bills will get out of hand.

Maintenance Expenses

Have you allowed enough money for maintenance expenses in an operating budget for each property that you are managing? Many landlords, and some property managers, fail to make accurate projections for their maintenance expenses. This is largely due to a lack of experience. It is hard for the average person to look at a water heater and know if it is going to have to be replaced within the next year. You can solve this puzzle by spending a little money on a professional inspection of your property.

There are companies that specialize in inspecting and evaluating the condition of buildings. These professional inspectors often provide a detailed report on all aspects of the property. Their report will cover everything from the foundation to the roof. By paying a few hundred dollars for a thorough, professional inspection, you can have a strong basis for setting your maintenance and repair budget. While you may not like finding out that a roof will need to be replaced within the next two years, it is better to know about it before the time comes to replace it. With advance warning you can begin to prepare for the costs involved to replace the roof, before it starts to leak. Now, let's take a tour of an average rental property, and see what you are likely to encounter with your maintenance and repair experiences.

The Lawns and Grounds

The lawns and grounds of a property include all of the exterior features of the property that are not a part of the building. This group of items could include the following:

- Lawns
- Parking area
- Driveways
- Sidewalks
- Landscaping
- Security lights
- Drainage systems
- Garbage disposal
- Snow removal

Keeping the exterior of a property in good repair improves it appearance, value, and performance. When the exterior of an investment property is neat and clean, it will attract more tenants. Traditionally, the tenants will be of a better quality than those housed in neglected properties. Existing tenants will remain happier if their rental unit is pleasant to come home to. No one wants to wade through puddles of standing water to get into their home. Neither do tenants enjoy coming home to a building where there is garbage scattered around the lawn. A well-kept building will be more impressive to an appraiser than a run-down one. The owner's interest in a property should be reflected in a higher appraised value. All of these reasons are motivation for you to maintain the lawns and grounds of a property.

The Lawn

If a property has a lawn, don't underestimate the affect it has on people. A shaggy lawn is not conducive to a good relationship with tenants. If the tenants see that the lawn is not cared for, they may not take care of a rental unit that they lease. Keep the grass cut and the leaves raked.

✔ FAST FACT

A manicured lawn goes a long way to making a good impression on all that view a property. And, exterior appearance can have an influence on the type of tenants a building attracts.

Drainage Problems

Drainage problems in a yard can make for bad feelings and they can add to the value of a building. When you have standing water in a lawn, tenants will not be happy. The puddles are a nuisance to walk around and they encourage insect population. If the drainage problems are near the foundation of a building, they can create other problems. The basement could flood. With a crawlspace foundation, mold may grow under the building and cause health problems for the tenants. The moisture may cause paint to peel off of a building. In some cases, the water can be responsible for damage to a foundation. If you encounter drainage problems, they should be addressed and corrected.

Driveways and Parking Areas

Driveways and parking areas are used by tenants daily. If these items fall into poor repair, tenants will become unhappy. The more you allow these areas to go unattended, the worst the cost of repairs become. For example, if you have a paved driveway with cracks or holes in it, winter freezing can make the cracks or holes larger. In graveled drives, insufficient gravel will lead to erosion. In both cases, repairing the driving surface will cost much more than maintaining it. By sealing paved areas and re-surfacing graveled areas you can preserve the owner's initial investment, without costly repairs.

Landscaping

If a property has landscaping features, keep them looking nice. Trim hedges and foundation shrubs to keep them below your first-floor windows. If the building looks to be overrun by wild bushes, people will not want to live in it. Dense greenery can contribute to crime. If shrubs are too tall and bushy, people can hide behind them. This can encourage burglary and vandalism. Exterior appearance is always an important part of a rental property.

Security Lights

Tenants feel more comfortable when their home is lighted with security lights. If property you are managing has security lights, keep them in working order. By allowing burned-out bulbs to remain in lights, you discourage tenants and encourage the criminal element. Protect lights from rocks with impact-resistant covers. If kids know they can't break the lights, they won't throw rocks at them. By discouraging the throwing of rocks, you reduce the number of broken windows in a building.

> ▶ *PRO POINTER*
>
> Security is an issue that seems to become increasing important from year to year. Tenants want to feel safe. Installing lights, security locks, closed-circuit cameras, and other security devices can pull tenants to the building that you are managing quicker than a competitor's building will, if it doesn't offer the security features.

Garbage Control and Removal

Garbage and trash scattered around a building is unhealthy and ugly. Make arrangements in your leases to have the tenants be responsible with their refuse. If necessary, provide metal containers for the tenant's use. By putting the trash cans in an enclosed area, you can remove the eyesore from view. In tough neighborhoods you can issue each tenant a key for access to the enclosure.

Snow and Ice Removal

In cold climates, snow removal is a part of every property manager's job description. If you expect to get snow in the winter, make arrangements for its removal by fall.

Tenants that cannot get their cars out of a building's parking lot cannot go to work. Tenants who do not go to work can not pay their rent. It is in your best interest to provide fast and efficient snow removal for your clients and their tenants.

If your exterior walkways and steps are covered in ice, someone may be in jeopardy from a potential lawsuit. If someone falls on the ice, you may find yourself in deep financial trouble. The property owner could also be affected. If ice is prevalent in your area, make arrangements to clear the ice before there is a problem. The small investment of sand or ice-removing chemicals is much easier to take than the cost of a lengthy legal battle.

▶ **PRO POINTER**

Protect yourself and your clients from lawsuits related to ice that forms in walking areas. Don't allow ice to build up. Take the proper precautions to avoid injuries that may result in lawsuits.

Dead Trees

Dead trees often go unnoticed, until they fall. When dead trees fall, they can land on a building, a tenant's car, or even a tenant. Obviously, this can cause severe damage with potentially expensive results. Inspect trees and limbs around your property. When you see a potentially hazardous situation, don't wait to cure it. Act quickly to avoid damages or injuries. Normally, you should call a professional to remove dead trees or limbs. Be sure that the contractor is properly licensed and insured for the work being done.

Exterior Maintenance

The exterior of a building is exposed to weather. Inclement weather has a way of deteriorating a building's condition. To guard against substantial damage from the elements, you must be willing to provide routine maintenance to the exterior of rental investments. The outside considerations for a building may encompass the following:

Exterior Maintenance Items
- Roofing
- Siding
- Paint
- Trim material
- Exterior doors

- Windows
- Porches
- Gutters
- Walkways
- Fences

The Roof

The roof on a building provides shelter and protection for the building and its tenants. If you allow the roof to go bad, you will have angry tenants and a damaged building. Nobody is going to be happy with you under these conditions. Water damage from a leaking roof can do serious structural damage. The damage can progress to dangerous levels before you know it exists.

✔ **FAST FACT**

When an attic is heavily insulated, it can take months for the water to stain ceilings. In the meantime, you could have rafters rotting or water entering electrical boxes.

Many factors influence the life of a roof. A roof's exposure to extreme heat can reduce its life. The type of roofing used will make a difference in the length of time the roof is good for. The untrained eye may not be able to tell a roof is bad. As an owner and manager, you should have your roof inspected by a professional. The report generated from such an inspection will tell you how long you can expect the roof to last. When the time comes to repair or replace a roof, don't procrastinate.

Your Siding and Exterior Trim

Siding and exterior trim is a building's skin. It is generally the largest exterior part of a building. When wood siding and trim is not properly maintained, it will rot. When the siding and trim has to be replaced, you may not be able to match the new materials with the existing materials. This will result in either great expense to replace more than you need to or a mismatched building.

▶ **PRO POINTER**

If a property is equipped with vinyl or aluminum siding, the siding may need to be washed periodically. Mold and mildew can build up on siding. To remove it, a good washing from a power-wash machine will get the job done. There are contractors available who specialize in power washing.

By inspecting siding and trim at regular intervals, you can catch problems in their early stages. If rot is detected early, you can make simple repairs. A key to the preservation of siding and trim is a good paint job. Having the proper flashing, caulking, and weather protection is another way to ensure a long life for siding and trim.

Chimney Maintenance

- If a property has a chimney, expect to give it some attention from time to time.
- The mortar joints on the masonry work may occasionally need to be pointed up.
- The flashing around the chimney should be inspected periodically for leaks.
- Depending upon the device connected to the chimney, the chimney should be cleaned annually, or on a regular, recommended basis.

Exterior Paint

Exterior paint serves two purposes. It prevents siding and trim from rotting and it gives a building more of a pleasing appearance. If paint is cracking or peeling, there may have a moisture problem. Moisture that collects around exterior walls, near the foundation, can cause a paint job to have a short life. If there is a habitual problem with paint cracking and peeling, check for high moisture content. If the moisture problem is severe, the wood in exterior walls and plates may be rotting. Keeping paint in good shape will help to protect the investment of a building while making it more attractive.

Outside Windows and Doors

Outside windows and doors can cost a property owner a lot of money when they are not up to par. For the person responsible for heating and cooling a building or rental unit, faulty windows and doors can drain their bank account. This is especially true in older buildings. If windows and doors do not seal properly, heating and cooling dollars will go right through the cracks.

In addition to energy losses, windows and doors are prime candidates for rotting wood. If the exterior trim around windows and doors is not protected, it will rot quickly. Water gathering in windows will rot the window trim and work its way into the walls. Door jambs and trim can also fall prey to rot. It is important that all these surfaces be properly caulked and painted.

Porches, Balconies, and Railings

Porches, balconies, and railings are frequently ignored by landlords. This is a mistake on the landlord's part. If porches or railings are in bad repair, a personal injury could result. If someone falls off a balcony, because of a rotted railing, you are probably going to be in trouble. The same could be true for an injury received due to a faulty porch.

Old buildings are particularly famous for bad porches, balconies, and railings. Many landlords prefer to look the other way, instead of replacing or repairing these items. While thousands of landlords get away with their shaky railings and porches, you may not be so lucky. Whether you are the property owner or the property manager, there is no reason to jeopardize your assets, or your tenant's health, by ignoring a dangerous situation. Inspect railings, porches, and balconies. If they need repair or replacement, have the job done or get permission for the building owner to have the repairs done.

> ▶ *PRO POINTER*
>
> When a building's porches, railings, and balconies are in good repair, keep them that way. Routine maintenance with paint and frequent inspections can prevent the need for spending large sums of money in replacements. It can also reduce the risks of lawsuits and injuries.

> ▶ *PRO POINTER*
>
> If a building is required to have a fire escape, be sure that it has one. Also be certain the fire escape is in good working order. You should never wait until human lives are in danger to discover that your fire escape is useless. If the fire inspector finds fault with your fire escape, you could be facing a heavy fine.

Common Areas

Common areas are the areas shared by tenants. These areas can include:

- Lawns
- Tennis courts
- Walkways
- Ponds
- Playgrounds
- Hallways

- Laundry rooms
- Basement area where storage facilities are located

The condition of common areas affects tenants. If light bulbs are missing or burned out, tenants will not appreciate it. If smoke detectors or fire extinguishers are stolen, they will have to replace them. When bags of garbage are left sitting in a hall, the smell may permeate an entire building. The rancid garbage will also attract rodents and other undesirable animals. All of these problems exist in many multi-family rentals. You can solve some of them by installing a security door.

Security Doors

If a property does not have security doors on the exits, you should consider having them installed. When you are acting as a manager for others, you can recommend such an improvement. By having access to the building restricted to authorized tenants, you reduce many maintenance headaches. After installing security doors, you can look to the tenants who have access for problems occurring in the common areas. Then, if light bulbs, fire extinguishers, or smoke detectors are missing, you can narrow the search to authorized tenants and their guests. This is not to say that an outsider couldn't be responsible for the trouble, but the odds are greatly reduced when good security doors are installed.

Security doors also please tenants. The tenants will be happy to know they are the only ones likely to be in the building. None of the tenants will enjoy leaving their apartment, only to trip over someone sleeping in the hall.

> ✔ *FAST FACT*
>
> Good exterior lighting and security doors can attract tenants who might have gone to another building.

Hallways

The hallways in a building can take a lot of abuse. When people move furniture in and out of a building, they are likely to damage the hall walls. The floors in a hall can be subjected to heavy use in all kinds of weather. Melting snow and water can damage the floors. Without security doors, outsiders are likely to visit the hallways. When they do, damage is likely to occur.

> ✔ *FAST FACT*
>
> Keep halls well lighted and free of clutter. When the code enforcement officer pays a building a visit, the hallways will be one of the first areas inspected.

As the property manager, you should inspect halls frequently. Test lights to be sure they work. Test smoke detectors to see that they are operating properly. If you find garbage in a hall, clean it up and find out who is responsible for the mess. When you find the guilty party, impress upon them not to dirty the halls again.

Basements

Many landlords use the basements of their buildings as a common area. The basement may house a laundry room or storage facilities. If the basement is not used as a common area, it should be locked to prevent prowling tenants from entering it. There are usually many ways for people to get hurt in basements. By restricting access to the basement, you reduce your chances of a lawsuit.

If the basement is a common area, make sure it is up to snuff. The stairs into the basement must be sturdy and equipped with a railing. There must be adequate lighting for the stairs and the basement. There should be partition walls to limit access to intended common areas. All mechanical equipment and non-common area should be behind locked doors to prevent the entry of unauthorized people.

If a basement is equipped with a sump pump, it should be checked on a regular basis. Sump pumps are installed to remove water below the basement floor. If the pumps fail, the basement can flood. Checking a sump pump monthly will reduce the risk of having a flooded basement.

Laundry Rooms

Laundry rooms that are open to all tenants are a potential trouble spot. If the tenants abuse your equipment, the repair bills can add up quickly. You should inspect laundry equipment on a regular basis. If you find a washer or dryer that is not working, have it repaired. When tenants become frustrated with a machine that won't work, they may abuse it. By keeping equipment in working condition, you lower the stress levels of the tenants. Happy tenants make for a building that runs smoother and keeps your job easier.

▶ **PRO POINTER**

If you are managing a building that does not have a coin-operated laundry and that doesn't have laundry facilities in each apartment, suggest that the owner consider adding a coin-operated laundry. The additional revenue can be substantial. If you are paid a percentage of the gross income, this can mean more money to you.

Inspect the hoses on washing machines frequently. These hoses can become worn, and break. When a washing machine hose breaks, a laundry area is likely to flood. Unless the valve controlling the water to the hose is cut off, there will be a steady stream of water blowing out of the hose. Regular inspections of hoses can reduce the chance of an unwanted flood. If the hoses appear cracked, worn, or tender, replace them.

Rarely Visited Areas

Rarely visited areas of a property are the attic and the crawlspace, if there is one. Since you do not regularly venture into these areas, you must make a note to inspect them occasionally.

The Attic

There should be little need for maintenance in a building's attic. While there shouldn't be much too worry about in the attic, there are a few things you should check on from time to time. By going into an attic you can check for roof leaks and insect damage. If the roof plywood has turned black, there is more than likely a moisture problem. If you notice small piles of sawdust in the attic, there may be an insect infestation.

When you are in an attic, check to see if it is ventilated. There should be gable vents, soffit vents, or a ridge vent to circulate air in the attic. A healthy attic needs proper ventilation. Ideally, there will be a ridge vent and either gable or soffit vents, or both. This will provide the best circulation and help to avoid moisture problems.

Crawlspace Foundations

When there is a crawlspace foundation, you should inspect it at least twice a year. Look for standing water that may damage the building. Standing water can cause mold, mildew, rot, and peeling paint. Insect activity could be a problem in the crawl-space. When you arrange annual pest inspections, the inspector will check the crawlspace, as well as the attic. If you have

✔ **FAST FACT**

Wood-eating insects can destroy a building. Arrange for a professional pest inspection at least once a year. These inspections are often done without charge. The inspector will look for any sign of pest and insect activity.

plumbing pipes in the crawlspace, they may need to be protected from freezing during cold weather.

Most crawlspace foundations will be equipped with air vents. These vents will be mounted in the foundation. It is important for the crawlspace to receive proper ventilation. In winter, if cold air can blow on your plumbing pipes, they may freeze. Protect the pipes from drafts. Insulation or even a heat tape may be necessary to prevent plumbing from freezing.

Inside the Rental Units

The interior of rental units is where most routine maintenance will be required. This is where tenants live and where most problems occur. The problems that can occur in a rental unit include the following:

- Plumbing
- Electrical systems
- Appliances
- Walls
- Ceilings
- Floors
- Interior doors
- Door hardware
- Interior trim
- Cabinets

Plumbing Problems

Plumbing problems are probably the most frequent cause of panicked calls from a tenant to their landlord or property manager. If you plan to manage your own property, be prepared for plumbing problems. When you manage buildings for others, have a list of dedicated plumbers who you can call and depend on. Problems

▶ *PRO POINTER*

When you manage buildings for others, have a list of dedicated plumbers who you can call and depend on.

range from dripping faucets to flooding toilets. Some of the calls will be emergencies. You must either be prepared to play plumber yourself or have a regular plumber you can depend on.

Plumbers can be an independent lot. They are expensive, and they are usually busy. If you plan to call an outside plumber when a property needs help with its plumbing, plan ahead. Establish a relationship with a dependable plumber before you need one. If you wait until you need a plumber to find one, you may not be able to. Plumbing emergencies know no boundaries. They may occur in the middle of the night or on a week-end. If you need a plumber after normal business hours, you can expect a hefty bill, if you can find a plumber.

If you have numerous rental units you may not have as much trouble finding, and keeping, a plumber. When you give them steady business, plumbers respond to your calls. If you only call for plumbing work now and then, getting a good plumber can be quite a job. One way to hedge your odds is to learn basic plumbing principals. If you are not handy, find and keep a good plumber within easy reach.

The routine maintenance of a rental unit's plumbing is a financial responsibility. If a toilet's flush valve is bad, causing the toilet to run constantly, it should be replaced. The person paying the water bill will see a noticeable increase in the bill

> ✔ **FAST FACT**
>
> Most landlords have provisions in their leases to hold tenants responsible for plumbing problems the tenants create. If a tenant's child tries to flush a rubber ducky down the toilet and the toilet floods, it should be the tenant's responsibility to pay for repairs and damages. By including the proper language in a lease the risk of out-of-pocket expenses for plumbing repairs can be reduced.

from the wasted water when the problem is ignored. The same is true for dripping faucets. It is a good idea to inspect a unit's plumbing at least twice a year. Tenants may not care if their bathtubs are dripping a steady stream of water, but the water bill will force someone to pay the price for the drip. Leases should include a clause that allows you to inspect the interior plumbing on a regular basis.

Failures in the Interior Electrical System

Bad plumbing can be messy and costly. Faulty wiring can be deadly. Inspect rental units regularly to check the electrical system at the same time you are inspecting the plumbing. If the unit has it own fuse panel, check the fuses to see that they are the proper size. If a tenant replaces a blown fuse, the tenant may install a fuse that is wrong for the circuit. An oversized fuse could lead to a fire. This is not a problem in buildings that have circuit breakers. Leases should have provisions in them to prevent tenants from creating electrical safety hazards. If you see extension cords being used all over the unit, insist that they be removed.

> **▶ P R O   P O I N T E R**
>
> When the property owner is supplying tenants with appliances, inspect them as warranted. It is in your best interest to keep all aspects of a rental property in good repair.

Other Interior Maintenance

Windows and doors that stick can aggravate tenants. Doorbells that don't work are a nuisance. Cabinet drawers that are hard to operate can put a tenant into a tailspin. These may be little items, but they can add up to make a hostile tenant. By going through rental units on a regular basis, you can control these little complaints.

> **✔ F A S T   F A C T**
>
> Many property managers subcontract all of their maintenance and repair work out to independents. Independent contractors are often the most cost effective way to handle the maintenance of a building.

Working with Independent Contractors

Most individuals retain independent contractors to perform at least some part of their property maintenance. Many property managers subcontract all of their maintenance and repair work out to independents. Independent contractors are often the most cost effective way to handle the maintenance of a building. It rarely pays to keep a maintenance person on the payroll. Between the wages, taxes, and employee benefits, the cost of employees is not feasible for most investors.

When you arrange for independent contractors to do your work, you are the general contractor. If your property was being managed by a professional management firm they would probably charge extra for their services as a general contractor. Many landlords resent these additional charges. Once you start acting as your own general contractor you will understand why management companies charge more for their contracting services. If you are operating as a professional property manager, you should charge for the time you invest in arranging and supervising subcontractors.

Being a general contractor is not easy. The job requires you to wear many hats. You must find reputable subcontractors. After finding suitable subcontractors you must learn to control and manipulate them. Subcontractors can be hard to deal with. A general contractor must be well organized, firm, in control, and confident. These qualities are not always easy to come by. This is especially true when you have a burly plumber staring you down into a corner. Subcontractors can be quite intimidating to an inexperienced general contractor.

As the general contractor, you will be assuming the final responsibility for the subcontractors work. If the subcontractor fails to perform, it is up to you to enforce your rules. To stay in control you need strong written agreements with your subcontractors. With written agreements you will have disputes, without written agreements, you will have lots of disputes. When you have a written agreement you have some power to control your subcontractors. Without a contract you have little hope of winning the shouting match. The subcontractor will have lien rights and may not hesitate to take you to court and lien the property where work was done and not paid for. When you can settle your disputes out of court you are money ahead. Let's look more closely at how you should prepare for working with subcontractors.

Finding Your Subs

Finding you subcontractors is the first step towards working with them. It will be easy to find names and phone numbers of subcontractors. The hard part will be finding good subcontractors who are dependable. No one advertises and says they are incompetent and unreliable. Advertisements give you a place to start, but they are not the end of your search. After generating a list of subs, you must qualify them and weed out the bad ones. To learn more about subcontractors, turn to Chapter 16.

CHAPTER FIFTEEN

Finding and Managing Contractors

Selecting the right contractors is like culling crops. You must disregard the weak, the camouflaged, and the unreliable. The first step in weeding out bad contractors is to go to the telephone. Telephones are the arteries of strong remodeling, mechanical, and home- improvement firms. These types of contractors are the ones that are most often needed by property managers. Communication is critical to a satisfying job. When you begin your search for contractors, you start with the telephone. There will be questions and concerns about projects that you are responsible for. When they arise, you will need to be able to contact your contractors. The phone can tell you much about a contractor before you ever talk to the business owner.

Answering Machines

Answering machines are disliked by almost everyone. When you take the time to call a company, you expect to get information right away, not after the beep. Recorded messages are offensive to many people. Others think it is rude to have a business phone answered electronically. If a machine answers your initial call to a contractor, what will your opinion be? Answering machines are used for many different reasons and do not necessarily indicate a bad or disreputable contractor. Maybe the contractor spends much of his or her time supervising or working on jobs. These are two qualities to look for in a good contractor. When the general is on the job, fewer problems occur.

A positive aspect of answering machines is that they keep overhead costs down. Receptionists and secretaries increase overhead significantly and may be unnecessary for small firms. As a customer you pay for increased overhead, which is passed on through higher prices. The contractor with an answering machine may be less expensive.

Some contractors use answering machines to screen calls. This is not a desirable trait. Contractors who screen their calls usually have dissatisfied customers or hounding creditors. There is a way to distinguish between the two purposes of an answering machine. Call early in the morning and again around 6:30 P.M. See if the contractor answers the phone. The contractor using a machine to keep costs low will probably be coordinating work at these times and should answer your call personally. The machine will answer the phone 24 hours a day, acting as a buffer for the undesirable contractor.

Regardless of their purpose, answering machines eliminate your ability to talk with the contractor immediately. Even if the contractor checks for messages regularly, you will not be able to reach the contractor right away. This can be a pivotal problem if something serious goes wrong on your job. All you can do is leave a recorded message, with no way of knowing when your call will be returned. This could be reason enough to disqualify the contractor from your consideration.

> ▶ *PRO POINTER*
>
> Look for contractors who can be reached quickly. Contractors who carry and answer cell phones and pagers will be of much more help to you during an emergency situation than contractors who you have to leave messages for and wait for hours, or even days, to hear from.

Keep a Log

When you begin the search for contractors, keep a log. Enter the contractor's name, phone number, the date, and the time you called. When the contractor returns your call, note the time and date in the log. This may sound excessive or silly, but it can tell you a lot about a potential contractor.

You might be surprised by how many contractors will never return your call. It continually amazes me how contractors can remain in business without returning phone calls. A successful contracting company depends on new business, and the refusal to return phone calls is business suicide. Some contractors will return the call, but only after two or three days. The phone log helps you spot these red flags.

PHONE LOG			
Date	Company Name	Contact Person	Remarks

FIGURE 15.1   Phone Log

If it takes this long to speak with the contractor, there is a problem. Slow response to a request for new work means no response to calls about work done poorly. Contractors should return your initial call within a few hours. If the contractor is working in the field, it may be evening before your call is reciprocated. A good contractor will tend to present clients first and then potential customers. Although your message may receive lower priority, you should not have to wait days for a return call.

Phone response is an important element in choosing any contractor. If a contractor uses a receptionist or personal answering service, he or she can be reached quickly. The answering service should be capable of paging the contractor or calling the contractor on a job site. Many contractors have a cell phone or truck radio and will check in with the service periodically.

In today's competitive market, most successful contractors utilize cellular technology. Ask the answering service when your message will be conveyed to the contractor and how long it will be before you can expect a call. Write the information in the log, then wait and see if the time estimate was accurate. You shouldn't base a job decision on the empty promise of a rapid response.

Two hours of turnaround time is acceptable when you are not an existing customer. Once your job is started, your calls should be returned within an hour or less. There should also be a way for you the reach the contractor immediately in a crisis situation. An answering service can promptly relay your call for help; an answering machine cannot. A cell phone is even better. Overhead costs for the contractor remains low with an answering service, and the phones can be tended 24 hours a day. For the small contractor this is the sensible solution to the phone challenge. For the property manager it is an acceptable arrangement, combining fast phone responses with lower contract prices.

> ✔ *FAST FACT*
>
> Contractors should return your initial call within a few hours. If the contractor is working in the field, it may be evening before your call is reciprocated.

> ✔ *FAST FACT*
>
> There should be a way for you the reach the contractor immediately in a crisis situation. An answering service can promptly relay your call for help; an answering machine cannot. A cell phone is even better.

A Sense of Security

Contractors with offices and administrative personnel and offer consumers a sense of security. The customer can go to an office and speak with the contractor or his office staff. Unless the contractor is doing a high volume of business, you will pay more for these conveniences. This secure, professional appearance can also be misleading. Offices and administrative assistants don't make good contractors.

▶ *P R O   P O I N T E R*

Do not be lulled into a false sense of security by outward appearances. It is possible that a contractor's office rent hasn't been paid for in months or the administrative staff is from a temporary service. The office furniture and equipment could be on a monthly lease. You can't judge contractors on appearance alone.

Finding the right contractor requires attention to detail and a well-conceived plan. A phone log is only the beginning, as it allows you to eliminate some contractors right away. If they don't perform well in your phone test, they won't perform well on your job. Delete contractors who don't promptly return your call; they obviously don't want or need your job. If they don't care enough to return your calls, forget them. You are looking for a good contractor with a desire to do your job. Ask them questions and record their answers on paper to keep in a file. Keep a list of the subcontractors with whom you may work.

The right contractor will understand your needs and strive to meet them. There are good contractors available, but finding them can be a challenge. Like any good result in life, locating the right contractor takes time. You will have to look hard to pinpoint exceptional contractors, and inducing them to do your job may take some creative maneuvering. These high-demand contractors have plenty of work. Don't despair; there are ways to attract the best contractors.

▶ *P R O   P O I N T E R*

Delete contractors who don't promptly return your call, as they obviously don't want or need your job. If they don't care enough to return your calls, forget them.

Where Should You Start Your Contractor Quest?

Where should you start your contractor quest? The advertising pages of your local phone book are a logical answer. Here you will find contractors who have been in

Your Company Name

Your Company Address

Your Company Phone and Fax Numbers

SUBCONTRACTOR QUESTIONNAIRE

Company name: _____

Physical company address: _____

Company mailing address: _____

Company phone number: _____

After-hours phone number: _____

Company president/owner: _____

President/owner address: _____

President/owner phone number: _____

How long has company been in business: _____

Name of insurance company: _____

Insurance company phone number: _____

Does company have liability insurance: _____

Amount of liability insurance coverage: _____

Does company have worker's comp. insurance? _____

Type of work company is licensed to do: _____

List business or other license numbers: _____

Where are licenses held: _____

If applicable, are all workers licensed? _____

Are there any lawsuits pending against the company? _____

Has the company ever been sued? _____

Does the company use subcontractors? _____

Is the company bonded? _____

With whom is the company bonded? _____

Has the company had complaints filed against it? _____

Are there any judgments against the company? _____

FIGURE 15.2   Questions to ask subcontractors

SUBCONTRACTOR LIST

Service	Vendor	Phone	Date

FIGURE 15.3   List of subcontractors

business for awhile. It takes time to get into the book, and the advertising rates are steep. If you really want to do your homework, check the phone company for back issues of their phone book. You can chronicle a contractor's business history by noting the size and style of the ad over a period of time. You must sift through the list to find suitable contractors for your job.

Your Local Paper

Advertisements in the classified section of your local paper are another good resource for names. These contractors are probably either hungry or starting in business.

Check to see if the contractor is also listed in the advertising section of the local phone book. Here is a quick tip on telephone advertising. If the contractor advertises in the paper as "John Doe Building," he should also be listed as "John Doe Building" in the phone book. If you find a listing in the white pages for "Mr. John Doe" and no Yellow Page listing, you can assume he operates from home without a business phone number. If you don't find "John Doe Building" in the line listings of the advertising section in the phone book, he is probably a rookie or part-timer. This isn't always bad. John Doe may have years of field experience with other contractors. This background can override the lack of business experience, and you might get your best deal from John Doe.

If Mr. Doe tells you he has ten employees and has been in business for fifteen years, be cautious. The phone company is not in the habit of allowing people to operate a business from their home without paying additional fees. Official businesses are customarily given a free line listing in the phone book. A little research can go a long way in testing the validity of a contractor.

Jobs In Progress

Another effective way to find contractors is by doing some undercover work around your neighborhood. Look for jobs in progress. When you see a contractor's sign or truck, write down the name and phone number. Jot down the address of the job where the work is being done. These jobs can be future references to check for potential contractors.

> ✔ **FAST FACT**
>
> Jobs under construction often yield easy access and allow you to see the contractor's work. If you like what you see, call the contractor and ask if he or she is interested in bidding your job.

Explain that your job is close to the one the contractor is working on and ask to walk through the job in progress with the contractor. Finished jobs are much more difficult to gain access to because customers don't appreciate a parade of people going through their property. Take advantage of your timing, and go see the work while you can. If you get the opportunity, ask the customers if they are satisfied with the contractor and the work.

Networking

Networking with other professionals is one way of finding good contractors through word-of-mouth referrals. This is absolutely one of the best ways to acquire top-notch contractors. However, do not take this information as the absolute solution to your contractor search. Before running out and signing a contract, ask yourself a few questions. Was the work done for your friends similar to the work you want done? If they had their bathroom remodeled, it

doesn't automatically qualify the contractor to build a garage for a multi-unit apartment building. A contractor capable of building exquisite decks isn't always the best candidate for extensive kitchen remodeling. Dig deep and do your homework to make sure that you are building a stable of the best contractors available.

Contractor Referrals

Contractor referrals are another way to find good contractors. Yes, many contractors will refer you to other contractors when asked. Make sure a contractor is qualified to complete the work you want done. If not, consider contacting the contractor and asking for references of other tradespeople in your specific area. Good contractors do not associate with unprofessional, amateurs who might tarnish their reputations. Networking among reputable contractors increases the chances of finding a good contractor for your job. Mentioning that you were referred by a fellow contractor or satisfied customer also carries a lot of weight.

Establishing Your Needs

A key step in finding the right contractor is establishing your needs. Make an outline of the type of work you want done. Do you plan to build a garage? A competent contractor in bath and kitchen remodeling may not be the best choice to construct your garage. The bath contractor works with existing interior conditions, as opposed to footings, site work, or rafters. Check out your contractors carefully and compare their qualifications to your specifications.

Many remodelers are specialists in their field. Remodeling has become increasingly complex and can be compared to medical services. Would you go to a pediatrician for advice on a heart condition? A dormer addition requires a specialist, experienced in cutting open a roof and the many structural changes involved. The knowledge required for work of this magnitude is different from the experience needed to finish a basement. The company that did a great job on your neighbor's

OUTLINE OF WORK TO BE DONE
GARAGE CONSTRUCTION

Choose style of garage desired.

Draw a rough draft of garage or obtain a pre-drawn plan.

Make or obtain a list of required materials.

Select materials to be used.

Price materials.

Make list of contractors needed or a list of general contractors.

Contact contractors.

Obtain labor quotes.

Evaluate budget needs and ability to afford the garage.

Make financing arrangements.

Make final decision on plan to be built.

Choose contractors and check references.

Meet with attorney to draw-up contracts and other documents.

Make commitments to suppliers and contractors.

Schedule work.

Start work.

Inspect work.

Obtain copies of code enforcement inspections.

Make required payments and have lien waivers signed.

Inspect completed job.

Make punch-list, if necessary.

Make absolute final inspection and approval.

Make final payments, except for retainages.

Make retainage payments.

CATEGORIES OF WORK TO BE DONE

Survey	Floor	Trim work
Blueprints	Framing	Painting
Permits	Windows	Electrical work
Site work	Doors	Insulation
Footing	Sheathing	Drywall
Foundation	Roofing	Electric door openers
Floor preparation	Siding	Landscaping

FIGURE 15.4 Garage outline

basement could prove to be a disaster for your dormer addition. Whenever possible, you want to compare apples to apples and to differentiate the knowledge and skill needed for the job at hand.

There is almost no comparison between building a dormer and finishing a basement. Basement work doesn't usually require any structural expertise. A contractor doesn't have to contend with inclement weather or rafter cuts. Finishing a basement has its own challenges with support columns and altering existing conditions. Proper care to control moisture is another skill necessary in finishing a basement. With a dormer, contractors have to know how to deal with rain, wind, and snow. Most of the work is new construction, and existing conditions only play a small role. The contractors who execute these jobs can be as different as the two types of work performed. A comparison will show both types of contractors are professionals in their field.

There may be a few contractors capable of doing both types of work well, but this is the exception rather than the rule. Finding a well-rounded, fully experienced contractor is rare. The majority of contractors specialize in closely defined areas of remodeling, which are determined by several factors. Some contractors concentrate on the jobs offering the highest profit, and others specialize in work they enjoy. You must determine a potential contractor's weaknesses and strengths. Usually the work a contractor does most often is the work he or she does the best.

The fields of specialization can cover any aspect of remodeling and improvements. Some examples include:

- Painting
- Plumbing
- Electrical work
- Heating work
- Drywall work
- Flooring work
- Tile work
- Plaster work
- Masonry work
- General carpentry
- Garages can be a specialty.
- Sunrooms are a common specialty.
- Dormers can be a specialty.

- Additions offer the opportunity for specialization.

- Kitchens are a natural specialty.

- Bathrooms are one of the most popular rooms to remodel and this type of work offers specialization experts.

Some companies stress their special talents through advertising. The bulk of newspaper ads consist of newer businesses. Many haven't been established long enough to get in the phone book. Newspaper ads and fliers are easy sources of effective advertising for young businesses.

New Businesses

New businesses need your work and will try very hard to win your job. Your negotiating power is stronger with these contractors. While they are new in business, they may be extremely good at what they do. They may have years of experience working for another company, and experience is what you are looking for. It doesn't matter where they learned to do the job as long as they do it right. The contractor who sits behind a desk for five years could have less experience than the tradesperson just starting a business. Your interest is in their work experience, not their business degree.

Rules of the Road

- Do not be afraid to use a new company; the savings often offset the risks.

- Maintain control.

- Don't give the contractor a large cash deposit.

- Put everything in writing.

- Inspect all work closely before advancing any money.

▶ *PRO POINTER*

Contractors just starting out can be an inexpensive alternative to get your job done. With the right precautions, new businesses can result in exceptional values.

✔ *FAST FACT*

There is some risk to a new company, since it is more likely to fail. This will result in trouble when a warranty problem arises. You could get well into a large job; say renovating three apartments, only to have the company close its doors. Getting another contractor to come in to finish someone else's work isn't easy, and it will be expensive. To reduce this problem, stay in control. Be prepared for the worst and never let the contractors have more money than has been earned.

- Insist on lien waivers when any money is paid.

- Ask for original certificates of insurance before any work is started; these should be provided to you without delay from the insurance company.

- Ask for three credit references.

- Obtain several job references.

- Follow up on the references and ask to see actual examples of the contractor's work. It's easy to give friends and relatives as job references, so check them out personally.

- Request evidence of the contractor's state and local license numbers.

- Ask for the contractor's address; this will make a bad apple squirm.

- Validate and investigate all the information to protect yourself against the unforeseen.

These basic rules should be used with any contractor. A company in business for ten years can be out of business in a day. The longer a company has been in business, the more time they've had to get into financial trouble. Businesses that grow too fast sink even faster. From the outside, a company can look extremely successful even when it is in deep trouble. Shiny new trucks, fancy offices, and large management staffs are impressive but expensive. A company with these expenses must compensate for its overhead with volume or higher prices. Any company with extensive overhead is a potential bankruptcy case. And this can be bad for you.

A contractor may have been successful for the last several years and still get in trouble fast. A growing business, with heavy overhead can be derailed by a slow economy. If the company's volume of business declines, it can't afford its overhead. Items such as a fleet of trucks and expensive offices quickly consume any reserve capital. When this happens, a once successful company fails. Don't be fooled by an impressive exterior appearance. Keep your guard up, and make all contractors play by the rules.

If you find a contractor from advertising, be selective. Call enough contractors to get a fair assessment of the talent available. Evaluate each contractor. Ask questions, get everything in writing, and don't assume anything. It is important to establish a position of control from the beginning. Reputable contractors will respect you for your knowledgeable business practices. If you know enough to ask the right questions,

✔ **FAST FACT**

You can be hurt by either an established company or a new one. You have to protect yourself at all times.

SUBCONTRACTOR SCHEDULE

Type of Service	Vendor Name	Phone Number	Date Scheduled

Notes/Changes:

_____

_____

_____

_____

_____

_____

FIGURE 15.5 Subcontractor schedule

the quality contractor will get your job. They don't have to worry about the fast-talking, hard-selling, low bidder. When you are ready to schedule your subcontractors, make a written record of the schedule.

Good contractors constantly fight the price-war battle with questionable contractors. They have to survive without using the slick tactics of less honorable companies.

▶ *PRO POINTER*

Experienced contractors will be happy to answer your questions, and they will put their answers in writing. This process will eliminate much of the competition, and reputable contractors appreciate an informed consumer.

Regardless of the game, playing by the rules is the hardest way to win. In the construction, remodeling, and mechanical arena there are a lot of people looking to win at the customer's expense. The best contractors are in business for the long haul, and your satisfaction will mean more business down the road. They know you will call again for future work or refer them to your friends. Word-of-mouth advertising is the best a contractor can have. It is inexpensive and produces a consistent flow of good work.

Contractors living on the dark side will not have these concerns. They are looking to make a fast buck. They aren't building a business. They're making money. Their objective is to get your money, and they operate on a one-shot basis. In larger cities they survive because of the turnover of residents. In many urban areas a contractor can get to you before his reputation does.

Large cities are a perfect breeding ground for shoddy work. The environment allows renegade contractors to run rampant. They know their present customers aren't likely to affect future business. All of these contractors concentrate on getting jobs so they can get the customer's money. Many contractors have refined this approach into an art. They utilize good advertising and trained salespeople to thrive in the city. They know all the ways to stay one step ahead of you.

Is this the kind of game you want to play? It shouldn't be, unless you are willing to lose. These sales-oriented professionals seldom have any field experience in the trades. It is likely that they use subcontractors for all the work. Their prices will be inflated to allow a hefty profit for their time; you are probably paying them a commission to sell you the job. Why should you keep them in expensive suits and luxury cars? Cut them out and enjoy the money yourself.

Calling a contractor you know nothing about is risky. A business card picked up from the community bulletin board could produce a good deal or a rip-off artist. Advertisements in free newspapers deserve a phone call, but be wary. There are unlimited ways to find good contractors. The tricky part is finding a suitable contractor for the type of work you want done. Not all contractors are created equal. Some are better than others in specialized areas.

✔ FAST FACT

Use common sense, and never allow yourself to be pressured or persuaded into a commitment.

▶ PRO POINTER

A call to the Better Business Bureau or Contractor Licensing Board can tell you if the contractor has been reported for adverse or illegal business practices.

Review the Documents

Don't sign anything without thinking or before you review the documents. Ask about material and work guarantees, and be sure to get them in writing. Requiring the contractor to use your contract will immediately weed through many of the sharks. Remove their fancy clauses and legal rhetoric and you pull their teeth.

Swing the pendulum in your favor in every way possible. Read books and research your project before dealing with any contractors. Try to get a referral if at all possible. Do your homework before having work done.

If you can find subcontractors by way of referrals your job will be easier. If you have a friend who has good luck with a contractor it stands to reason that you might expect similar results. Look for all your contractors before you need them. The best contractors will have regular customers that keep them busy. Check references supplied by the contractors and check with any agency that would have knowledge of legitimate complaints against the contractor. Do enough homework to reduce your risks of getting less than you expect from your contractors.

Agreements

As a property manager and general contractor you will do best when all of your agreements are in writing. While verbal contracts are legal, they are usually unenforceable. If you ask an independent contractor to perform a service for you, the terms of the request should always be in writing. If there will be a deviation from the outline of the contract you should insist on having a written change order executed. When you pay your contractors for services rendered, have them sign a lien waiver. Lien waivers protect you from having mechanic and materialman liens placed against the property where work is done.

Once a contractor has started work on a building the contractor has lien rights. Too many property managers learn the importance of well documented agreements through bad experiences. You have the opportunity to learn from this book. If you follow good business principals in your dealings with contractors you eliminate many potential risks.

Certificates Of Insurance

Obtain certificates of insurance from all of your independent contractors before they work for you. If you fail to keep a contractor's certificate of insurance on file, you may be penalized at the end of the year. Your insurance company may charge you additional money for allowing uninsured contractors to work for you.

Letting Contractors into Rental Units

If you have contractors going into occupied rental units, be careful. Even if the contractors don't do anything wrong, the tenant may make accusations. If contractors will be working in occupied units they should be bonded. It is best if the tenant can be present while the work is being done. If the tenant can't be there, you should consider accompanying the contractors while they are in the property. This can reduce your level of exposure to claims against you.

Be Prepared to Make Calls At Night

Many of the best contractors do not have large businesses. They work alone or with just a small crew. Most of these contractors don't have fancy offices or full-time secretaries. When you call during the day you are likely to reach an answering service. Since these contractors are in the field during the day, they return calls at night. If you are unwilling to talk business after hours, you will have trouble connecting with many of the best contractors. It may be inconvenient to have to deal with night calls, but it can save you money. Since these contractors have low overhead, their prices are often better than those of larger companies.

Getting Bids

If the work you need done will be expensive, you should solicit bids from several contractors. This can be a pain, but it can also save you a lot of money. When putting your job out to bids, keep all of the bid packages identical. If the contractors are not bidding exactly the same work, the prices you get will be meaningless. Beware of substitution clauses in the contractor's quote or estimate. When you specify a particular brand of an item, see to it that the contractor is bidding with that item. It is common for contractors to put in a clause to avoid providing the specified materials. They do this with an "or equal" clause. When you see this clause in a quote, be suspicious. Substituting materials can make a huge difference in the cost of a job. Be certain the prices you are getting are based on the materials you want. Also scrutinize the quote for omissions. Some sly contractors will purposefully forget to include an aspect of the job to make a quote more attractive. When you are just starting out as a property manager you are easy prey for unscrupulous contractors.

Protecting Yourself from Contractors and Vendors

Protecting yourself, and your clients, from contractors and vendors is a major responsibility for professional property managers. All rental buildings require routine maintenance, and this often involves the use of contractors and vendors. Many buildings are improved from time to time. Again, contractors and vendors are brought in for work and goods. Keeping yourself in control of these people and companies will be essential to a successful project.

Get it in writing! These four words convey the most important message in dealing with contractors and vendors. The significance of having everything in writing cannot be stressed enough. Written documents solve problems before they happen and eliminate confusion. Concise written agreements protect your investment and assure your satisfaction. Without these agreements, you are exposed to a variety of uncontrollable, potentially devastating problems.

The Outline

The first form you will use before a significant project is an outline. This form gives you the ability to document and organize your intended improvements in writing. No signatures or legal jargon are required in this form. It is simply an orderly list of your desires. A good outline should be arranged in chronological order. The categories create an overview of the scope of the work to be done. The information should focus on of the types of work you want done, not the products you intend to use. If you

COST ESTIMATES OUTLINE

Cost Projections For Bathroom Remodeling

Item/Phase	Labor	Material	Total
Plans			
Specifications			
Permits			
Trash container deposit			
Trash container delivery			
Demolition			
Dump fees			
Rough plumbing			
Rough electrical			
Rough heating/ac			
Subfloor			
Insulation			
Drywall			
Ceramic tile			
Linen closet			
Baseboard trim			
Window trim			
Door trim			
Paint/Wallpaper			
Underlayment			
Finish floor covering			
Linen closet shelves			

(continues)

FIGURE 16.1 Cost Estimates Outline

want to convert a closet or make room for a laundry area, this is where you define the project. This outline will be helpful when you define your anticipated costs. You and the property owner can review the outline and refine it before you solicit bids from contractors.

Keeping a written report of your project requirements will make your life simpler.

Item/Phase	Labor	Material	Total
Closet door & hardware			
Main door hardware			
Wall cabinets			
Base cabinets			
Counter tops			
Plumbing fixtures			
Trim plumbing material			
Final plumbing			
Shower enclosure			
Light fixtures			
Trim electrical material			
Final electrical			
Trim heating/ac material			
Final heating/ac			
Bathroom accessories			
Clean up			
Trash container removal			
Window treatments			
Personal touches			
Financing expenses			
Miscellaneous expenses			
Unexpected expenses			
Margin of error			
Total estimated expense			

FIGURE 16.1   Cost Estimates Outline *(continued)*

You won't forget to price work in the bidding stage, because the outline reminds you to request quotes. Put everything on the outline. Include the faucets you want replaced, the location of carpets to be installed, and the new door handle you are considering. This is not a bid sheet, so put everything you want on it. You can edit the list later. It is only for proposed work.

CONTRACTOR QUESTIONNAIRE

PLEASE ANSWER ALL THE FOLLOWING QUESTIONS, AND EXPLAIN ANY "NO" ANSWERS.

Company name _____

Physical company address _____

Company mailing address _____

Company phone number _____

After hours phone number _____

Company President/Owner _____

President/Owner address _____

President/Owner phone number _____

How long has company been in business _____

Name of insurance company _____

Insurance company phone number _____

Does company have liability insurance _____

Amount of liability insurance coverage _____

Does company have Workman's Comp. insurance _____

Type of work company is licensed to do _____

List Business or other license numbers _____

Where are licenses held _____

If applicable, are all workman licensed _____

Are there any lawsuits pending against the company _____

Has the company ever been sued _____

Does the company use subcontractors _____

(continues)

FIGURE 16.2   Questions to ask contractors

Contractor Selection Form

When your outline is complete, move onto the contractor selection form. This form is designed to aid during the contractor selection process. All the major groups of contractors are listed on the form, and you should note those you will need on your job. When you get to the bidding process, this list will be very helpful. Knowing which contractors to call will be obvious, and omissions are less likely. The contractor selection form can also remind you of a phase of work previously forgotten.

Is the company bonded _____

Who is the company bonded with _____

Has the company ever had complaints filed against it _____

Are there any judgments against the company _____

Please list 3 references of work similar to ours:

#1 _____

#2 _____

#3 _____

Please list 3 credit references:

#1 _____

#2 _____

#3 _____

Please list 3 trade references:

#1 _____

#2 _____

#3 _____

Please note any information you feel will influence our decision:

_____

ALL OF THE ABOVE INFORMATION IS TRUE AND ACCURATE AS OF THIS DATE.

DATE:_____ COMPANY NAME: _____

BY:_____ TITLE: _____

FIGURE 16.2   Questions to ask contractors *(continued)*

You will know the types of contactors you may need to call, some of which could include:

- Carpenter
- Plumber
- Heating contractor
- Electrician
- Insulator
- Drywall contractor

CONTRACTOR RATING/COMPARISON SHEET

Job name: _____   Date: _____

Category	Contractor 1	Contractor 2	Contractor 3
Contractor name			
Returns calls			
Licensed			
Insured			
Bonded			
References			
Price			
Experience			
Years in business			
Work quality			
Availability			
Deposit required			
Detailed quote			
Personality			
Punctual			
Gut reaction			

Notes: _____

_____

_____

_____

_____

_____

_____

FIGURE 16.3   Contractor rating/comparison sheet

CONTRACTOR SELECTION FORM

TYPE OF SERVICE	VENDOR NAME	PHONE NUMBER	DATE SCHEDULED
Site Work	N/A		
Footings	N/A		
Concrete	N/A		
Foundation	N/A		
Waterproofing	N/A		
Masonry	N/A		
Framing	J. P. Buildal	231-8294	7/3/04
Roofing	N/A		
Siding	N/A		
Exterior Trim	N/A		
Gutters	N/A		
Pest Control	N/A		
Plumbing/R-I	TMG Plumbing, Inc.	242-1987	7/9/04
HVAC/R-I	Warming's HVAC	379-9071	7/15/04
Electrical/R-I	Bright Electric	257-2225	7/18/04
Central Vacuum	N/A		
Insulation	Allstar Insulators	242-4792	7/24/04
Drywall	Hank's Drywall	379-6638	7/29/04
Painter	J. C. Brush	247-8931	8/15/04
Wallpaper	N/A		
Tile	N/A		
Cabinets	N/A		
Countertops	N/A		
Interior Trim	The Final Touch Co.	365-1962	8/8/04
Floor Covering	Carpet Magicians	483-8724	8/19/04
Plumbing/Final	Same	Same	8/21/04
HVAC/Fina	Same	Same	8/22/04
Electrical/Final	Same	Same	8/23/04
Cleaning	N/A		
Paving	N/A		
Landscaping	N/A		

NOTES/CHANGES _____

_____

FIGURE 16.4   Sample contractor comparison sheet

- Painter
- Wallpaper contractor
- Flooring contractor

This form serves as a reminder of which trades will be needed to complete the work. You will need competitive bids for each phase of the job to plan your budget. A budget loses its effectiveness if you forget that you will need a tile contractor for your bathroom remodel. There are spaces on the form to list the name and phone number of the company you choose to do each phase of work. This allows you to use the form as a quick reference sheet during the project. The more you have in writing, the less you will forget.

Professional Services Directory

Now that you know the work you want done and the type of contractors you need to complete the job, the next document to use is the professional services directory. This form is similar to the contractor guide in that it lists all the services you will require. Use this form to reduce the risk of forgetting professionals who may be needed and

PROFESSIONAL SERVICES DIRECTORY

TYPE OF SERVICE	VENDOR NAME	PHONE NUMBER	DATE SCHEDULED
Survey	All-Pro Surveyors	555-9976	6/3/04
Attorney	B. C. Warden, Esq.	555-1738	6/5/04
Financing	Home Loans, Inc.	555-0080	6/27/04
Blueprints	Design Options, LTD.	555-2589	6/11/04
Accounting	A. G. Marks, CPA	555-3756	6/6/04
Appraisal	Valuall Appraisers	555-1789	6/12/04
Insurance	Quick-Claims Mutual	555-7898	7/2/04

FIGURE 16.5   Sample professional directory

who may not be at the top of your thoughts. Some examples of these types of professionals may include:

- Surveyors
- Architects
- Drafters
- Attorneys
- Insurance agents
- Home inspectors

Query Letter

Your next written tool will be the Query Letter, which requests prices and inquires about the availability of services. Mailing this form letter to all the professionals you anticipate needing will save you time and money. The letter saves hours of phone calls to answering services.

Product Information Sheet

The next form you will need is a product identification sheet. This sheet is divided into construction phases. It will detail all the specifics of the products you are interested in. The sheet lists information such as:

- Brand name
- Model number
- Color
- Size
- Other pertinent information

Do you feel like you are being buried in paperwork? These forms don't have to be used, but the results without them are unpredictable at best. At this point you

know the work you want done and the
people required to do it. You even have
your product list ready for bids. Are you
ready to start the job? No, there is still
work to be done in the office before the
fieldwork is started.

Estimated Cost Sheet

Review the information you have assembled. Create files for all the suppliers and contractors. These files will help you during your negotiations and final decision. Using
an estimated cost sheet is the next logical approach. This worksheet will give you a
rough idea of the costs required to complete your remodeling project. The estimate
sheet will be divided into phases of work, such as:

- Framing
- Siding
- Trim
- Electrical
- HVAC
- Plumbing

These phases are considered hard costs. In addition, your estimated cost sheet
should include soft costs. These are professional fees, loan application fees, interest
charges, and other broad-based costs.

The estimated cost sheet should include all expenses. You have to know what the
total cash requirements will be before committing to a project. If you forget to include
soft costs, you could run out of money before the job is finished. Review the sample
cost sheets and add categories as needed. Some hidden expenses could be related to
a loan to make the improvements. These loans can require points, title searches, application fees, closing costs, and other financial expenses. Be aware of these potential
costs and allow for them in your estimate.

Fine-Tuning the Preliminary Design

With your estimating done, you can move on to the next step. This involves fine-
tuning your preliminary design. Refer to the specifications sheet you have created.

It should detail all the proposed materials for the job. It is time to begin to cross-reference the information in the stack of paperwork you have generated. The specifications sheet should be accompanied by a revised contractor list. Perhaps you found that you cannot afford a quarry tile floor. These types of changes need to be reflected in your spec sheet. Adjust the estimated costs in accordance with your proposed changes. At this stage you are getting ready to get final quotes.

Bid Request Form

The bidding process is the financial backbone of your job. A Bid Request Form is an intricate part of the bidding process. Without it, you are dealing with ambiguous, bulk numbers.

Contractor Questionnaire

When you are ready to start making commitments, you need to tie down the details. A contractor questionnaire can help with this important procedure. Some questions to ask potential contractors include:

- Do the contractors you plan to use have liability insurance?
- Do they provide worker's compensation insurance for their employees?
- Are their workers properly licensed?

▶ *PRO POINTER*

The changes you make within the specifications sheet may affect your contractor selection list. Changing the scope of the work may eliminate the need for some subcontractors. Make these notations on your contractor selection form. Don't waste time contacting contractors you don't need.

✔ *FAST FACT*

Every job should start with good written agreements and a strong production plan. Predicting an accurate financial budget is vital to completing a successful job.

▶ *PRO POINTER*

It is easy for a contractor to side-step your verbal questions or even to answer the questions with lies. Questionable contractors will think twice before answering with lies in writing. They could be charged with fraud. This is a proven way to cull the crop of bad contractors. Don't feel bad about asking them to complete forms. If they are good contractors, they will have no problem answering the questions in writing. The bad ones will disappear and save you a lot of trouble.

- Does the contractor have the required business licenses?
- Is the contractor licensed to do the work you are requesting?
- Will the work performed be done by employees or subcontractors?
- Is the contractor bonded?
- Have the contractors and subcontractors ever had complaints filed against them by other customers?

These are questions you should answer before signing a contract. The questionnaire is designed to ask these questions without embarrassing you. When a contractor is asked to complete a form, they know you are requesting the same information from other contractors. This competition will provide the motivation for the contractor to answer the questions. The form also gives you the opportunity to get a contractor's answers in writing.

Contracts

Once you find the right contractors, you are ready to proceed with your contracts. There is no reason to limit written contracts to tradespeople. While it not routine business practice to contract with suppliers, it is a good idea. You can achieve additional assurances of your prices and delivery dates with a solid contract. Don't be afraid to ask for a contract from everyone involved in the project. Everything you have in writing reduces your risks.

A written contract is the last word in your job. It answers all the questions and calls all the shots. The contract is for your benefit, and you should have some input in its structure. Don't leave the contract preparation in the hands of a lawyer without providing your personal input. Lawyers know law, but they don't necessarily know your business needs and desires.

✔ *FAST FACT*

A written contract with your general contractor or subcontractors is absolutely necessary. Contracts are an accepted requirement in business. The contract should be strict but fair.

▶ *PRO POINTER*

If you slant a contract too heavily to your advantage, contractors will not sign it. Most contractors will want you to sign their proposal or contract. They will have pre-printed forms, with the information regarding your job filled in the blank spaces. Contracts ultimately protect those who write them, so try to avoid using a contract supplied by others. Contractors may resist at first, but they will sign your contract if it's fair. Use contracts prepared by your attorney.

SAMPLE SUBCONTRACTOR SUPPLIED CONTRACT

Anytime Plumbing & Heating
126 OCEAN STREET
BEACHTOWN, ME 00390
(000) 123-4567

PROPOSAL CONTRACT

TO: Mr. and Mrs. Homeowner   Date: 8/17/04

ADDRESS: 52 Your street Beachtown, ME 0039

PHONE: (000) 123-9876

JOB LOCATION: Same   JOB PHONE: Same

Plans: Drawn by ACS, 4/14/04

ANYTIME PLUMBING & HEATING PROPOSES THE FOLLOWING:

Anytime Plumbing & Heating will supply and or coordinate all labor and material for the work referenced below:

PLUMBING

Supply and install a 3/4", type "L", copper water main from ten feet outside the foundation, to the location shown on the attached plans for the new addition.

Supply and install a 4", schedule 40, sewer main to the addition, from ten feet outside the foundation, to the location shown on the plans.

Supply and install schedule 40, steel gas pipe from the meter location, shown on the plans, to the furnace, in the attic, as shown on the plans.

Supply and install the following fixtures, as per plans, except as noted:

1 ABC Venus one piece, fiberglass, tub/shower unit, in white.

1 CF 007_222218 chrome tub/shower faucet.

1 ABC 900928 water closet combination, in white.

1 CBA 111 cultured marble, 30" vanity top, in white.

1 CF 005-95011 chrome lavatory faucet.

1 PKT 11122012 stainless steel, double bowl, kitchen sink.

1 CF 908001 chrome kitchen faucet.

1 DFG 62789 52 gallon, electric, 5 year warranty, water heater.

1 WTFC 20384 frost proof, anti-siphon silcock.

(Page 1 of 4) Initials_____

FIGURE 16.6   Sample subcontractor-supplied agreement

SAMPLE SUBCONTRACTOR SUPPLIED CONTRACT
(CONTINUED)

1 AWD 90576 3/4" backflow preventer.

1 FT66754W white, round front, water closet seat.

1 plastic washer box, with hose bibs.

Connect owner supplied dishwasher.

All fixtures are subject to substitution with fixtures of similar quality, at Anytime Plumbing & Heating's discretion.

All water distribution pipe, after the water meter, will be Pex tubing, run under the slab. This is a change from the specifications and plans, in an attempt to reduce cost.

If water pipe is run as specified in the plans, the pipe will be, type "L" copper and there will be additional cost. Any additional cost will be added to the price listed in this proposal.

All waste and vent pipes will be schedule 40 PVC.

Anytime Plumbing & Heating will provide for trenching the inside of the foundation, for underground plumbing. If the trenching is complicated by rock, unusual depth, or other unknown factors, there will be additional charges. These charges will be for the extra work involved in the trenching.

All plumbing will be installed to comply with state and local codes. Plumbing installation may vary from the plumbing diagrams drawn on the plans.

Anytime Plumbing & Heating will provide roof flashings for all pipes penetrating the roof, but will not be responsible for their installation.

All required holes in the foundation will be provided by others.

All trenching, outside of the foundation, will be provided by others.

All gas piping, outside the structure, will be provided by others.

The price for this plumbing work will be, four thousand, eighty seven thousand dollars ($4,087.00).

HEATING

Anytime Plumbing & Heating will supply and install all duct work and registers, as per plans.

(Page 2 of 4) Initials_____

FIGURE 16.6 Sample subcontractor-supplied agreement *(continued)*

SAMPLE SUBCONTRACTOR SUPPLIED CONTRACT
(CONTINUED)

Anytime Plumbing & Heating will supply and install a BTDY-P5HSD12NO7501 gas fired, forced hot air furnace. The installation will be, as per plans. The homeowner will provide adequate access for this installation.

Venting for the clothes dryer and exhaust fan, is not included in this price. The venting will be done at additional charge, if requested.

No air conditioning work is included.

The price for the heating work will be, three thousand, eight hundred dollars ($3,800.00).

Any alterations to this contract will only be valid, if in writing and signed by all parties. Verbal arrangements will not be binding.

PAYMENT WILL BE AS FOLLOWS:

Contract Price of: Seven thousand, eight hundred eighty-seven dollars ($7,887.00), to be paid; one third ($2,629.00) at the signing of the contract. One third (@2,627.00) when the plumbing and heating is roughed-in. One third ($2,629.00) when work is completed. All payments shall be made within five business days of the invoice date.

If payment is not made according to the terms above, Anytime Plumbing & Heating will have the following rights and remedies. Anytime Plumbing & Heating may charge a monthly service charge of two percent (1%), twenty four percent (12%) per year, from the first day default is made. Anytime Plumbing & Heating may lien the property where the work has been done. Anytime Plumbing & Heating may use all legal methods in the collection of monies owed to Anytime Plumbing & Heating. Anytime Plumbing & Heating may seek compensation, at the rate of $50.00 per hour, for their employees attempting to collect unpaid monies. Anytime Plumbing & Heating may seek payment for legal fees and other cost of collection, to the full extent that law allows.

(Page 3 of 4) Initials_____

FIGURE 16.6   Sample subcontractor-supplied agreement *(continued)*

SAMPLE SUBCONTRACTOR SUPPLIED CONTRACT
(CONTINUED)

If Anytime Plumbing & Heating is requested to send men or material to a job by their customer or their customer's representative, the following policy shall apply. If a job is not ready for the service or material requested, and the delay is not due to Anytime Plumbing & Heating's actions, Anytime Plumbing & Heating may charge the customer for their efforts, in complying with the customer's request. This charge will be at a rate of $50.00 per hour, per man, including travel time.

If you have any questions or don't understand this proposal, seek professional advice. Upon acceptance this becomes a binding contract between both parties.

Respectfully submitted,

H. P. Contractor
Owner

PROPOSAL EXPIRES IN 30 DAYS, IF NOT ACCEPTED BY ALL PARTIES

ACCEPTANCE

We the undersigned, do hereby agree to and accept all the terms and conditions of this proposal. We fully understand the terms and conditions and hereby consent to enter into this contract.

Anytime Plumbing & Heating

by _____

Title_____Date _____

(Page 4 of 4)

FIGURE 16.6   Sample subcontractor-supplied agreement *(continued)*

Your Company Name
Your Company Address
Your Company Phone and Fax Numbers

SUBCONTRACTOR AGREEMENT

This agreement, made this _____ day of _____, 20__, shall set forth the whole agreement, in its entirety, between Contractor and Subcontractor.

Contractor: _____, referred to herein as Contractor.

Job location: _____

Subcontractor: _____, referred to herein as Subcontractor.

The Contractor and Subcontractor agree to the following.

SCOPE OF WORK

Subcontractor shall perform all work as described below and provide all material to complete the work described below.

Subcontractor shall supply all labor and material to complete the work according to the attached plans and specifications. These attached plans and specifications have been initialed and signed by all parties. The work shall include, but is not limited to, the following: _____

_____

_____

_____

_____

COMMENCEMENT AND COMPLETION SCHEDULE

The work described above shall be started within _____ (___) days of verbal notice from Contractor, the projected start date is _____.

The Subcontractor shall complete the above work in a professional and expedient manner by no later than _____ (___) days from the start date. Time is of the essence in this contract. No extension of time will be valid without the Contractor's written consent. If Subcontractor does not

(Page 1 of 3. Please initial _____.)

FIGURE 16.7 Typical subcontractor agreement

SUBCONTRACTOR AGREEMENT
(CONTINUED)

complete the work in the time allowed, and if the lack of completion is not caused by the Contractor, the Subcontractor will be charged _____ ($_____) dollars per day, for every day work extends beyond the completion date. This charge will be deducted from any payments due to the Subcontractor for work performed.

CONTRACT SUM

The Contractor shall pay the Subcontractor for the performance of completed work subject to additions and deductions as authorized by this agreement or attached addendum. The contract sum is

_____($_____).

PROGRESS PAYMENTS

The Contractor shall pay the Subcontractor installments as detailed below, once an acceptable insurance certificate has been filed by the Subcontractor with the Contractor. Contractor shall pay the Subcontractor as described: _____

All payments are subject to a site inspection and approval of work by the Contractor. Before final payment, the Subcontractor shall submit satisfactory evidence to the Contractor that no lien risk exists on the subject property.

WORKING CONDITIONS

Working hours will be _____ a.m. through _____ p.m., Monday through Friday. Subcontractor is required to clean work debris from the job site on a daily basis and leave the site in a clean and neat condition. Subcontractor shall be responsible for removal and disposal of all debris related to the job description.

CONTRACT ASSIGNMENT

Subcontractor shall not assign this contract or further subcontract the whole of this subcontract, without the written consent of the Contractor.

(Page 2 of 3. Please initial _____.)

FIGURE 16.7 Typical subcontractor agreement *(continued)*

SUBCONTRACTOR AGREEMENT
(CONTINUED)

LAWS, PERMITS, FEES, AND NOTICES

Subcontractor shall be responsible for all required laws, permits, fees, or notices, required to perform the work stated herein.

WORK OF OTHERS

Subcontractor shall be responsible for any damage caused to existing conditions or other contractor's work. This damage will be repaired, and the Subcontractor charged for the expense and supervision of this work. The Subcontractor shall have the opportunity to quote a price for said repairs, but the Contractor is under no obligation to engage the Subcontractor to make said repairs. If a different subcontractor repairs the damage, the Subcontractor may be backcharged for the cost of the repairs. Any repair costs will be deducted from any payments due to the Subcontractor. If no payments are due the Subcontractor, the Subcontractor shall pay the invoiced amount within _____ (_____) days.

WARRANTY

Subcontractor warrants to the Contractor, all work and materials for _____ from the final day of work performed.

INDEMNIFICATION

To the fullest extent allowed by law, the Subcontractor shall indemnify and hold harmless the Owner, the Contractor, and all of their agents and employees from and against all claims, damages, losses, and expenses.

This agreement, entered into on _____, 20____, shall constitute the whole agreement between Contractor and Subcontractor.

_____   _____
Contractor   Date   Subcontractor   Date

(Page 3 of 3)

FIGURE 16.7 Typical subcontractor agreement *(continued)*

Your Company Name
Your Company Address
Your Company Phone and Fax Numbers

SUBCONTRACTOR CONTRACT ADDENDUM

This addendum is an integral part of the contract dated _____,
between the Contractor, _____, and the Customer(s),
_____, for the work being done
on real estate commonly known as _____.

The undersigned parties hereby agree to the following: _____

_____

_____

_____

The above constitutes the only additions to the above-mentioned contract,
no verbal agreements or other changes shall be valid unless made in
writing and signed by all parties.

_____   _____
Contractors   Date   Customer   Date

                                         _____
                                         Customer   Date

FIGURE 16.8   Example of an addendum for a contract

Now it's done; you have all your contracts signed. You probably thought you would never see the end of the paperwork. Well, you haven't. The job is only about to begin. There are reams of paper yet to be used. A successful job runs on paper. Without it you will suffer in the end. What else could you possibly need to put in writing? Some suggestions include, change orders, lien waivers, and completion certificates.

▶ *PRO POINTER*

Legal documents such as contracts should be prepared by attorneys. Attorneys have the skill and knowledge to write contracts capable of standing the test of the courts.

Your Company Name
Your Company Address
Your Company Phone and Fax Numbers

NOTICE OF BREACH OF CONTRACT

Date: _____

To: _____

From:_____

TAKE NOTICE that under Contract made _____, 20 _____,
as evidenced by the following documents:
_____, we are hereby holding you IN
BREACH for the following reasons: _____
_____

   If your Breach is not cured within _____ days (i.e., cure must be
completed by _____, 20 _____), we will take all further
actions necessary to mitigate our damages and protect our rights, which
may include, but are not necessarily limited to, the right to Cover" by
obtaining substitute performance and chargeback to you of all additional
costs and damages incurred.

   This Notice is made under the Uniform Commercial Code (if applicable)
and all other applicable laws. All rights are hereby reserved, none of which
are waived. Any forbearance or temporary waiver from enforcement shall
not constitute permanent waiver or waiver of any other right.

   You are urged to cure your Breach forthwith.

_____

Contractor

By: _____
      Authorized Signatory

FIGURE 16.9   Example of a notification for breech of contract

Change Order

Once the job is started, it is sure to produce unexpected results. When these problems arise, you need to adapt your plans and agreements to accommodate any necessary changes. Use a written change order for every deviation from the contract. You must maintain consistency in your management. Written change orders reinforce your dedication to have every aspect of the work clearly defined in black and white.

Contractors will be less likely to take advantage of you when change orders are used, and there will be fewer misunderstandings. Requiring the use of written change orders prevents unexpected price increases. Your contract should mention that change orders will be required for any changes or additional work. In this way a contractor is not entitled to payment for extra work unless you first authorize it in writing. By requiring written change orders, you will be better prepared if you find yourself in court.

▶ *PRO POINTER*

During the job, you will be tempted to avoid all of this paperwork, especially change orders. You will gain a comfort level with your contractors, which will make change orders seem unnecessary. If you get a phone call at the office regarding mandatory alterations, you will be tempted to give verbal authorization for changes over the phone. Resist these urges. If the situation demands immediate verbal authorization, follow it up with a change order as soon as possible. It is important to maintain continuity. If you start making exceptions, your paperwork will become almost useless.

✔ *FAST FACT*

Going to court is never a planned part of remodeling. It is an activity you want to avoid. The best way to bypass the courts is to maintain clear, concise, written agreements.

Code Compliance Forms

As work progresses, contractors will want to be paid. When the work being done is substantial, local code- enforcement inspections will be required on the work done. Don't advance any payments until these inspections are completed and accepted. The codes office will provide written evidence of satisfactory inspections. Insist on a copy of each inspection certificate from the contractor. This protects you from code-violation problems. If a code officer turns down an inspection, complete a code violation notification and give it to the appropriate contractor. This notification gives the contractor a specific period of time to have the work corrected and approved by the code officer. In this way you avoid delays, which may affect other trades and throw your

Your Company Name
Your Company Address
Your Company Phone and Fax Number

CHANGE ORDER

This change order is an integral part of the contract
dated_____, between the customer _____, and
the contractor, _____, for the work
to be performed. The job location is _____. The following
changes are the only changes to be made. These changes shall now
become a part of the original contract and may not be altered again
without written authorization from all parties.
Changes to be as follows:

_____

_____

_____

These changes will increase / decrease the original contract amount.
Payment for theses changes will be made as follows:
_____. The amount of
change in the contract price will be
_____ ($_____). The new total
contract price shall be _____ ($_____).

The undersigned parties hereby agree that these are the only changes to
be made to the original contract. No verbal agreements will be valid. No
further alterations will be allowed without additional written authorization,
signed by all parties. This change order constitutes the entire agreement
between the parties to alter the original contract.

_____   _____
Customer   Contractor

_____   _____
Date   Date

FIGURE 16.10 Typical change order

CODE VIOLATION NOTIFICATION

CUSTOMER NAME: Mr. & Mrs. J. P. Homeowner
CUSTOMER ADDRESS: 192 Hometown Street
CUSTOMER CITY/STATE/ZIP: Ourtown, MO 00580
CUSTOMER PHONE NUMBER: (000) 555-1212
JOB LOCATION: Same
DATE: July 25, 2004
TYPE OF WORK: Electrical
CONTRACTOR: Flashy Electrical Service
ADDRESS: 689 Walnut Ridge, Boltz, MO 00580

OFFICIAL NOTIFICATION OF CODE VIOLATIONS

On July 24, 2004, I was notified by the local electrical code enforcement officer of code violations in the work performed by your company. The violations must be corrected within two business days, as per our contract dated July 1, 2004. Please contact the codes officer for a detailed explanation of the violations and required corrections. If the violations are not corrected within the allotted time, you may be penalized, as per our contract, for your actions, delaying the completion of this project. Thank you for your prompt attention to this matter.

_____   _____
J. P. Homeowner   Date

FIGURE 16.11   Sample code violation notification

project way off schedule. Stipulate in the contract your desire for a photocopy of all permits and inspection results.

> ✔ *FAST FACT*
>
> Never advance money to a contractor until the work passes the inspection of the local code officer.

Lien Waver Form

Before paying anyone, you should complete a lien waiver form. One of these should be signed by any vendor receiving money for services or materials related to your job. Require the lien waiver to be signed at the time you make payment for the service or material. The lien waiver is like your receipt for issuing payment and will protect you, your client, and the rental property from mechanic's and materialman's liens.

Punch List

A punch list is a written notice to contractors of items left to be completed or repaired. These lists come into play at the end of the job. When contractors are finished, you should inspect all the work before final payment is made. Use the punch list form to note all unsatisfactory or incomplete workmanship or materials. After your inspection and before final payment, present a copy of the punch list to the contractor. Have the contractor agree to the list by signing it and allow a reasonable time for corrections to be made. When the punch work is done, inspect the job again. If there are still deficiencies, complete another punch list. Continue this process until the work is done to your satisfaction.

Here is some advice about the proper usage of the punch list:

- Remember that, throughout the work process, we have stressed the need to be fair.
- Be realistic about the work you demand on the punch list.
- Don't require the contractor to replace an entire roll of wallpaper just because there is a tiny wrinkle down by the floor.
- Do not allow a contractor to bully you into accepting work with obvious or offensive flaws.
- Be very thorough when you make the first punch list. Contractors will be quickly angered if they repair everything on your list only to have you find additional items that you missed in your initial inspection.
- Only add items to the list that were caused by the punch work.

You can use a retainer system when dealing with a punch list. Your contractor will want some payment before doing the punch list, and this is okay. But make sure that you retain enough money to pay some other contractor if necessary to have the problems corrected.

Certificate of Completion

Certificates of completion document the conclusion dates of all work performed. This form is important in determining your warranty period. Contractors normally offer one-year warranties on their major work, and the manufacturer's warranty applies to

PUNCH LIST
BATHROOM REMODELING PROJECT

ITEM/PHASE	O.K.	REPAIR	REPLACE	FINISH WORK
Demolition				
Rough plumbing				
Rough electrical				
Rough heating/ac				
Subfloor				
Insulation				
Drywall				
Ceramic tile				
Linen closet				
Baseboard trim				
Window trim				
Door trim				
Paint/Wallpaper				
Underlayment				
Finish floor covering				
Linen closet shelves				
Linen closet door				
Closet door hardware				
Main door hardware				
Wall cabinets				
Base cabinets				
Countertops				
Plumbing fixtures				
Trim plumbing material				
Final plumbing				
Shower enclosure				
Light fixtures				
Trim electrical material				
Final electrical				
Trim heating/ac material				
Final heating/ac				
Bathroom accessories				
Clean up				

NOTES _____

FIGURE 16.12 Bathroom punch list

SAMPLE CERTIFICATE OF COMPLETION AND ACCEPTANCE

CONTRACTOR: _Willy's Drywall Service_

CUSTOMER: _David R. Erastus_

JOB NAME: _Erastus_

JOB LOCATION: _134 Faye Lane, Beau, VA 29999_

JOB DESCRIPTION: _Supply and install drywall in new addition, as per plans and specifications, and as described in the contract dated, 6/10/04, between the two parties. Hang, tape, sand, and prepare wall and ceiling surfaces for paint._

DATE OF COMPLETION: _August 13, 2004_

DATE OF FINAL INSPECTION BY CUSTOMER: _August 13, 2004_

DATE OF CODE COMPLIANCE INSPECTION & APPROVAL: _August 13, 2004_

ANY DEFICIENCIES FOUND BY CUSTOMER: _None_

NOTE ANY DEFECTS IN MATERIAL OR WORKMANSHIP: _None_

ACKNOWLEDGEMENT

Customer acknowledges the completion of all contracted work and accepts all workmanship and materials as being satisfactory. Upon signing this certificate, the customer releases the contractor from any responsibility for additional work, except warranty work. Warranty work will be performed for a period of one year from August 13, 2004. Warranty work will include the repair of any material or workmanship defects occurring after this date. All existing workmanship and materials are acceptable to the customer and payment will be made, in full, according to the payment schedule in the contract, between the two parties.

_____   _____

Customer   Date   Contractor   Date

FIGURE 16.13   Sample completion certificate

SAMPLE DAMAGE CLAUSE

CONTRACTOR LIABILITY FOR DAMAGES TO EXISTING CONDITIONS

Contractor shall be responsible for any damage caused to existing conditions. This shall include work performed on the project by other contractors. If the contractor damages existing conditions or work performed by other contractors, said contractor shall be responsible for the repair of said damages. These repairs may be made by the contractor responsible for the damages or another contractor, at the discretion of the homeowner.

If a different contractor repairs the damage, the contractor causing the damage may be back-charged for the cost of the repairs. These charges may be deducted from any monies owed to the damaging contractor, by the homeowner. The choice for a contractor to repair the damages shall be at the sole discretion of the homeowner.

If no money is owed to the damaging contractor, said contractor shall pay the invoiced amount, from the homeowner, within seven business days. If prompt payment is not made, the homeowner may exercise all legal means to collect the requested monies.

The damaging contractor shall have no rights to lien the homeowner's property, for money retained to cover the repair of damages caused by the contractor. The homeowner may have the repairs made to their satisfaction.

The damaging contractor shall have the opportunity to quote a price for the repairs. The homeowner is under no obligation to engage the damaging contractor to make the repairs.

FIGURE 16.14   Sample damage clause

individual products. These warranties should start with the date on the completion certificate. These simple forms take the guesswork out of warranty claims. They clearly establish the date all work was completed, inspected, and approved. This little piece of paper can make a big difference if you have a major malfunction or problem.

Many of the problems in working with contractors and vendors are not caused by intentional deceit. They are caused by confusion. You are thinking one thing, and the contractor or vendor is thinking something else. You both have good intentions, but the conflict can get out of hand. Neither of you will want to give ground in the dispute when money is involved. With oral agreements there is no way to determine who is right. Written agreements eliminate the source of confusion. Each party knows exactly what is expected from a contractual relationship. It is also a good idea to include a clause about any damage that a contractor may cause during a job. Many problems arise when contractors damage personal property or the work of others.

Working with close friends can be the worst experience of your life. Business is business, and it can become a true threat to relationships. Friends don't want to insult each other; consequently, they avoid written contracts. Trust is not a factor, and the lack of a good contract can ruin your friendship. Financial disputes can turn into an all-out battle. The friend you golf with every week can become your worst enemy over a simple misunderstanding. Written contracts protect you and your friends.

Are You Ready?

Are you ready to hang out your shingle as a professional property manager? There is no time like the present. Enter the business with your eyes wide open. Invest in yourself with as much education as you can obtain for your new position. Your new venture is full of humps and bumps. To make your move smoothly into property management, you will have to dedicate yourself to your goals. Going into business for yourself is not all fun and games. There is a tremendous amount of time and effort required to open and run your own business. If you want it badly enough, the rewards are wonderful. I wish you the best in your new career.

Index

Entries in italics indicate figures